WITH HONOUR AND GLORY

WITH HONOUR AND GLORY
Five Great Artillery Battles

MAJOR GENERAL A.J.S. SANDHU, VSM (RETD.)

(Established 1870)

Centre for Military History and Conflict Studies

United Service Institution of India

New Delhi

Vij Books India Pvt Ltd

New Delhi (India)

ABOUT THE UNITED SERVICE INSTITUTION OF INDIA

The United Service Institution of India was founded in 1870 by a soldier scholar, Colonel (later Major General) Sir Charles MacGregor. The story of its growth is the story of the growth of the Indian Armed Forces. It was founded for 'furtherance of interest and knowledge in the art, science and literature of the Defence Services.'

The USI's Centre for Military History and Conflict Studies (Formerly CAFHR), was established in December 2000 with an aim to encourage the objective study of all facets of Indian military history in general and the history of the Indian Armed Forces in particular.

Published by
Vij Books India Pvt Ltd
(Publishers, Distributors & Importers)
2/19, Ansari Road
Delhi – 110 002
Phones: 91-11-43596460, 91-11-47340674
Mob: 98110 94883
e-mail: orders@vijpublishing.com
web: www.vijbooks.in

Copyright © 2021, United Service Institution of India, New Delhi

ISBN: 978-93-90917-41-9 (Hardback)
ISBN: 978-93-90917-42-6 (Paperback)
ISBN: 978-93-90917-47-1 (ebook)

Contents

Illustrations

under Gen. Joshi's command during the Kargil War

70. (Top) The Indian Express war correspondent, Vikram Jit Singh (in fawn trousers), in a tricky spot on the western cliff face of Khalubar ridge, Batalik, and coming under fire from UMGs and RPGs directed by Pakistanis lodged on the flanking Kukarthang ridge, July 7, 1999. He was accompanied by soldiers of the 12 JAK Light Infantry. (Below) During the climb to Tololing Top on July 6, 2019, as part of a 2 Rajputana Rifles commemorative expedition: Kargil War veterans, Hav. Rajinder Singh (Kirti Chakra) and Sub. Surender Kumar, along with the Times of India Defence correspondent, Vikram Jit Singh.

CREDITS

Images 16 and 20: Canada War Museum, Ottawa

Images 14, 17, 19: Canadian Army and the Library and Archives Canada

Images 21 to 27: The Army Museum Halifax Citadel.

Images 28, 29 and 35: 2 Medium Regt (SP)

Image 39: 2nd (Royal) Lancers

Images 42 and 49: Brig A N Suryanarayanan

Image 47: Brig AS Bal

Image 55: Lt Gen Mohinder Puri

Image 56: Maj Gen Lakhwinder Singh

Images 57 to 65: Dte Gen of Arty

Image 70: Maj. M. Indrabalan, then BM, 70 Infantry Brigade, for the 1999 War photograph, and Arpit Seth for the 2019 commemorative expedition photograph (69)

MAPS

Foreword

It gives me great pleasure to write the Foreword to this book titled With Honour and Glory: Five Great Artillery Battles'. This study, undertaken by a former gunner and well-known author and military historian with the support of the Directorate General of Artillery, will help to educate young officers about the role and importance of artillery in battle. We have very few qualified military historians in India and this contribution by Maj Gen AJS (Abdo) Sandhu, VSM (Retd.) will prove to be an invaluable didactic tool for familiarising the officer fraternity with the central role of artillery in battles throughout history. I am sanguine that this book is going to be the first of its kind in more ways than one.

I was commissioned into the Indian Army in the year 1967. I shared five of my initial glorious years with Abdo, who went on to become the Additional Director General (Artillery) at Army Headquarters, New Delhi. Few can claim such unparalleled expertise and experience in artillery operations, given his service in the Punjab Sector during the 1971 war, the Siachen conflict as well as the unforgettable Kargil war.

With his previous book, **Battleground Chhamb: The Indo-Pakistan War of 1971,** Maj Gen Sandhu has detailed the most hard-fought battle of the 1971 war. He is as hard-hitting with his words as he is on the battlefield. And this time, he is back with another important contribution towards the development of artillery in warfare.

Artillery has been used as the final arbiter of battle for over 750 years. Maj Gen Sandhu has picked out five of the most important artillery battles from the overall history of artillery combat, starting from The Battle of Gettysburg in 1863 to the Battles of Tololing & Tiger Hill during Operation Vijay in 1999.

This book will prove to be a very good source of information and knowledge for service officers, gunners, and artillery combat enthusiasts alike.

Lt. Gen. PK Singh, PVSM, AVSM (Retd.)
Director, United Service Institution of India, New Delhi
Former GOC-in-C South Western Command &
Colonel Commandant, Regiment of Artillery

Preface

The idea of writing a book on Great Artillery Battles was germinated by Lieutenant General P. R. Shankar (then Director General of Artillery), and his deputy and later successor, Lieutenant General Pankaj Srivastava. After toying with the idea of making it an 'in house' project, the United Services Institution of India (USI) was requested to undertake this venture on their behalf. Consequently, the Centre of Armed Forces Historical Research (CAFHR) of the USI approached me, and since I had just finished writing the manuscript of my book Battleground Chhamb: The Indo-Pakistan War of 1971, I readily accepted.

I did not realise at the time that it would turn out to be so challenging and in fact a rather onerous task! The reason was that when I commenced my research of some famous battles, in all of the material I went through, I found very little mention of the role of the artillery! This was somewhat surprising because ever since the advent of guns and cannons, artillery has been a battle-winning factor in the conduct of military operations. I soon realized that when it comes to writing battle accounts, the artillery generally gets short shrift, with the focus being mainly on the infantry and armour; it therefore took me some time to initially shortlist ten battles and later, after some more research, finalise the five that appear in this book. The battles selected by me span continents and are almost a century and a half apart, and I have attempted to flesh out the role played by artillery in each one of them.

In this journey there were many people who provided me encouragement, guidance and assistance in different ways. I wish to thank Lieutenant Generals P.R. Shankar and Pankaj Srivastava (both former Director Generals of Artillery) and Lieutenant General P.K. Singh (Director USI and former Army Commander), for giving me the opportunity to research and write this book. My gratitude to Squadron Leader Rana

Chhina (of the CAFHR) who was my guiding force, offering me valuable advice through my research. Ms Aaliya Khan, also of the CAFHR, helped in getting the images for the various battles. Major Kendall Hynes, Chief Curator, The Army Museum Halifax Citadel, Canada and Ms Gurinder Kaur were kind enough to send me pictures of Vimy Ridge. My thanks to Colonel (now Brigadier) Binuraj, Colonels D.K. Sen and Amit Verma, and Lieutenant Colonel P.S. Dhanoa of the Artillery Directorate who helped in getting research material, as well as the battle accounts of the Indian Artillery regiments which fought in Chhamb and Kargil. I also wish to thank Colonel Suraj Bhan, then commanding officer of 2 Medium Regiment (SP) who provided me with the Regimental War Diary of the Battle of Bir Hacheim (Point 171), Lieutenant Colonel Sachin Wakankar who visited the National Archives in London to procure the documents pertaining to the this battle and my sister Jessie Sidhu who helped in getting research material on the role of artillery in the Battle of Gettysburg.

I am grateful to veteran gunner officers who fought in the Battle of Chhamb 1971, and spared their valuable time to speak with me on telephone and later were kind enough to send me their accounts of the 'gunner battle' via email. These include Major Generals J.R.K. Bhatacharjee, S.V. Thapliyal and Virpal Singh, Brigadiers A.N. Suryanarayanan, A.P. Deo, V.K. Chopra and Jitender Dhasmana, and Colonels R.I. Singh and Prakash Pande. Brigadier AN Suryanarayanan was also kind enough to send me his articles and unpublished notes of the Battle of Chhamb. I am also thankful to Colonel Mahesh Chadha, then ADC to GOC 10 Infantry Division, for sharing his perspective of the performance of the artillery in this battle. My thanks to Major General Lakhwinder Singh for sending me his unpublished note on artillery in Kargil, and Ms Aastha Tandan and Gunner (OPR) Rohit Solanki of 218 Medium Regiment for preparing or adapting maps for this book. I wish to thank the indefatigable Havildar Clerk Amit Kumar Yadav for typing my numerous drafts and the final manuscript. I am also extremely grateful to Major General K. Manmeet Singh, (former Major General Artillery of Western Command) for going through my drafts and giving valuable inputs, as well supporting me in different ways. I would like to thank Ms Shefali Oberoi of the CAFHR, for seeing this volume to press.

Mr Vikram Jit Singh who covered the Kargil War from the frontline for the Indian Express newspaper, was kind enough to send me his first-hand account of the artillery operations as he saw them – this account appears as a 'Tail Piece' in Chapter 6.

Finally, I wish to thank my wife Ameeta who, as always, was my pillar of support and encouragement right through my project.

MAJ. GEN. A.J.S. SANDHU (RETD.)

CHAPTER 1

Introduction

Great battles are won with artillery.

NAPOLÉON BONAPARTE

Artillery has come a long way since its evolution many centuries ago. The following two quotes, in a way, sum up the importance of artillery in warfare. *'Ultima Ratio Regum'*, a Latin phrase meaning: The last argument of kings. King Louis XIV of France had this motto engraved on all cannons manufactured during his reign. The second quote is attributed to Joseph Stalin who described artillery as the *'God of War'*. The Russians were known to employ massed artillery in all their battles during the Second World War. The artillery today continues to retain its role as a battle-winning factor.

It is difficult to pin-point the exact dates of the origins of artillery. There are records of primitive artillery weapons (precursors to the cannons) being used during wars in the medieval period such as *ballistas* (mounted cross bows), *magonels* (catapults) and *trebuchets* (which were an advanced form of *magonels)*. These mechanical devices were designed to fling or throw projectiles at longer ranges. The 'gun powder using cannon' is said to have made its advent sometimes in the 12th century, as there is evidence of its use in China during this period. In Europe there is documented evidence which shows that cannons were employed in the Battle of Crecy in 1346 during the Hundred Years War. Such cannons were used very effectively in both the anti-siege and anti-infantry role. Gradually, the cannon made its appearance in other countries such as Russia, Sweden, France and the Middle East.

The cannon, with its ability to strike at the enemy at longer ranges, brought in a new dimension to warfare. In spite of the emergence of this very potent and destructive weapon of war, the development of artillery in the 15th and 16th centuries proceeded at a slow pace. It was during this period that King Gustavus Adolphus (who ruled Sweden from 1611 to 1632), brought in the concept of lighter and more mobile artillery in order to keep pace with the cavalry and infantry elements. He ordered the manufacture of lighter cannons (4 and 9 Pounders) which could be operated by fewer men. Major General D. K. Palit, the Indian military historian, has written:

The first man to appreciate the correct role of artillery in battle was the Swedish King Gustavus Adolphus. He realized the importance of artillery - and invented the first light field piece - weighing 650 lbs and firing a 4 lb shot, as lightly mounted that two men could handle it in battle. This was a momentous achievement, because it is from the mobile use of the light field piece that artillery tactics as we understand it today eventually emerged - though it took nearly two more centuries before the fullest tactical use could be made of artillery on the battlefield. It is to Napoleon that we owe the modern concept of artillery in battle.[1]

Simultaneous development of the use of cannon in naval ships continued, giving a new dimension to war at sea. The 18th and 19th centuries saw a steady improvement in the design of the cannons, giving better accuracy and longer range. It was during this period that Napoleon (himself an artilleryman) organised them into cohesive units (battalions and batteries), and employed them to bring massed fire on the targets. Artillery soon became an important (and sizable) component of armies around the world. This period also saw the very effective use of artillery in the Crimean War (October 1853-March 1856). In faraway United States of America, the artillery also had its nascent beginnings during the Revolutionary War against the British colonialists. However, after independence, the expansion of artillery in the USA slowed down due to change in threat perceptions. In her book, The Organizational History of Field Artillery: 1775-2003, Janice E. Mckenney writes:

After the Revolutionary War, the new nation viewed security from foreign aggression and Indian depredations as the main mission of its armed forces. The United States, while spending more effort on harbour defence programs to protect the coastline against enemy assault, paid scant attention to field artillery because it was expensive to maintain and not usually necessary on the frontier. As the dramatic successes of Napoléon Bonaparte's artillery corps became well known, Army leaders made a concerted effort to increase the effectiveness of their own field artillery, and a small number of such units fought with great distinction during the Mexican War.[2]

It was during the U.S. Civil War (1861-1864) that the artillery came into its own. The Union and Confederate armies employed artillery with great effect during the various battles. The artillery actions in the famous Battle of Gettysburg are covered in Chapter 2 of this book. By the time of the First World War, the guns and howitzers, as well as munitions had developed further. With longer ranges, the guns could now fire well into the depth areas, with projectiles that packed more lethality. The artillery organizations too were well structured to ensure complete integration with the infantry corps, divisions and brigades. The Great War saw the use of 'massed artillery barrages' for the first time; the Battles of Somme and Vimy Ridge being good examples of this. The Battle of Vimy Ridge is narrated in Chapter 3 of this book. Further development of artillery continued in the intervening period between the two World Wars. By the time of the Second World War, the concept of indirect fire had fully matured and Observation Post (OP) officers were affiliated with the infantry and cavalry units, to bring down accurate and effective artillery fire on the enemy at long distances. Heavier calibre guns were now in the arsenals of major armies. There were guns for anti-aircraft (Ack Ack) and Anti-tank rules. The Germans, in fact, used their 88mm Ack Ack guns in the anti-tank role against the allied armour with devastating effect. Although heavier calibre guns made their advent in this war, the main-stay of the British field artillery were the 25 Pounder guns. These guns were used with telling effect against Rommel's Afrika Korps (the German term for Africa Corps) by the Indian Gunners of 2 Indian Field Regiment, during the Battle of Bir Hacheim (Point 171) which is narrated in Chapter 4.

The seven decades since the end of the Second World War have seen immense technological developments in the artillery weapons, equipment and munitions. Such advancements have brought in longer range guns, better gun fire control systems, precision guided munitions, long range rockets and missiles.

Furthermore, the advent of Unmanned Aerial Vehicles (UAVs), drones (and their armed versions) have resulted in an enhanced capability of target acquisition and damage assessment well beyond the Tactical Battle Area (TBA). Although these advancements have enhanced the role of artillery to include destruction and degradation of the battlefield, the original task of providing close support to the manoeuvre arms (infantry and armoured corps) will continue to hold primacy, since only the gunners can help them close-in into the enemy. In the words of Janice E. Mckenny,... if the ground soldier remains a critical element of warfare, so the services of the field artillery – the King of Battle – will remain critical as well'.[3]

As far as the evolution of artillery in the Indian sub-continent is concerned, although it is commonly (but erroneously) believed that Mughal Emperor Babar first employed artillery at Panipat in 1526, there is documented evidence of the use of cannons by the Bahamani kings a couple of centuries earlier. Major General D.K. Palit has noted in his book *History of Regiment of Artillery: Indian Army*:

> The Persian historian Ferishtah (who served in the armies of both Ahmednagar and Bijapur during the sixteenth century) records that at the Battle of Adoni in 1368, Mohammed Shah Bahmani had collected a train of artillery (he used the Portuguese word tope) - the guns being served by Persians, Abyssinians and Arabs; Turks and Europeans being attached to the train as advisers. The tactics was to open the battle with a cannonade which disrupted the formations of the Vijayanagar troops, followed by the coup de grace of a cavalry charge.[4]

It was, however, at the First Battle of Panipat in 1526 that Babar used a vast array of cannons to defeat the overwhelmingly superior forces of King Ibrahim Lodi, ushering centuries of Mughal rule in India. The lethal fire of Babar's artillery created utter chaos and disarray amongst Lodi's elephants, horses as well as infantry (he had no guns). The artillery remained an important component of the armies of successive Mughal emperors. Meanwhile, the rise of Chhatrapati Shivaji in the Deccan region of India, led to the establishment of the Maratha Kingdom in the 17th century. Since the Maratha tactics were based on speed and mobility, they relied more on lighter artillery cannons. Although the growth of artillery continued in the Peshwa period, it was under Madhavji Sindhia (also called Scindhia), that a cohesive organisation was formulated for the artillery units. Major General D.K. Palit notes:

The trained artillery battalions in Sindhia's army had their contingent of artillery. The artillery personnel of a battalion consisted of one sergeant major (European), and five European gunners, one jemadar, one havildar, five naiks, thirty-five golandaz, five tindals, thirty-five Klassis, twenty bildars, thirty gariwans, four ironsmiths and four carpenters. Every battalion had 408 stand of arms, four field-pieces, one howitzer, five tumbrils, 120 bullocks and two native carts. Every gun had, constantly ready with it, 300 rounds of shot and 100 rounds of grape. Besides the battalion complement of guns mentioned above, the brigade had attached to it three battering guns and two mortars with a compliment of gunners to serve them.[5]

Another ruler of southern India who gave importance to artillery was Tipu Sultan, the Sultan of the Mysore Kingdom (from 1782 to 1799). He fought numerous battles against the Marathas and the British. He organized his army on western models, with artillery being an important component. His father Haidar Ali introduced artillery rockets in India, which were later improved upon by Tipu and employed during the Anglo-Mysore wars, and were later improved upon by Sir William Congreve. Brittanica.com notes that 'The Congreve Rocket developed by Sir William Congreve was first used by Haidar Ali, prince of Mysore, against the British in India in the 1790'[6]. About Tipu's artillery, Major General D.K. Palit writes in his book:

The size of Tipu's artillery can be gauged from the fact that on the capture of Seringapatam, nine hundred and twenty seven pieces were found in the fort, including 287 mounted on the walls. Out of 373 brass guns, 202 were from Tipu's own foundry and the rest were of European make. The workmanship of iron guns does not appear to have been so well developed by Tipu as was the case of brass guns, for out of 466 iron guns only six were from Tipu's foundry. Nearly all the captured mortars had been manufactured in Seringapatam.[7]

Meanwhile in the late 18th and early 19th centuries in north-west India, Maharaja Ranjit Singh was busy consolidating his Sikh Empire. He had a formidable *Khalsa* army which he used to invade places as far away as Afghanistan and Tibet. He had a vast arsenal of guns, and a well-structured artillery organisation. The Department of Artillery was organised into two sections - *Topkhana Kalan* (siege guns) and *Topkhana Khurd* (field guns), under command of a different *Darogha* (Chief Officer)[8]. He established artillery workshops at Lahore, Amritsar and Kotli - Lahoran for the manufacture of guns. His foreign artillery generals included Paolo Di Avitable (Italian) and Claude Auguste Court (French). It was Maharaja Ranjit Singh who bought artillery into pre-eminence in his army. His death in 1839 led to the two Anglo-Sikh wars, and the downfall of the Sikh Empire and the annexation of Punjab by the British. The Sikh artillery played a dominant role in the battles of both the Anglo-Sikh Wars. Maj Gen D.K. Palit has recorded: 'Whatever may have been the outcome of the final battles, the guns proved their worth during the Sikh wars, and many Sikh gunners were enrolled by the British in their artillery after the annexation of the Punjab'[9].

Concurrent with the above developments, the British East India Company (EIC) had begun to raise artillery companies. According to Major General (later Lieutenant General) Anjan Mukherjee, formal orders were issued by the Board of Directors of EIC to raise one artillery company for the Bengal, Madras and Bombay Presidencies, and the first company was raised in Calcutta the following year. He notes that: 'A captain was appointed to command all the three Presidency artillery companies with his residency at Calcutta. Each company was to be composed of one second-captain, one captain-lieutenant, three lieutenant fireworks, four sergeants, four corporals, three drummers and 100 gunners[10].' Gradually, the strength of these artillery companies (sometimes referred to as 'artillery trains') grew in each of the Presidencies. Some of these native 'artillery trains' later became mountain batteries. These mountain batteries acquitted themselves very creditably in military campaigns in North West Frontier Province, Afghanistan Burma, Gallipoli as well as the First World War. The Indian Artillery celebrates its Gunners Day (Regimental Day) on 28 September every year; this is the date of raising (28 September

1827) of the No. 1 Company Native Artillery, renamed as No. 1 Bombay Battery in 1876, and yet again as 5 Bombay Battery in 1890. This mountain battery can claim to be the oldest Indian mountain battery, having an 'unbroken' record since 1827[11]. Special mention must be made of 1st Kohat (F.P.) and 6th (Jacobs) Mountain Batteries which fought in Gallipoli as part of the 7th Indian Mountain Brigade. They gave artillery support to the Australian and New Zealand Army Corps (ANZAC Corps) during their attack on Turkish positions, and suffered heavy casualties, i.e. 23 killed (two officers) and 278 wounded (including five officers). They also won 45 gallantry awards.[12] The ANZAC Corps Commander, Lieutenant General Sir W. Birdwood sent the following message to the Commander of the 7th Mountain Brigade:

...I want, however, to thank you, both your batteries and all your officers and men for the really magnificent work they have done for us during the months when, I am glad to say, we were all together at ANZAC, I think you will all have realized what a very high regard the Australian troops have for your two batteries, and I am so delighted that this is the case, for they have thoroughly deserved their high reputation....[13]

Till the beginning of the 20th century, the mountain batteries were officered by British officers. In the early 1930s it was decided to 'Indianise' the Indian artillery, consequent to which 'A' Field Brigade was raised in Bangalore on 15 January 1935, and the first Indian artillery officers to be posted were Captain P.S. Gyani and 2/Lt P.P. Kumaramangalam, followed after a few months by 2/Lt A.S. Kalha. 12 more Indian Officers joined this regiment between 1935 and 1939. Later, on 15 May 1940, 'B' Field Brigade was raised in Bangalore. These two regiments were later re-designated as 1 and 2 Indian Field Regiments, and covered themselves with glory in the Second World War; the former at Meiktila in Burma, and the latter in Bir Hacheim (North Africa) and Letse (Burma), earning Honour Titles for their gallant actions. As mentioned earlier, the brave and courageous stand of 2 Indian Field Regiment at Bir Hacheim (Point 171) is narrated in Chapter 4. It is not within the ambit of this chapter to cover the post 1935 growth of Indian artillery in detail; however it must be mentioned that the artillery played decisive roles in the various battles of the Second World War, and all the post Independent conflicts which the Indian Army has fought since 1947. Two battles fought against Pakistan, i.e. Battle of Chhamb in 1971, and the Kargil Operation (Tololing and Tiger Hill) of 1999 are covered in Chapters 5 and 6.

The five battles narrated in this book were fought in four different continents over a wide span of time; the first in 1863 and the fifth in 1999. One battle each has been selected from the US Civil War, First World War and Second World War, while two are from the India-Pakistan conflicts of 1971 and 1999.

The *Battle of Gettysburg* (1 to 3 July 1863) was a turning point of the US Civil War. The artillery, although still a 'direct firing' weapon and referred to as the 'long arm', played a dominant role from both sides. It is also famous for the *Great Cannonade* fired by the Confederate artillery onto the Union forces on 3 June 1863.

The *Battle of Vimy Ridge* (9 to 12 April 1917) is a famous battle of the First World War, in which the Canadian Corps (consisting of four Canadian Divisions) fought as an entity for the first time. This battle was part of the wider Arras Offensive launched by the Allies against the Germans in the spring of 1917, (just five months after the Battle of Somme), in which the Canadians managed to capture the massive ridge in only four days. Once again the artillery played a decisive role in the victory. In fact the battle began with the greatest barrage in history (till then) being fired; a total of 983 guns opened up at 0530 hours on Easter Monday 9 April 1917, shattering window panes of nearby towns.

The *Battle of Bir Hacheim (Point 171)* took place on 27 May 1942 in North Africa's Libyan Desert. The 'defensive box' held by 3 Indian Motor Brigade at Point 171 came under attack in the morning of 27 May 1942, when Field Marshal Erwin Rommel launched his *Panzerarmee Afrika* to capture Tobruk. Standing no chance against such a formidable assault by the German and Italian tanks, the brigade position was overrun in a matter of hours. However, the gunners of 2 Indian Field Regiment fought stubbornly, knocking out 56 enemy tanks by the 'direct firing' of their 25 pounder field guns. This battle has been immortalised in a painting by the German artist Walter Langhammer and appears on the cover of the book.

The Battle of Chhamb (3 to 17 December 1971) was indisputably the bloodiest and most intensely fought battle of the Indo - Pakistan War of 1971. This was Pakistan's biggest land offensive of the war for which it had mustered a formidable force. A less known fact is that the artillery employed by Pakistan to support this offensive was more than they had to defend themselves in the entire East Pakistan (now Bangladesh)! They had concentrated 31 artillery batteries (186 guns/mortars), against which India had 18 batteries (108 guns). Thus it was that in the first three days of the battle (3 to 6 December), there were almost 300 guns of assorted calibres firing into a small area of 12 by 8 kilometres, making it the highest 'per square kilometre' concentration of artillery of that war. The artillery was used to good effect by both sides, and maximum casualties were caused due to shrapnel. Due to the stubborn fight put up by 10 Infantry Division, the Pakistani Forces were stopped along the west bank of the Manawar Tawi River, and were unable to achieve their military aim of capturing Akhnur.

The *Battles of Tololing and Tiger Hill* were amongst the many battles fought during the short and successful campaign by the Indians against the Pakistani troops in summer of 1999, in the Kargil District of Ladakh. The Infantry attacks on the Pakistanis occupying the icy mountain peaks were supported by large concentrations of artillery fire. At Tololing and Tiger Hill, each battalion was supported by over 100 guns and one troop of 122mm GRAD Multi Barrel Rocket Launchers (MBRLs); 155 mm Bofors guns and MBRLs were also used in the 'direct firing role' to engage enemy targets as high as 16000 feet. In many ways *Operation Vijay* (the Kargil Operation) was a gunner's battle.

NOTES

1. Maj Gen D.K. Palit, *History of the Regiment of Artillery: Indian Army,* Palit and Dutt, Dehradun, 1971, pp. 1-2.
2. Janice E. McKinney, *The Organizational History of Field Artillery: 1775 - 2003,* Center of Military History, United States, Washington D.C, 2007, p.17.
3. Ibid., p.323.
4. Maj Gen D.K. Palit, *History of the Regiment of Artillery: Indian Army,* p.2.
5. Ibid., p.9.
6. http://www.brittanica.com/technology/congreve-rocket, accessed on 27 August 2019.
7. Maj Gen D.K. Palit, *History of the Regiment of Artillery,* pp. 12-13.
8. Ibid., p.14.
9. Ibid., p.17.
10. Lt Gen Anjan Mukherjee, Thesis titled : *Evolution of Indian Artillery and its impact on India's Comprehensive Military Power,* University of Madras, 2013, p.61.
11. Maj Gen C.A.L. Graham, *The History of the Indian Mountain Artillery,* Gale and Polden, Aldershot, 1957, p. 37.
12. Ibid., p.p. 132-4 gives details of casualties and gallantry awards.
13. Ibid., p. 134.

CHAPTER 2

Battle of Gettysburg
(1 July to 3 July 1863)
U.S. Civil War

A battery of field artillery is worth a thousand muskets.

GENERAL WILLIAM TECUMSEH SHERMAN
Major General of the Union Army during The Civil War,
later Commanding General of the United States Army.

INTRODUCTION

The Battle of Gettysburg took place over three days between
1 July and 3 July 1863. It was fought between the Confederate
Army of North Virginia led by Lieutenant General Robert
E. Lee and the Union Army of the Potomac commanded
by Major General George G. Meade, in and around the
town of Gettysburg in Pennsylvania. This bloody, three day
engagement was a defining moment of the U.S. Civil War, and
is considered by many historians as the 'turning point' of that
internal conflict. It is also considered to be the 'most written
about battle in American military history'.[1]

Buoyed by his recent success over the Union forces at
Chancellorsville in May 1863, Lee led his Confederate
Army into the second invasion of Pennsylvania, with a view
to decisively defeat the Federals (as the Union Army was
also referred) in their home ground, so as to get the Lincoln
administration to stop the prosecution of war and sue for
peace. Unfortunately for Lee, this battle ended in defeat, and
heralded the gradual downfall of the Confederacy. It was also
a very bloody battle, with the number of dead, wounded or
taken prisoner totaling around 51,000.

By the middle of the Civil War, the artillery had matured
as a fighting arm. Although still a 'line of sight' weapon on

account of the short range guns, it wielded a very potent threat to the enemy both in offensive and defensive operations. Both sides used it with great effect in Gettysburg, and to date the battleground near the city continues to display the artillery guns, limbers, caissons and other support equipment used by the artillery during the battle.

With the deployment of over 600 guns, the artillery played a key role in this epic battle. In the words of U.S. historian Bradley M. Gottfried, 'Artillery played a major role in the Battle of Gettysburg, and some historians go so far as to claim that Federal artillery's superiority in numbers, placement, handling, and better ammunition made victory possible'.[2]

CIVIL WAR IN THE UNITED STATES : AN OVERVIEW

The American Civil War, also known as the 'War Between The States', was fought over a four year period (1861 to 1865) between the United States on one side, and the 11 Southern States which seceded from the Union to form the Confederate States of America, on the other. After years of growing differences between the 'North' and the 'South' over various issues such as slavery (the chief cause), state's rights and western expansion into new territories, the election of President Abraham Lincoln (of the recently formed Republican Party), known for his abolitionist views on slavery, acted as a trigger for the Civil War. His election on 6 November 1860 set the course for the secession of seven states of the South. The secession started with South Carolina's Ordinance of Secession on 20 December 1860 and ended with Texas's secession on 1 February 1861. These seven states were South Carolina, Mississippi, Florida, Alabama, Georgia, Louisiana and Texas.

'A Provisional Congress of their delegates met on 4 February at Montgomery, Alabama and speedily adopted a Provisional Government with Jefferson Davis of Mississippi as President and Alexander Stephens of Georgia, Vice-President'.[3] This in itself did not provoke war. However, in his inaugural address on 4 March 1861, President Lincoln pronounced all secessionist ordinances invalid and declared his intention to hold, occupy, and possess, the property and places belonging to the government.[4]

This was construed by the Confederate States as a virtual threat of war, and they responded by a call-up of 1,00,000 volunteers for twelve months service.

The Civil War commenced with the bombardment of Fort Sumter by the Confederate forces in April 1861. This Union Fort located in Charleston, South Carolina was held by the Federal forces under Major Robert Anderson. Lincoln had ordered the relief of Fort Sumter by sea. Before any relief could arrive, Jefferson Davis ordered an attack on the fort. The first shots of the Civil War were thus fired on 12 April 1861, with the Confederate forces under P.G.T. Beauregard launching an artillery bombardment on Fort Sumter. Two days later Major Anderson surrendered. This action started the Civil War.

President Lincoln immediately issued a call for recruitment of 75,000 militia for three-month service. Meanwhile, in the second wave of secession, four more states seceded from the Union, viz. Virginia, Tennessee, Arkansas and North Carolina. The stage was now set for the deadliest war in US history. It pitted the 23 states of the Union against the 11 secessionist states of the South (Confederacy). The northern states had a population of 21 million as against nine million of the south (of whom around four million were slaves). The north also had an edge in every field – manpower, industry, armed forces strength, commercial and financial resources. Over the next few years many battles were fought between the two armies; some of the more famous are Fort Donelson, Second Bull Run, Antietam, Stones River, Shiloh, Chancellorsville, Spotsylvania Court House, Chickamauga and Gettysburg. The war effectively ended with the capture of Confederate President Jefferson Davis on 10 May 1865, although some Confederate troops continued to fight for a few more weeks.

With regards to the casualties suffered by both sides, *Britannica.com* notes: 'Traditionally, historians have put war deaths at about 3,60,000 for the Union and 2,60,000 for the Confederates. In the second decade of the 21st Century, however, a demographer used better data and more sophisticated tools to convincingly revise the total death toll upward to 7, 27,000 and indicated that it could be as high as 8,51,0000... roughly 2 percent of the 1860 US population dead in the war...'[5]

This was indeed a 'transitional war' bridging the gap between the so called 'old-fashioned wars' and 'modern wars'. There were several firsts in this war. Once again to quote *Britannica.com*:

It was the *first* in history in which *ironclad* warships clashed; the *first* in which telegraphs and railroad played significant roles; the *first* to use extensively, rifled ordnance and shell guns and to introduce the machine gun (the Gatling gun); the *first* to have widespread newspaper coverage, voting by servicemen in the field in national elections, and photographic recordings; the *first* to organize medical care of troops systematically; and the *first* to use land and water mines and to employ a submarine that could sink a warship. It was also the *first* war in which armies widely employed aerial reconnaissance (by means of balloons)[6]

The above overview of the US Civil War is to give a backdrop to the Battle of Gettysburg, which was fought roughly half way through the Civil War, from 1 to 3 July 1863.

UNION AND CONFEDERATE ARTILLERY

In the mid-nineteenth century the artillery was still evolving as an arm of decision. The formulation of artillery organizational structures, chain of command and principles of employment were in the transitional stage. Philip Cole states that each army's artillery branch entered the war with little or nothing in the way of adequate manpower levels, trained officers, equipment necessities and a reliable organization.[7] There was also no previous experience of artillery employment at the scale that the Civil War battles were going to be fought. While the Union (or Federal) Army did have a functional artillery branch, the Confederates had to start from scratch to form a structural artillery organization as the war commenced. However, by the end of the Civil War the artillery of both sides had indeed transformed into a battle-winning arm.

FEDERAL (UNION) ARTILLERY OF THE UNITED STATES

The US government had an advantage in as much that it already had a standing army. Though small in numbers, the Union army had a proper organizational structure, was well equipped and had a trained manpower of officers and men. Its main challenge was to quickly expand and transform into a wartime mode.

Its Artillery branch was however quite small and not suited to large scale operations which were to unfold during the Civil War. Fortunately for the Union, most of the foundries, factories and other manufacturing resources were located in its territory, making it easier to equip the artillery batteries with guns, carriages and ammunition. In his book, *Civil War Artillery At Gettysburg*, Philip M Cole notes : 'While the North (Union) enjoyed a superior capacity for making Artillery pieces and projectiles, there was even greater difference with the South (Confederacy) in production capacity for making gunpowder. In the North many pre-civil war powder mills were already in place within its territory; existing facilities were due to the high demand for gunpowder's use in civilian development'.[8]

In spite of the above-mentioned advantages enjoyed by the Federal Army, its Ordnance Department which was responsible for procuring, distributing, maintaining and repairing ordnance and ordnance stores, as well as developing and testing new types of ordnance, was found wanting. In fact the Joint Select Congressional Committee on Ordnance, formed after the end of the Civil War, found several deficiencies in its performance.

At the functional level, the Union Artillery was organized into batteries, and brigades. Each battery was composed of six guns, and five such batteries formed a brigade (of 30 Cannons). Typically one artillery brigade was assigned to an infantry corps (there were seven of these which fought at Gettysburg), two brigades were allotted to the cavalry corps, while five brigades formed the general artillery reserve.

CONFEDERATE ARTILLERY

Whereas the Union already had a permanent army, the Confederacy started to establish its own army as the prospects of a war became imminent. So also was the case with its artillery organization which continued to evolve during the early years of the Civil War. It faced great difficulty in equipping the fledgling Army, and especially its artillery. As a compared to the North, it had negligible resources. Cole writes that 'Without the plentiful resources and foundries to manufacture artillery pieces like those in the North, the southern government faced great difficulties in equipping its artillery branch'.[9]

He further writes that : 'As secession spread, the Confederate government seized the Federal navy yards at Norfolk, Virginia, and Pensacola, Florida. Even though hundreds of cannons were captured, almost none were suitable as field pieces. Ultimately there were three main sources of arms for the Confederate army: those manufactured in the Confederacy; those captured as result of operations against Federal armies; and those that were imported. Private foundries, such as the Tredegar Iron Works in Richmond, expanded or converted from peacetime enterprises to making sorely needed artillery pieces. The rapid transition produced deficiencies in artillery weapons, often beyond control of the foundries. "Bad Iron" or inferior raw materials were blamed for the barrel failure by some'.[10] Thus, the Confederate artillery was disadvantaged not only by inferiority in numbers, but also poor quality equipment.

Inspite of the inadequacies mentioned above, the Ordnance Bureau of the Confederate War Department played a very positive role in ensuring the manufacture and supply of guns, ammunition and allied equipment to their army. The Chief of Confederate Ordnance, Josiah Gorgas organized many arsenals, powder mills and foundries to meet the demands of the quickly expanding army.

Organizationally the Confederate artillery differed from the Union, in that it organized itself into batteries and battalions (rather than brigades). Also, its battery consisted of four guns as against six in the Union artillery battery; this configuration was borne more out of necessity since the Confederates did not have an adequate number of guns. Also some of batteries were equipped with guns of mixed calibre. Although one of the reasons was the scarcity of equipment, the other was that quite often captured Union guns were handed over in a random manner to the Confederate batteries. Four batteries formed an artillery battalion (of sixteen guns), one battalion was allocated to an infantry division and one to the cavalry corps. Each infantry corps was also allotted one 'Artillery Reserve' consisting of two artillery battalions, i.e. 32 guns. A major failing in the Confederate army was that it did not have any dedicated Artillery Reserve at the disposal of the Army Commander, since all its artillery batteries and battalions were already allotted to various formations; in contrast, the Union Army of the Potomac had an independent Artillery Reserve of five brigades, which was almost one-third of its total artillery. This Reserve was used decisively in the Battle of Gettysburg.

For details of Union and Confederate Artillery, please see Tables 2.1, 2.2 and Appendices A and B.

ARTILLERY GUNS

The type of artillery guns employed in the Battle of Gettysburg can be classified in different ways[11]. The first is by the design of barrel, i.e. Smoothbores and Rifled guns. The smoothbores were so called, because the inner surface of the barrel was smooth. On the other hand the Rifled guns had spiral grooves running down the length of the barrel. These grooves imparted a spin to the projectile as it left the barrel thereby imparting stability during its flight. The Rifled Guns also had greater range as compared to the Smoothbores. The second classification was that of Howitzers and Cannons. The Howitzers in use during the Civil War were generally short barreled guns which mostly fired hollow shells. [11]

The range of the various artillery pieces employed in the Battle of Gettysburg at five-degrees elevation is given at Appendix C.

AMMUNITION

There were four types of ammunition which wasused in this battle; the selection of type of projectile depended upon the type of target and the terrain. These four types were:

(a) Shot. The shot was a solid projectile or cannonball

TABLE 2.1 : ARMY OF THE POTOMAC ARTILLERY ORGANISATION*

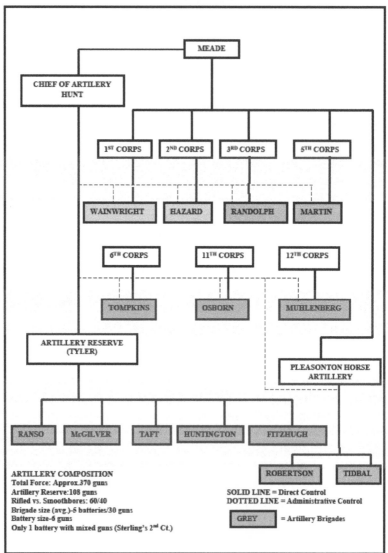

ARTILLERY COMPOSITION
Total Force: Approx.370 guns
Artillery Reserve:108 guns
Rifled vs. Smoothbores: 60/40
Brigade size (avg.)-5 batteries/30 guns
Battery size-6 guns
Only 1 battery with mixed guns (Sterling's 2ⁿᵈ Ct.)

SOLID LINE = Direct Control
DOTTED LINE = Administrative Control

GREY = Artillery Brigades

* Note: Sourced from Philip M. Cole, Civil War Artillery at Gettysburg, Colecraft Industries, Orrtanna, 2002, p.69.

TABLE 2.2 ARMY OF NORTH VIRGINIA
ARTILLERY ORGANIZATION*

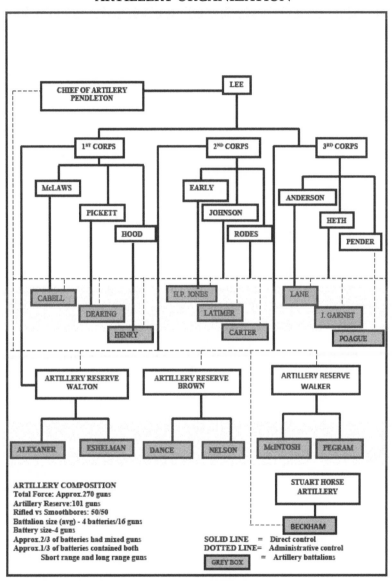

* Note: Sourced from Philip M. Cole, *Civil War Artillery at Gettysburg*, Colecraft Industries, Orrtanna, 2002, p.70.

which was used to the have a 'battering' effect or the enemy defences. Due to its weight and high kinetic energy, it was ideal against guns, limbers, caissons, wagons etc.

(b) Case Shot (Also referred to as Shrapnel). This was an explosive projectile, loaded with lead or iron balls, and designed to explode in the air just above the target; a 12-pounder case shot had as many as seventy eight balls. Upon bursting, it showered down its small pieces with telling effect. Its bursting noise and flash had a very unsettling effect on men and horses.

(c) Shell. Like the case shot, this too was an explosive projectile; however it was less lethal than the former due to fact that upon bursting it broke up into much fewer pieces.

(d) Cannister. This round was a metal cannister in which a large number of lead or iron balls were packed in sawdust. It was a close range ammunition, effective upto four hundred yards; beyond that range the dispersal of balls did little damage. It was indeed a very potent and deadly ammunition. In his book *Civil War Artillery Gettysburg,* Cole writes:

Cannister was the deadliest kind of artillery ammunition. It did not explode when fired; when it left the barrel the balls packed within broke and disintegrated the metal wrapping... When flung out of the barrel, the load spread the widest path of destruction of any ammunition. Adding to this ammunition's lethality, cannister rounds could be loaded and fired more rapidly since aiming was almost unnecessary; and gun crews did not have to contend with fuze preparations ...[12]

GUN DETACHMENTS

A typical gun system consisted of an artillery piece, limber and caisson. A limber was a two-wheeled support vehicle, containing one ammunition chest, that pulled an artillery piece or a caisson or other support vehicle. A caisson was also a two wheeled support vehicle, which contained two ammunition chests and a spare wheel, pulled by a limber and accompanying the artillery piece. Typically, each artillery piece had two limbers and one caisson. While one six-gun horse team pulled the gun hitched to a limber, another such team pulled a limber – caisson combination. Each ammunition chest could carry about 500 pounds of ammunition or supplies. Typically, a gun crew consisted of nine gunners, though they were often understaffed.

PRELUDE TO THE GETTYSBURG CAMPAIGN

The seeds of the Gettysburg campaign were sown two months earlier at Chancellorsville. It was here that between 2 and 4 May 1863, Lee had decisively defeated Lieutenant General Joseph Hooker's Army of the Potomac. Although Lee would spend the next few weeks reorganizing his army, many options for future operations had been thrown up after this victory. Lee's army could either be moved westward towards Mississippi (and Vicksburg), or to Tennessee (both of which were Confederate territories embroiled with Union Forces), or to take the battle into the enemy camp by launching an invasion of Pennsylvania; Lee favoured the latter option. In his book *The Battle of Gettysburg* written over a century ago, Jesse Bowman Young has analyzed the reasons which prompted Lee to undertake this second invasion of Pennsylvania (the first having ended the previous September in Antietam). A *summary* of what he writes is given below:

(1) 'One of the distinctive aims of General Lee, as indicated in his first report of the campaign (dated July 31, 1863, official *Records, XXVIII, 2:305*, was to place, if possible, the Army of the Potomac in such straits by his advance that the authorities at Washington would be led to "draw to its support troops designed to operate against other parts of the country".

(2) The hope of securing by a victorious campaign on Northern Soil the recognition of the Confederacy by England and France, was a distinctive element in the campaign.

(3) It was, of course, in Lee's mind by his proposed campaign, to relieve for the time being war-worn Virginia from the burdens she had been bearing for two years...

(4) A further reason urging Lee to undertake an offensive policy is to be found in the scarcity of food supplies in the South, occasioned by the partial collapse of the whole system of railroad transportation in that section... A little over hundred miles to the north from Fredericksburg were the bountiful harvest-fields of Pennsylvania, her full granaries, her farms with their stock of horses and cattle, and - this was

a point to be heeded - her towns and cities with an ample
supply of boots and shoes.

(5) The political and financial situation in the North, in 1863
inspired Lee and his generals, as well as the Confederate
authorities, with hope. Dissensions were prevalent in the
United States; and here and there men openly advocated
the doctrine that the war was a hopeless enterprise, that the
Union could never be restored, and that it would be better
to agree upon a treaty of peace with the South and let the
Confederacy by common consent be established... under
these circumstances it was hoped on the part of the South
that a crushing defeat administered upon the Union Forces on
Northern Soil... would... ensure the success of the factions
which were opposing Mr Lincoln's administration and
advocating peace at any cost....

(6) ...Gen. A.L. Long, Lee's military secretary, in his
Memories of Lee, indicates that one aim in the campaign
was to frustrate the Union advance to Richmond (the capital
of the Confederacy - author), and delay at least for a time
the attack on that city... Long further writes that Lee felt
'...that the Federal Army, if defeated in the pitched battle,
would be seriously disorganized and forced to retreat across
the Susquehanna River [in case the engagement occurred
in the neighbourhood of York or Harrisburg or possibly
Gettysburg], an event which would give him control of
Maryland and western Pennsylvania, and probably of West
Virginia...

(7) A further element... was the almost contemptuous estimate
which the Southern leader and his officers and men had come
to cherish concerning the fighting ability of the Army of the
Potomac and the skill of its successive commanders"[13]

The afore-mentioned detailed analysis by Jesse Bowman
Young clearly indicates a combination of factors–
military, political, diplomatic and economic–which led
to the Confederate invasion of the North, culminating
in the bloodiest combat of the Civil War in and around
the town of Gettysburg.

REORGANIZATION OF THE ARMY OF NORTH VIRGINIA

Up to the Battle of Chancellorsville, Lee's Army had consisted of two infantry corps [1st Corps, (five divisions) under Lieutenant General James Longstreet and 2nd Corps (four divisions) under Lieutenant General T.J. 'Stonewall' Jackson], besides the Cavalry Corps under Major General J.E.B Stuart. Unfortunately, Lee lost his ablest and best-known general, 'Stonewall' Jackson at Chancellorsville, when he was accidently shot by his own troops and succumbed to his injuries a few days later. Lee now decided to reorganize his infantry into three corps, each comprising three divisions. Retaining Longstreet as the commander of 1st Corps, Lee promoted Major Generals Richard S. Ewell and Ambrose P. Hill to head the re-organised 2nd and 3rd Corps respectively. The re-organisation of these Corps entailed a re-distribution of troops including re-shuffling some brigades and divisions, as well as appointing new brigade commanders to make up losses at Chancellorsville. This re-organisation, barely a month before Gettysburg battle, did not allow the troops to settle down to the new commands.

At the same time a re-organisation of artillery was also carried out on both sides. On the Confederate side, the general Artillery Reserve was done away with, and batteries were re-distributed to form artillery battalions - four guns to a battery, and four batteries to a battalion. Five Battalions were allotted to each corps at the scale of one per division (three division in all), and two to the corps reserve. A Corps Chief of Artillery was designated to coordinate the employment of these battalions. In addition, six batteries of 'horse artillery' were allotted to Stuart's Cavalry Corps. The erstwhile Chief of Lee's Artillery Reserve, Brigadier General William N. Pendleton was now appointed as Chief of Artillery of the Army of North Virginia. He, however, did not have any 'unattached' artillery resources (in the form of reserves) under his direct authority (unlike his counter-part in the Union Army of the Potomac). This handicap greatly constrained his actions later at Battle of Gettysburg.

The Union Army of the Potomac too re-organised its artillery, but somewhat differently. It organised five batteries (of six guns each) into artillery brigades, allotting one brigade per Corps. However, they also created an 'unattached' Artillery Reserve of five brigades of four batteries each; this asset of 108 guns (some batteries had less guns) was under the direct control of its Chief of Artillery, Brigadier General Henry Hunt and was to play a decisive role at Gettysburg. In addition, forty four guns of 'horse artillery' (i.e. eight batteries divided into two brigades) were allotted to Major General Alfred Pleasanton's Cavalry Corps.

PRELIMINARY MOVES

General Lee's invasion army set out towards Pennsylvania on 3 June 1863 through the Shenandoah and Cumberland valleys, with a view to reach the Susquehanna near York and Harrisburg, posing a credible threat to the northern cities of Baltimore and Washington. With this turning movement around General Hooker's forces, he hoped to draw the Union Army of the Potomac into the battle and defeat it. With this crushing defeat, it was hoped that the North would sue for peace.

Ewell's 2nd Corps was in the lead, with Longstreet's 1stCorps and Hills 3rd Corps following. By 8 June, the former two corps had concentrated near Culpeper, while Hill was left to hold position at Fredericksburg in order to mask the Confederate infantry movement from Hooker. On 10 June, the largest cavalry engagement of the war took place between the opposing armies at Brandy Station. Unsure of Lee's future intentions (or his movements), Hooker had sent Brigadier General Pleasanton's cavalry force to carry out a reconnaissance across the Rappahannock river. The sudden appearance of the Northern cavalry took Stuart by surprise, and there ensued a major battle between the two sides. Although forced to retreat, Pleasanton's forces conducted themselves very well and in fact 'came into their own'. This skirmish also alerted Hooker about Lee's northern movement.

Lee recommenced his forward movement through the Shenandoah Valley on 11 June, with Ewell's 2nd Corps in the lead. Capturing the garrisons of Winchester and Martinsburg enroute, Ewell crossed the Potomac at Williamsport on 15 June and reached the area of Chambersburg, Pennsylvania on 25 June. Having got wind of Lee's movement after the clash at Brandy Station, Hooker had also started his northward movement on 11 June, crossing the Potomac river at Frederick City between 25 / 26 June. Meanwhile, Stuart's Cavalry Corps which was supposed to shield Lee's movement from Hooker, somehow moved further east, thus placing Hooker between Lee and Stuart. Meanwhile due to difference of opinion with Gen Halleck, the General-in-Chief of the Union Army, Hooker offered his resignation on 28 June, which was immediately accepted. He was replaced by Major General. George G. Meade as the new commander of the Army of the Potomac. Meade immediately ordered his army to move towards the Susquehanna river, with a view to prevent Lee's force from crossing it. Both the armies were now marching northwards, in order to reach favorable positions for the ensuing battle. At that point of time neither side had envisioned a battle at Gettysburg. In their book *the Civil War in the United States,* W. Birbeck Wood and Brigadier General Sir James Edmonds write:

Neither Lee nor Meade originally planned to fight at Gettysburg. Both desired a defensive battle, Lee at Cashtown, eight miles west of Gettysburg, and Meade on Pipe Creek (a tributary of the Monocacy river), ten or twelve miles east... Behind this stream, Meade proposed to make his stand, if as he was inclined to anticipate, Lee came from the south from the Susquehanna to attack Baltimore. Close in his rear he would have Parr's Ridge which would secure his retreat in case of defeat in the same way as South Mountain secured Lee's. He was not, however, any more than Lee irrevocably committed to a defensive. He was prepared to take the offensive, if a favourable opportunity offered. Two forced marches had brought the Federal left wing near Lee's main body on the evening of the 30th June, and chance made Gettysburg the battlefield.[14]

The Order of Battle (ORBAT) of the Union Army of the Potomac and the Army of North Virginia is given in Appendix D.

UNION AND CONFEDERATE POSITIONS:
30 JUNE 1863

On the eve of the battle, i.e. on 30 June 1863, the general dispositions of the Union and Confederate armies is as given below.[15]

UNION ARMY OF THE POTOMAC

* HQ of Major General George C. Meade	- Tanneytown
* HQ of Major General John F. Reynolds (Over all Commander of 1st, 3rd & 11th Corps)	- Marsh Run; troops located between Marsh Run and Bridgeport (near Emmetsburg)
* 5th Corps	- Union Mills (east of Tanney town)
* 2nd Corps	- Uniontown (south of Tanney town)
* 6th Corps	- Manchester
* 12th Corps	- Littletown (south - east of Gettysburg)
* Cavalry troops	- Located at various points on the flanks; Buford's Division after conducting a reconnaissance-in-force, and having located the Confederate Forces, was in Gettysburg.

CONFEDERATE ARMY OF NORTH VIRGINIA

* HQ of Lieutenant General Robert Lee	- Greenwood.
* Hill's Corps	- Cashtown.
* Ewell's Corps	- On the way from Carlisle to wards Cashtown (along with Rhode's division)
* Longstreet's Corps	- Near Chambersburg (along with Johnston's Division of Ewell's Corps).
* Stuart's Cavalry Corps	- After the battle with Kirkpatrick at Hanover, were on the move towards Carlisle.

TOPOGRAPHY OF THE BATTLEFIELD AREA

The area of Gettysburg is shown in Map 1. Gettysburg is a city located in Pennsylvania. The city had a 'spoke and wheel' configuration on account of a large number of roads converging from virtually all directions. In the words of Mackubin Thomas Owens: 'A glance at the map of south-central Pennsylvania records that "all roads lead" to Gettysburg. The town resembles the hub of a wheel with spokes converging from all directions...'[16] There were 10 roads which connected Gettysburg with nearby towns in Pennsylvania and Maryland (the state line with Maryland was barely 10 miles away.) The roads converging into Gettysburg were:

(a)	From the north	- Carlisle Road.
(b)	From the north-east	- Harrisburg Road.
(c)	From the east	- Bonaughtown Road and York Pike.
(d)	From the south	- Emmitsburg Road, Tanney town Road and Baltimore Pike.
(e)	From the south-west	- Hagerstown / Fairfield Road.
(f)	From the north-west	- Chambersburg Pike.
(g)	From the north-north-west	- Mummasburg Road.

Astride these roads were many hill features, knolls and ridges which provided natural defence lines. To the west of the town

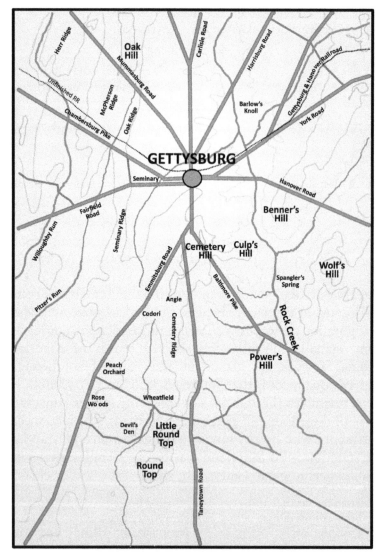

Map 1: The Area Around Gettysburg

Note : Adapted from the Map by Hal Jespersen, www.cwmaps.com.

flowed the Willoughby Run through two ridgelines; the one to its east (towards Gettysburg) was the Seminary Ridge. Towards the north-west of this ridge, were the McPherson Ridge, Herr Ridge and Oak Hill. In the north-east lay Barlow's Knoll. To the south of the town was an interesting configuration of hilly features in the shape of a 'fish hook'. Starting from in the south and going towards the north were Round Top, Little Round Top, Cemetery Ridge and Cemetery Hill, after which the ridge turned east towards Culp's Hill, thereby giving it the 'hook' shape. To the west of Little Round Top was Devil's Den, and further (along the Emmitsburg road) lay Rose Woods and Peach Orchard. All these were to become the battlefield points in the coming three days, i.e. 1 to 3 July, 1863.

THE FIRST DAY: 1 JULY 1863

INFANTRY OPERATIONS

Before coming to the events of 1 July 1863, it needs to be reiterated that even upto the 30 June, neither of the two commanders had envisaged Gettysburg as the site of the battle. Lee had all along looked at the area around Cashtown as the place he intended to give battle to Meade. With the mountains protecting his rear, the woods and rolling hills affording good defensive positions and a road of retreat (were it to occur) leading towards Chambersburg, Lee was inclined to lure Meade to attack him and then defeat him piecemeal. On the other hand, Meade favoured giving battle near the Pine Creek Line. It was however a chance sighting of Confederate Forces by Buford's Cavalry the evening before, that lead to the commencement of the battle on 1 July 1863 (See Map 2).

Buford's force, which had been tasked to cover the left of the Union Army, made its way towards Gettysburg in order to locate the reported movement of the Confederate army. He reached Gettysburg in the afternoon where he encountered Pettigrew's advance elements (the North Carolina Brigade) who were about to enter the town looking for boots and other supplies. Although the Confederates withdrew, both sides were now aware of each other's positions and information was accordingly passed on to their respective Corps Commanders (Hill and Reynolds). Buford (with around 3,500 Cavalry) decided to occupy the ridges on the west of Gettysburg, till the arrival of reinforcements from Reynold's corps. It was in the

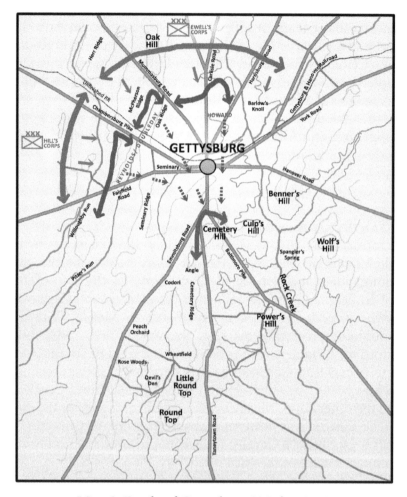

Map 2: Battle of Gettysburg (1 July 1863)
Note : Adapted from the Map by Hal Jespersen, www.cwmaps.com.

early morning of 1 July, around 5.30 a.m, that Heth's Division (of Hills Corps) clashed with Buford's Cavalry deployed on McPherson's Ridge; the cavalry had taken up *dismounted* positions on the ridge. In his article *the Great Battle of Gettysburg*, Mackubin Thomas Owens, narrates that, 'Heth's Divisions deployed from column into line and advanced against Buford's dismounted troops on McPherson's Ridge. Despite being outnumbered the cavalrymen, armed with repeating carbines, were able to deliver a high volume of fire and gave ground only grudgingly'[17]. These cavalrymen then fell back towards Seminary Ridge. Meanwhile, Major General John F Reynolds of 1st Corps (having been alerted of the Confederate troops by Buford), arrived with reinforcements. Unfortunately, he was killed early in the battle by a snipers bullet. His 1st Corps had occupied positions along Seminary Ridge and adjoining high ground. Hill's Corps continued to press its attack on the Union forces. Meanwhile, the Union 11th Corps had also arrived and taken up positions north of the town, where they were attacked by Ewell's Corps. In the afternoon the Union forces were attacked from the West as well as North, by Hills and Ewell's corps; the former against the flank of 1st Corps, and the latter against 11th Corps. The Union lines gave way and retreated towards the line of Culp's Hill, Cemetery Hill, and the Big and Little Round Top.

Then came a lull, which gave the Union forces time to dig in. Had the Confederate attack continued, it is possible that they could have defeated the Union forces. Lee, who had arrived at the edge of Gettysburg by late afternoon, did indeed sense this opportunity, and gave the senior of his two corps commanders, i.e.. Ewell, the orders to attack, but with a caveat 'if practicable'. This gave Ewell the discretion of whether or not to launch the offensive; in the event he chose not to press home the attack. What would have been the outcome of the Battle of Gettysburg, had the Confederate forces launched their attack, is debated to this day[18]. It was a missed opportunity.

Lee, however, had reason to be satisfied. His forces had got the better of two Union Corps (1st & 11th). Out of the 9000 casualties (including 3000 prisoners) of the Union forces, 1st Corps alone accounted for 5700 (of which 1500 were captured). One of the units, the 24th Michigan Regiment of the famous 'Iron Brigade' lost as many as 399 of its 496 soldiers - a very heavy price indeed[19]. Just by counting the number of troops engaged, the first day would rank as the 23rd biggest battle of the Civil War!

ARTILLERY OPERATION

When A.P. Hills 3rd Corps was ordered by Lee to move forward from the Fredericksburg area, Heth's Division was in the lead followed by Pender's Division. In a strange turn of events, since Heth lacked Cavalry, he ordered an artillery battalion to lead the advance - a task it is unsuited for! It was Captain Edward A. Marye's Fredericksburg Battery of Major William A. Pegram's artillery battalion which was in the forefront of the Confederate march towards Gettysburg, Upon reaching the outskirts in the west of the city, they encountered Buford's troops and had the distinction of firing the first rounds of the battle in the morning of 1 July. A two-gun section of Marye's battery was unlimbered and fired on Buford's Cavalry sending them scurrying for safety. Soon the Confederates deployed the five batteries of Pegram's artillery battalion (17 guns out of his 20) along Herr's Ridge; this was a mix of Napoleons, 12-Pounder howitzers as well as ordnance rifles.

On the Union side, the only artillery available to Buford was Lieutenant John H. Calef's 2nd US Battery, consisting of six ordnance rifles, which were deployed in two-gun sections over a 600 yards frontage along McPherson's Ridge. This was a very famous battery, having fought earlier in the Mexican War as well as many battles in the first two years of the Civil War; Gottfried notes that: 'It also had the distinction of being the first to play "Taps" at a military funeral[20]. It was Calef's battery which was the first artillery unit to open fire from the Union side. Although outnumbered by the 17 confederate guns, Calef's battery held its own and provided admirable support to Buford's Cavalry in the early skirmishes of the 1 July morning, until re-enforcement arrived. Buford was effusive in his praise of Calef; he noted in his report that: 'Lieutenant Calef, Second US Artillery, fought on this occasion as is seldom witnessed. At one time the enemy had a concentrate fire upon this battery from twelve guns, all at short range. Calef held his own gloriously, worked his guns deliberately with great judgment and skill, and with wonderful effect upon the enemy"[21].

As the skirmishing progressed, both sides received additional artillery. On the Confederate side, it was Captain Thomas Brander's Letcher Virginia Battery, consisting of two Napoleon and two 10-Pounder Parrotts; this battery was essentially composed of men from Richmond's notorious Castle Thunder prison. They quickly opened fire on the Union troops, and in turn were engaged by Calef's guns. On the Union side, Captain James A Hall's 2nd Maine Battery (of 1st Corps) joined the fray and immediately swung into action by engaging Pegram's battalions. Gottfried writes: 'Hall observed that the first six shots fired at Pegram's battalion were exceptionally accurate, causing two of the enemy's pieces to take cover of a nearby barn. The battery continued banging away at Pegram's artillery for what Hall thought to be about 25 minutes'[22].

It was then that he saw the approaching Confederate infantry (42nd Mississippi) very close to his position. He immediately engaged them with cannister, causing them to spread out to avoid causalities: This battery came under another attack from the right, injuring some of his men and horses. He immediately ordered his guns to fire double-shotted cannister on to the advancing infantry, causing them to break the attack. Most of the morning it was Hall (from McPherson's Ridge) and Calef (from Seminary Ridge) who continued to engage the Confederate infantry as well as artillery positions. Around mid-day, Colonel Charles S. Wainright arrived with four batteries (22 pieces); his fifth battery (Hall) was already there. On the Confederate side, Major David McIntosh arrived on the scene with his artillery battalion (3rd Corps artillery reserve) consisting of four batteries (16 guns). Amongst these guns, were two Whiteworth guns of Hurt's battery which were really deadly in fire; these were the latest technology weapons which had been imported from England.

Although now built up to a fairly reasonable strength, the Confederates did not use this artillery decisively in the morning of 1 July. In his book, Gottfried notes that military historian Jennings Wise is very critical of the artillery employment since he feels that the thirty-three guns of Pegram's and McIntosh's battalions, 'though well up, were unable to gain positions from which to prepare the attack before Heth launched his brigades, and batteries were left to act as best as the could without any definitive plan or objective,.... He further states that: 'Wise (a Confederate historian - author) believed that had the 3rd Corps commander A.P. Hill placed and utilized his artillery to its best advantage, the guns could have smashed Buford's cavalry before Reynolds 'infantry arrived'[23]. Once again it was an opportunity lost.

In the early stages the Union artillery was not employed fruitfully. It is reported that there was difference of opinion between Colonel Wainright and his infantry commanders. Whereas the infantry wanted the batteries to support their troops, the artillery officers preferred counter-battery action. It was really a matter of conflicting priorities which was soon put right.

Meanwhile, the Confederate's Pender's division had launched their attack towards Seminary Ridge. This advance was met with heavy fire from the eighteen guns amassed along a thousand-yards line. The federal guns initially held their fire as their own infantry withdrew in the wake of the advancing enemy, and then opened up with all their guns when they were just 100 yards away. An artillery officer is quoted: 'Almost at the same moment, as if every lanyard was pulled by the same hand, this line of artillery opened, and Seminary Ridge blazed with a solid sheet of flame, and the missiles of death that swept its western slopes no human beings could endure'[24]. One gun is reported to have *fired as many as fifty - seven rounds in a matter of moments* (italics by author).

In the afternoon, Rode's Division of Lieutenant General Ewell's 2nd Corps arrived and took up positions north of Oak Hill. He had brought with him Lieutenant Colonel Thomas Carter's artillery battalion (four batteries comprising sixteen guns). They quickly opened fire on McPherson's Ridge to their south causing the enemy infantry to change positions. The Federal artillery quickly responded by firing on Carter's guns. In the late afternoon, Early's Division also arrived on the scene, and quickly his artillery too went into action. In the remaining daylight hours, both sides' artillery played a dominant role in support of their respective forces. Soon the Union troops had to retreat from Oak Ridge towards Cemetery Ridge.

During the first day's battle, the ten batteries of the Union 1st and 11th corps, lost eighty three men and eight officers killed or wounded. The Confederates also captured three federal guns and disabled seven. Although the artillery of both sides remained in action throughout the day, it was the Confederate's who performed better. In this regard, Gottfried writes : 'Overall, July 1 was not a good day for Federals, particularly their artillery. In the absence of their chief, Brigadier General Henry Hunt, the infantry commanders exercised undue influence on the batteries, often placing them in untenable positions for the sole purpose of supporting the infantry. According to two historians, there was "little coordination, no choice of terrain, no cross-fire". This would change with the arrival of Hunt later that evening.[25]

THE SECOND DAY: 2 JULY 1863

SITUATION

Even as the first days battle was being fought, the remaining infantry of both sides continued their march towards Gettysburg; i.e. 2nd, 3rd, 5th, 6th and 12th Corps of the Union Army, and two of Longstreet's divisions of the Confederates (Pickett's Division was still further behind). Most of these troops were in position by the morning.

The Union line commenced from Round Top in the south and moved upward along Little Round Top, Cemetery Ridge, Cemetery Hill and then turning westwards to Culp Hill, before bending towards the southern slopes of this hill. It thus resembled a 'fish hook'. Along these ridges, South to North were deployed the union 3rd Corps (Sickles), 2[nd]Corps (Hancock), 11th Corps (Howard) 1st Corps (Newton) and 12th Corps (Slocum). Sykes' 5th Corps was roughly in the centre of this inverted 'U'. Before, the battle commenced on this day, Sickles decided to move his 3rd Corps forward to positions astride the Emmitsburg Road in the area of Wheat Field and Peach Orchard.

The Confederate forces, approximately one mile away

opposite the Union Line, were disposed as follows:

(a) Longstreet's 1st Corps – To the west of Emmitsburg Road, opposite Devil's Den, Wheat Field and Peach Orchard.

(b) AP Hill's 3rd Corps -Along the Seminary Ridge.

(c) Ewell's 2nd Corps – Opposite the area of Culp's Hill.

As can be seen from Map 3, the Union line had the advantage

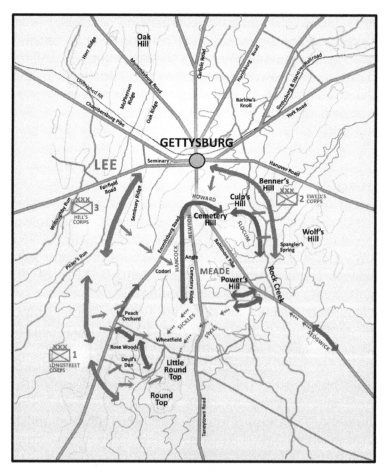

Map 3: Battle of Gettysburg (2 July 1863)

Note : Adapted from the Map by Hal Jespersen, www.cwmaps.com.

of operating under 'interior lines' giving it a great advantage over a much longer Confederate deployment, which was operating along 'exterior lines' with its attendant problems. Furthermore, in most places, the Confederate attacks would be 'up-hill'. In his first-hand account of the battle, Frank A. Haskell, who was a young officer in the Union 2nd Division of the 2nd Corps during this battle writes:

Our line was more elevated than that of the enemy; consequently our artillery had a greater range and power than theirs. On account of the convexity of our line, every part of the line could be re-enforced by troops having to move a shorter distance than if the line were straight; further, for the same reason, the line of the enemy must be concave, and consequently, longer, and with an equal force, thinner, and so weaker than ours. Upon those parts of our line which were wooded, neither we nor the enemy could use artillery; but they were so strong by nature, aided by art, as to be readily defended by a small, against a very large body of infantry. When the line was open, it had the advantage of having open country in front; consequently the enemy here could not surprise as we were on a crest, which besides the other advantages that I mentioned, had this: the enemy must advance to the attack up an ascent, and must therefore move slower and be, before coming upon us, longer under our fire, as well as more exhausted. These, and some other things, rendered our position admirable - for a defensive battle.[26]

Thus, before a great battle, was deployed the Army of the Potomac.

THE ATTACK COMMENCES

Lee, having tasted success on 1 July, had decided to renew his attack across the Union line the following day. His plan was to launch Longstreet's Corps on the left flank of the Union defences to work its way northward, with Hills' Corps attacking Cemetery Ridge from the west and Ewells Corps on to Culp's Hill from the north – east. Longstreet argued with Lee to move his army further south of Meade's line (towards Washington) and take up defences in order to get Meade to attack instead. Lee over-ruled him, However, although verbal orders had been given earlier, Lee finally gave orders to Longstreet around 11 a.m. as 2 July. Since his division was still not in position, Longstreet's attack got going only at 3 p.m. This delay gave time to Meade's army to re-adjust their defences. Had the

Confederate attack been launched in the morning as envisaged by Lee, it had a fair chance of success.

Hood and Mclaw's Divisions of Longstreet's Corps launched their attack on the left flank in the area of Little Round Top, Devil's Den, Wheat Field and Peach Orchard. While the Confederates managed to push the Union troops back from the latter three positions, Little Round Top held on. It was at Little Round Top that 20th Maine led by Colonel Joshua Chamberlain, launched their now famous counter-attack against the Confederates. With his troops running out of ammunition, he ordered them to fix bayonets and charge the surprised enemy, breaking up their attack and even capturing a few prisoners.

Meanwhile, a few hours later Hill's corps, followed in late evening, by Ewells Corps had also gone into action against the Union defences on Cemetery Ridge, Cemetery Hill and Culp's Hill. Although the Confederates did reach the Union line on the Cemetery Ridge, they were unable to take it. It was a question of 'so close and yet so far'. It was when the situation had become very precarious and re-enforcements were still on their way, that Hancock ordered 1st Minnesota to charge the enemy. In this suicidal charge, 1st Minnesota lost 215 men (killed and wounded) out of the 262 it had, i.e. 4/5th of its strength. It was a devastating loss, but the Union line held on.

At the end of the second day's fighting, although Lee's army had got the better measure of the Union forces, even capturing some ground on the Union flanks, he had not been able to defeat them. The delayed start of the attack, and piece-meal launch of his Corps denied him success. Had he launched his attacks simultaneously, all along the Union line early in the morning, the outcome could have been different.

ARTILLERY OPERATIONS

On the night of 1 July and the morning of 2 July, troops from both sides kept arriving on the battle field. On the Union side, the Artillery Chief Brigadier General Henry Hunt had arrived in the evening of 1 July, and immediately got involved in coordinating the deployment of federal artillery. Their artillery was deployed as follows:[27]

    (a) 1st Corps Artillery   - Culp's Hill

    (b) 12th Corps Artillery- South-west of 1st Corps position

    (c) 11th Corps Artillery   - Along Baltimore Pike

    (d) 3rd Corps Artillery   - South of the Federal line (Little Round Top, Wheat Field and Peach Orchard)

    (e) 2nd Corps Artillery   - In the centre of the Federal line, between 3rd and 11th Corps.

    (f) Reserve Artillery - Hunt supplemented the seventeen cannons of 11th Corps, by rushing thirty-two guns from his Artillery Reserve, taking the total in this area to forty nine. Thus, the Central Sector of the Cemetery Ridge was now a well-fortified artillery position, destined to play a key role on the final day. (The balance reserve was deployed in the area of Tanneytown Road).

The Confederate artillery had re-deployed as under:

    (a) 3rd Corps Artillery   - Along Seminary Ridge (generally west and opposite of Cemetery Hill)

    (b) 2nd Corps Artillery   - Their batteries were deployed in the north and north-west, facing Cemetery Hill and Culp's Hill from the north.

    (c) 1st Corps Artillery   - Longstreet's Corps was the last to arrive in the battlefield, and deployed in the south, opposite Sickle's 3rd Corps (which was in the area of Peach Orchard, Wheat Field, Devil's Den and the two Round Tops).

With both sides now in position, the die was cast for the actions of 2 July. With interior lines of communication, Hunt's artillery was well placed to take on any attack both from the north and west. They were somewhat weak in the south due to Sickle's Corps having moved forward towards the Chambersburg Pike. But the ratio of fire power had now clearly shifted in favour of the Union Army of the Potomac, who had a superiority in the number of cannon now deployed in the battlefield.

Just prior to Longstreet's attack being launched, the Confederate artillery opened fire with a view to soften the enemy positions, as also direct counter-battery fire on the Federal artillery. The latter soon replied in kind. In this artillery battle, Gottfried writes: 'Eleven Confederate batteries sporting forty-eight guns battled ten Federal batteries with fifty-six guns. Not only did the latter have numerical advantage, they also deployed more effective weapons - thirty four Napoleons, perfect for this type of fighting. While both sides suffered heavily, it appears that the Confederate took the worst beating... Most important, the Confederate long-arm had not achieved its mission: disabling and driving back the Federal artillery prior to the infantry attack. As a result, Confederate infantry losses mounted as they dashed across the open fields.[28]

In the battles in the Little Round Top, Devil's Den, Wheat Field and Peach Orchard area, the artillery batteries of both sides played a key role in support of their infantry. As mentioned, in this phase of attack the Confederates employed forty-eight guns (eleven batteries) as against the union's fifty – six guns (ten batteries); the latter once again had a technological edge in the form of employing thirty four superior Napoleons vis-a-vis only eleven such cannon of the confederates. It is not possible to detail the actions of so many batteries, but Gottfried has a fulsome account of such actions in his book *the Artillery of Gettysburg*. He notes that Colonel E. P. Alexander (the 1st Corps Artillery Reserve Commander) has been criticized for not employing *all* available artillery. Haskell gives a very interesting account of the Confederates action against 3rd Corps:

The enemy opened slowly at first, and from long range; but he was square upon Sickle's left flank...

As the enemy opened fire upon Sickles with his batteries, some five or six in all, I suppose, firing slowly, Sickles with as many replied and with much more spirit. The artillery fire became quite animated, soon; but the enemy was forced to withdraw his guns farther and farther away, and ours advanced upon him. It was not long before the cannonade ceased altogether, the enemy having retired out of range, and Sickles, having temporarily halted his command, pending this, moved forward again to the position he desired, or nearly that. It was now about five o'clock, and we shall soon see what Sickles gained by this move.

First we hear more artillery firing upon Sickle's left-the enemy seems to be opening again, and as we watch the Rebel batteries seem to be advancing there. The cannonade is soon opened again, and with great spirit upon both sides. The enemy's batteries press those of Sickles, and pound the shot upon them, and this time they in turn begin to retire to positions nearer the infantry. The enemy seems to be fearfully in earnest this time. And what is more ominous than the thunder or the shot of his advancing guns, this time, in the intervals of his batteries, far to Sickles left, appear long lines and the columns of Rebel infantry, now unmistakably moving out into the attack. The position of Third Corps becomes at once of great peril, and it is probable that its commander by this time began to realize his true situation.

All was astir now on our crest. Generals and their staffs were galloping hither and thither - the men were all in their places, and you might have heard the rattle of ten thousand ramrods as they drove home and "thugged" upon the little globes and cones of lead. As the enemy was advancing upon Sickles flank, he commenced a change, or at least a partial one, of front, by swinging back his left and throwing forward his right, in order that his lines might be parallel to those of his adversary, his batteries meantime doing what they could do to check the enemy's advance; but this movement was not completely executed before new Rebel batteries opened upon Sickle's right flank - his former front - and in the same quarter appeared the Rebel infantry also.

Now came the dreadful battle picture, of which we for a time could be but spectators. Upon the front and right flank of Sickles came sweeping the infantry of Longstreet and Hill. Hitherto there had been skirmishes and artillery practice - now the battle began; heavier smoke and larger tongues of flame of the batteries, now began to appear the countless flashes and the long fiery sheets of the muskets, and the rattle of the volleys, mingled with the thunder of guns. We see the long grey - lines come sweeping down upon Sickle's front, and mix with the battle smoke; now the same colours emerge from the bushes and orchards upon his right, and envelope his flank in the confusion of the conflict.[29]

With the withdrawal of Sickle's 3rd Corps from his forward positions, the focus shifted towards Cemetery Ridge (2nd Corps), Cemetery Hill (11th Corps) as well as later in the evening on Culp's Hill (12th Corps). In each of these battles the artillery batteries of both sides were used with devastating effect. Each side suffered many casualties of men and material, much of it by cannon shells.

With Sickles 3rd Corps having withdrawn, the Confederates continued their attack on to 2nd Corps. Once again, the Union artillery came into play. In his eye-witness account, Haskell notes:

The whole slope in our front is full of them; and in various formations, in line, in column, and in masses which are neither, with yells and thick volleys, they are rushing towards our crest. The Third Corps is out of the way.

Now we are in for it. The battery men are ready by their loaded guns. All along the crest is ready. Now Arnold and Brown - now Cushing, and Woodruff and Rosy- you three shall survive today! They drew the cords that moved the friction primers, and gun after gun, along the batteries, is rapid succession, leaped where it stood and bellowed its canister upon the enemy. The enemy still advances. The infantry open fire - first the two advance regiments, the 15th Mass and 82nd NY- then here and there throughout the length of the long line, at the points where the enemy comes nearest and soon the whole crest, artillery and infantry, is one continued sheet of fire. From Round Top to near the Cemetery stretches an uninterrupted field of conflict. There is a great army upon each side, now wholly engaged.

To see the fight, while it went on in the Valley below us (against Sickle's 3rd Corps –author), was terrible - what must it be now, when we are all in it, and it is all around us in all its fury?

All senses for the time being are dead but one of sight. The roar of the discharges and the yells of the enemy all pass unheeded; but the impassioned soul has all eyes, and sees all things, that the smoke does not hide. How madly the battery men are driving home the double charges of cannister in those broad-mouth Napoleons, whose fire seems almost to reach the enemy.

...Lieutenant Brown is wounded among his guns - his position is a hundred yards in advance of the main line - the enemy is upon his battery, and he escapes, but leaves three of his six guns in the hands of the enemy.[30]

At sundown of 2 July, the Confederates and Federals got down to counting their losses, readjusting positions and getting ready for the next day's fighting. Amongst the many casualtiessuffered by both sides, were two senior officers - one from each side. Just as the Confederate Major General Hood launched his attack against Sickles 3rd Corps in the south, an Artillery shell exploded above him sending fragments into his arm, injuring it so badly, that it had to be amputated later. He had to leave the field immediately and was succeeded by Brigadier General E.M. Law who proved largely ineffective. Later, the same day, Major General Sickles (3rd Corps Commander) was hit on the knee by a Confederate artillery solid shot; he too left the field and had his leg amputated!

3 JULY 1863: THE THIRD DAY

THE PLAN

Lee believed that his best chance now lay by attacking with force at the centre of the Union line by Longstreet's Corps, coupled with a demonstration by Ewell on its right flank at Culp's Hill. He also intended to employ Stuart's Cavalry Corps (which had finally arrived on the battle scene the evening before) to engage the Union's rear. For his main weight of the attack in the centre Lee had fresh troops in the form of Pickett's Division, and six additional brigades of Hill's Corps, i.e. Pettigrew's Division, two brigades of Pender's Division, as well as Anderson's brigade.

Early in the morning however, it was the Union which launched an attack against Johnson's Division at Culp's Hill on the right flank pushing him back. Lee had no option now but to concentrate his attack in the Centre. This was to be preceded by a heavy bombardment of Union positions on Cemetery Ridge by the Confederate artillery (See Map 4).

Writing about the difficulties of the attackers, Mackubin Thomas Owens notes in his article: 'The attackers would have to cross nearly 2000 yards under enemy fire. They would have to climb over a rail fence along the Emmitsburg Road, an obstacle that would be break the momentum of the attack. From that point, depending on where they crossed the Emmitsburg Road, the attacking Confederates would have to advance another 200 to 300 yards to reach the Union position. As they advanced, their ranks would be ripped apart by musket fire and artillery'[31].

THE INFANTRY ATTACK

This attack, now more famously known as Pickett's Charge (although it was launched by a total of nine brigades from different formations), began with the firing of the 'great cannonade' at 1 p.m. Around 150 to 170 Confederate guns opened up the artillery bombardment of Union positions and carried on for almost two hours. This was followed at 3 p.m., by the attack by the Confederate forces (numbering nine brigades). As the Confederate infantry closed on to the Cemetery Ridge, they were fired upon by Union Artillery followed by musket fire. The Confederate attack line which was in the open, were like dead ducks. Although men kept falling, the line kept moving and in fact Armistead's Brigade of Picket's Division even breached the Union defences. But with no reinforcements coming, they were forced to withdraw.

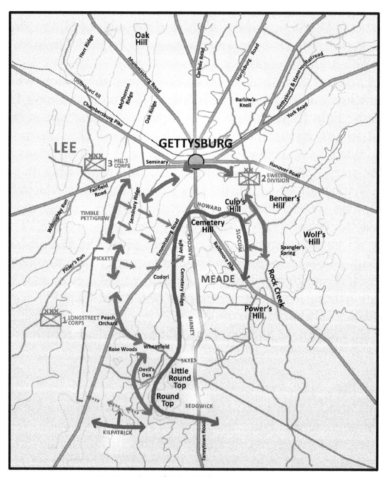

Map 4: Battle of Gettysburg (3 July 1863)
Note : Adapted from the Map by Hal Jespersen, www.cwmaps.com.

In this article in the Washington Post, Joel Achenbach sums ups this Confederate charge thus:

At the point of the spear would be a division led by the dashing General George Pickett. When Pickett asked, General, shall I advance? the despondent Longstreet could not speak. He could only nod his head.

At 3 p.m. the charge began. The men did not run. They marched, in a line roughly a mile long, almost as if performing a parade drill. At first, the Union soldiers held their fire.

Then the guns opened up - first the cannon, then the muskets. From Little Round Top came enfilading fire, Perhaps is an earlier age such an advance would have succeeded, but the weapon of the Civil War were more accurate and devastating, and the rebels were shredded. Some units reached the crest of the Cemetery Ridge and briefly pierced the Union line - the so-called High Water Mark of the Confederacy - but Federals proved too strong. Of 13,000 men who charged that ridge, half were killed, wounded or captured. All of Pickett's 15 regimental commanders were killed or wounded, as were three of his brigadier generals. When Pickett returned to the Confederate line, Lee told him to organize the division.

General Lee, I have no division now Picket said. Later in life, he would say bitterly that his division had been destroyed by Lee.

It was my fault Lee said as his men stumbled back to the rebel line.

That night, he was heard to say, "Too bad' 'Too bad' Too bad!" And the skies opened a torrential rain that washed away the blood into the soil.[32]

ARTILLERY OPERATIONS

The night of 2/3 July, as well as the next morning, was spent by both armies to replenishment of ammunition and readjustment of gun positions to prepare for the days battle. Lee's plan has already been mentioned above; the Confederate Artillery deployment was done in consonance with this plan.

Longstreet's 1st Corps artillery batteries were deployed along a thirteen-hundred yards front, extending from Peach Orchard in the south up to the area of Spangler's Wood on Seminary Ridge - a total of 83 guns. To his north were deployed the sixty guns of 3rd Corps artillery. Due to the terrain considerations, 2nd Corps had been able to deploy only thirty - three guns in support of the cannonade. The Confederate Artillery was essentially deployed in three distinct groups over a six-mile frontage, as compared to the Federal's line which was only half as long. Thus, not only did the latter have a better gun density (120 guns per mile as compared to Lee's 45 guns per mile), but their 'interior lines' gave them the benefit of easier and quicker enforcements and replacements. The Federal guns also had the advantage of being on higher ground.

The stage was now set for the massive preparatory bombardment, or the 'Great Cannonade' as it has been called. Brigadier General William Pendleton's instruction to his gunners was very clear: '...to give the enemy the most effective cannonade possible. It was not meant simply to make noise, but to try and cripple him – to tear him limbless, as it were, if possible;[33]

The Cannonade commenced with the firing of two 'signal guns' of Major Benjamin F. Eshleman's Washington Artillery Battalion of Longstreet's 1st Corps Reserve. As if on cue, more than 140 guns (some figures by different historians differ marginally) opened fire on the centre of the Federal line on Cemetery Ridge - the 'Great Cannonade' had begun. The Confederate guns aimed their fire on the Centre of the union line with devastating effect. In the words of a Federal gunner who was at the receiving end of this hail of shells: 'There appeared to be but one flash, and those simultaneous reports pealed out deafening salvos, and were grand and impressive beyond description... The heavens had opened, and the Union soldiers found themselves in a pitiless storm of shot and shell which burst and tore up the ground in all directions, dealing out death and destruction on every side. So terrific was the Cannonade... (that) the air was darkened by the heavy clouds of smoke white washing the sky.'[34]

Gottfried further quotes a Union Divisional Commander Major General John Gibbon, himself an artillery man, as saying that: 'It was impossible to count the shots; and, along with these reports came every kind of bustle, whirr, whistle and shriek that man has heard or can imagine... and the worst of it was that every shot seemed to be coming straight to hit you between the eyes'.[35]

The Federal artillery immediately opened retaliatory fire

with around fifty guns initially, choosing deliberately to hold the firing of the remaining artillery in order to conserve their ammunitions for the infantry attack which would surely follow. This was Hunt's idea, primarily to conserve ammunition as also to have fresh batteries to deal with the infantry onslaught.

Though estimates very about the duration of the cannonade from 45 minutes to almost two hours – it is reasonable to assume that it was over by around 3 p.m.. Gottfried estimates that although the Confederate batteries... 'succeeded in taking out most of 2nd Corps guns at the point of attack...', the casualties to the infantry were a mere 350 men, or 5 to 6 percent of the Federal infantry deployed in this sector.[36]

It was now the time of the Confederate infantry to launch their attack. Though more commonly known as 'Pickett's Charge'; as mentioned earlier, it was actually infantry brigades of three divisions; south to north, these were the infantry troops of Major General George E. Pickett, Brigadier General James J. Pettigrew and Major General Isaac R Trimble. Thus it is more appropriate to call it the 'Pickett - Pettigrew -Trimble charge'.

The Federal artillery initially opened fire cautiously on the advancing long line of the Confederates, but soon began to wreak havoc and destruction. A Confederate officer of Brigadier General. James L. Kemper's Brigade (of Pickett's Division) recalled: "Shot, shell, spherical case, shrapnel, canister - thousands of deadly missiles racing through the air to thin our ranks'.[37]

In spite of this devastating fire, the Confederate line did not waver but kept moving. A Confederate officer of Armistead's Brigade noted: 'The crash of shell and solid shot, as they came howling and whistling through our lines, seemed to make no impression on the men. There was not a waiver, but all was steady as if on parade'.[38]

Even an enemy officer was struck by the stoic resolve of the advancing infantry; this Federal officer is quoted as saying that, 'I can see no end to the right nor left to the line that is coming... Men are being mowed down with every step. And men are stepping into their places. There is no dismay, no discouragement, no wavering'.[39]

Pickett's men continued their advance, crossing two wooden fences and a stone wall before beginning their ascent in to the ridge. On his left (towards the north) the six brigades under Pettigrew and Trimble were also advancing. It was a match between the advancing Confederate infantry and the Federal artillery and infantry musketeers spewing fire on them. This was an unequal battle. Although some of the advancing infantry did breach the Union line in the centre of the ridge, no re-enforcements fetched up. Finally the attack was called off, and the Confederates started their withdrawal. The much vaunted Confederate charge had failed. Although the Confederate artillery had continued to support its advancing infantry, even moving many of their guns forward, their fire was too dispersed and misdirected to have the desired effect. Hunt is said to have written in his After-Action Report that, 'their artillery fire was too much dispersed, and failed to produce the desired effect'. He further noted that, 'most of the enemy's projectiles passed overhead, the effect being to sweep all the open ground in our rear, which was of little benefit to the Confederates - a mere waste of ammunitions...'.[40]

Even General Lee stated that, 'Our (artillery) having nearly exhausted their ammunition in the protracted cannonade... were unable to reply, or render the necessary support to the attacking party. Owing to this fact, which was unknown to me when the assault took place, the enemy was enabled to throw a strong fence of infantry against our left, already wavering under a concentrated fire of artillery form the ridge in front, and from Cemetery Hill on the left'.[41]

The Union artillery was employed very effectively by Brigadier General Hunt, who was all over the battlefield ensuring the replacement of ammunition, as well as bringing up fresh batteries from his reserve. Although, the artillery of both armies played a key role on this final day of the Battle of Gettysburg, it was the Union artillery which overshadowed the Confederate gunners.

One Union Artillery Officer, First Lieutenant Alonzo H. Cushing, displayed outstanding gallantry above and beyond the call of duty, while defending Cemetry Hill against Pickett's Charge. However the official acknowledgement of his valour came 151 years later, when US President Barak Obama conferred the posthumous award of the Medal of Honor on him on 6 November 2014. During the investiture ceremony Obama stated 'This Medal of Honor is a reminder that no matter how long it takes, it is never too late to do the right thing'. Cushing's Official Citation is given at Table 2.3.

REVIEW OF ARTILLERY OPERATIONS

Organisation
As mentioned earlier, the artilleries of the Union and Confederate armies differed in the manner they were organized. It must be mentioned that the re-organization of the artillery of both sides took place in 1863, based upon the lessons which had been learnt in the earlier battles.

The Union artillery's re-organization was done in the aftermath of the defeat of the Army of the Potomac under General Joseph Hooker, in the Battle of Chancellorsville on 2/3 May 1863. In his book *the Artillery of Gettysburg*, Brian Gottfried notes:

Realizing the error of his ways after the battle, Hooker permitted Brigadier General Henry Hunt who nominally commanded the artillery, to reorganize his batteries into a brigade system. Five batteries, usually numbering thirty guns, formed a brigade. Each infantry corps was assigned an artillery brigade. Two other artillery brigades reported to the cavalry, and five artillery brigades formed the reserve. While artillery brigade commanders continued to report to the commanders of infantry corps, Hunt maintained direct control over the Artillery Reserve, which contained 21 batteries, boasting 118 guns, or about one-third of the army's cannon.[42]

Unlike the Union artillery, the Confederates preferred organizing their batteries into battalions, rather than adopting the brigade structure. Gottfried writes in his book:

Robert E. Lee modified the Confederate Army of Northern Virginia command system on February 15, 1863. Prior to this date, batteries were allocated to infantry brigades. Now he created artillery battalions and assigned one to each infantry division. Two additional artillery battalions formed the reserve in each corps. Each battalion usually contained four batteries of four guns each. The battalion commanders in turn reported to the Chief of Artillery assigned to the corps. The biggest difference from the Federal system was that reserve battalions were assigned to each corps, not to Lee's artillery chief Brigadier General Pendleton.[43]

Table 2.3 - FIRST LIEUTENANT ALONZO H. CUSHING

OFFICIAL CITATION

The President Of The United States Of America, Authorized By Act Of Congress, March 3, 1863, Has Awarded In The Name Of Congress The Medal Of Honor To

FIRST LIEUTENANT ALONZO H. CUSHING UNITED STATES ARMY

For conspicuous gallantry and intrepidity at the risk of his life above and beyond the call of the duty:

First Lieutenant Alonzo H. Cushing distinguished himself by acts of bravery above and beyond the call of duty while serving as an artillery commander in Battery A, 4th U.S. Artillery, Army of the Potomac at Gettysburg, Pennsylvania on July 3, 1863 during the American Civil War. That morning, Confederate forces led by General Robert E. Lee began cannonading First Lieutenant Cushing's position on Cemetery Ridge. Using field glasses, First Lieutenant Cushing directed fire for his own artillery battery. He refused to leave the battlefield after being struck in the shoulder by a shell fragment. As he continued to direct fire, he was struck again, this time suffering grievous damage to his abdomen. Still refusing the abandon his command, he boldly stood tall in the face of Major General George E. Pickett's charge and continued to direct devastating fire into oncoming forces. As the Confederate forces closed in, First Lieutenant Cushing was struck in the mouth by an enemy bullet and fell dead beside his gun. His gallant stand and fearless leadership inflicted severe casualties upon Confederate forces and opened wide gaps in their lines, directly impacting the Union forces' ability to repel Pickett's charge. First Lieutenant Cushing's extraordinary heroism and selflessness above and beyond the call of duty, at the cost of his own life, are in keeping with the highest traditions of military service and reflect great credit upon himself, Battery A, 4th U.S. Artillery, Army of the Potomac, and the United States Army.

Thus, structurally, the Federal artillery was better organized than the Confederate artillery. There was a central authority in Hunt, who also had direct control of one-third of the guns. On the other hand, Pendleton had no direct control over the artillery, and could move his guns only in consultation with the division and corps commanders. This superior artillery command and control system was a significant factor of the Federal victory at Gettysburg.

MIXED BATTERY CONCEPT
Although similar in nomenclature, the Union batteries packed more punch as they were equipped with six guns each, as compared to the Confederate's four gun batteries. The primary reason for this was scarcity of resources in the Confederacy. They simply did not have sufficient number of cannon or horses to equip their artillery batteries with six guns. This was further compounded by the Confederates by having mixed calibre guns within a battery. Whereas the Union batteries were equipped with guns of uniform calibre (with the exception of one battery, i.e. the 2nd Connecticut Battery), the Confederate batteries were mostly equipped with two types of pieces; in some cases there were even three different types of guns. While having different types of cannon did indeed confer the Confederates with greater flexibility in employment, the disadvantages clearly outweighed the advantages, the chief problem being that of re - supply of varied types of ammunition to the batteries. At times it also resulted in the gun being loaded with the wrong ammunition. Mixed batteries having a combination of both short and long range guns, also affected the placement of artillery pieces within the battery deployment.

Philip M. Cole has written in his book *Civil War Artillery at Gettysburg:* 'For the Confederate army, mixing guns within the same battery was a natural occurrence as a result of engagements with the enemy when Yankee guns were captured or abandoned in the field. The Confederate artillery branch somewhat depended on subsisting off the Union army by capturing its highly desirable, better quality, Northern manufactured guns. Such guns were treated as war trophies by southern artillerymen and they resisted the idea of trading them for others to achieve uniformity'.[44]

This 'mixed battery' concept certainly affected the efficient employment of the Confederate artillery in the Battle of Gettysburg.

RESERVE ARTILLERY

Realizing the need for having some 'unattached' firepower to provide flexibility during changing situations in battle, both sides had earmarked artillery reserves for this purpose; however, they differed diametrically in terms of organization and control. The Union's artillery reserve was a centralized asset under the direct command of Brigadier General Robert Tyler, and consisted of five brigades, four of which had four batteries each, while the fifth brigade had five batteries. These 21 batteries totalled 108 guns, which was a formidable asset to be used at critical stages of a battle. In his book, Cole notes: 'One advantage of a single reserve, particularly useful at Gettysburg was the Union's fish-hook-shaped line that allowed easy internal movement of Federal reserve guns from a central location to any part of the field. An even greater advantage was having an independent reserve that allowed rapid massing of artillery. This unattached firepower streamlined the Union army's ability to move guns around without characteristic interference created in the chain of command'.[45]

The Artillery Reserve of the Army of Northern Virginia on the other hand, differed significantly from that of the Union, in that it was divided into three separate components, each being assigned to its three infantry corps. Each reserve consisted of two battalions. The total number of guns amounted to 101, only marginally less when compared to the 108 of Union Army's Artillery Reserve. However, whereas the Artillery Reserve of the Union Army of Potomac, under one commander had the freedom to be employed en masse at critical points, the Confederate Artillery Reserves organization did not permit such flexibility in its employment.

This difference in the command and control structure of the Artillery Reserves of the opposing forces, gave a clear edge to the Union Artillery in effecting their deployment without any delay or hindrance. Thus it was that while the Confederate Artillery Chief Brigadier General William N. Pendleton could move guns of his artillery reserve only after consulting the corps commanders, his counterpart in the Union Artillery Brigadier General Henry J. Hunt had the authority to employ his reserves as he wished. To quote Brigadier General Robert Tyler, commander of the Union's Artillery Reserve: 'I believe it almost unnecessary to speak of the value of the services rendered by the Artillery Reserve during the last two days of this action, and the great share it had in the glorious result. The one –hundred and eight guns which were on the field were all in position, their fire being concentrated and felt wherever the battle was hottest'.[46]

Artillery Leadership

The Chief of Artillery of the Confederate Army of Northern Virginia at Gettysburg was Brigadier General William Pendleton. He joined the United States Military Academy on 1826 and graduated in 1830, upon which he was assigned to the 2nd U.S Artillery. After three years he resigned and briefly taught mathematics at the Bristol College, Bucks County, Virginia, before turning to priesthood and serving as Rector of the Episcopal Church at Richmond. Upon the outbreak of the U. S. Civil War he volunteered for service and rejoined the Confederate Artillery. Quickly rising up the ranks, he was in July 1861, appointed as the Chief of the Artillery to Lieutenant General Robert E. Lee.

The Chief of Artillery of the Union Army of the Potomac at Gettysburg was Brigadier General Henry Jackson Hunt. After his training at the United States Military Academy, West Point, he graduated in 1839 and was (like Pendleton earlier) assigned to the 2nd U.S. Artillery. Prior to the Civil War, his claim to fame was that he was part of a three member board (along with William H. French and William F. Barry) which was formed to revise the artillery drills and tactics, and enunciate a new Artillery Doctrine. This manual titled *The Instructions for Field Artillery* was released by the War Department in

1861 and was the *Bible* for the Union Artillery during the Civil War. Hunt had also served with distinction in the Mexican War earlier in his career.

Most historians of the Civil War have rated Hunt's performance at Gettysburg as far superior to Pendleton. However, to be fair, it is not very easy to make a direct comparison due to the varying degree of authority and control they exercised during the Battle of Gettysburg. First, Brigadier General Hunt had *direct* control of the Artillery Reserve of the Union Army of the Potomac *totalling* 108 guns, i.e. 30 percent of the artillery which was at his disposal, to deploy at the critical points. On the other hand, although the Artillery Reserves of the Confederates totalled 101 guns (marginally less than those of the Union), these were attached to the infantry corps, and hence Pendleton could not move these without the permission of the corps commanders. This was indeed a major handicap. Second, whereas the Union Army fighting a defensive battle was operating on interior lines, the Confederates had a much longer front line to contend with. Hunt exploited these two factors to his great advantage, especially on the crucial third day of the battle (3 July 1863).

Notwithstanding above, Hunt's leadership was evident in the battlefield. Cole is effusive in his praise of Hunt and writes that : 'Hunt's valour in battle was inspirational'. He was seen riding on his horse all over the front line ensuring that his guns were kept supplied with ammunition to ensure they remained in action. He also moved the artillery reserves when required to boost up the Union firepower during the famous Pickett's charge following the Confederate Cannonade. Brigadier General Henry Hunt, widely regarded as the foremost artillerist of his time, has been rightly credited with the successful direction of the Union artillery in the defeat of the Confederate forces. On the other hand, most historians have found Pendleton wanting in his performance, quite disregarding the constraints of his authority – In fact one of the Confederates Artillery Battalion Commanders, Colonel Edward P. Alexander has been quite scathing in his criticism of Pendleton on the disappointing performance of the artillery. He states '... The fault of this day primarily with General Pendleton, General Lee's chief of artillery. He was too old and had been too long out of army life to be thoroughly up to all the opportunities of his position'.[47]

THE GREAT CANNONADE

The artillery fire unleashed by the Confederate artillery on to the Union defences on Cemetery Ridge in the afternoon of 3 July 1863, has come to be known as the *Great Cannonade*. It was a classic case of the employment of massed artillery fire to soften the enemy defences, prior to launching the attack. The simultaneous unleashing of fire of over 140 guns for a period of close to two hours (the exact timings continue to vary) had the necessary shock effect.

The effects of this massed artillery fire have been recounted by Frank A. Haskell, who was present as Cemetery Hill :

We sprang to our feet. In the briefest time the whole Rebel line to the west was pouring out thunder and its iron upon our crest. The wildest confusion for a few moments obtained amongst us. The shells came bursting all about. The servants ran terror-stricken for dear life and disappeared. The horses, hitched to the trees or held by the slack hands of the orderlies, neighed out in fright and broke away and plunged riderless through the fields...

...I had time to see one of the horses of our mess wagon struck and torn by a shell. The driver has lost the reins - horses, driver and wagon go into a heap by a tree. Two mules close at hand, packed with boxes of ammunition, are knocked all to pieces by a shell. General Gibbon's groom has just mounted his horse and is starting to take the General's horse to him, when the flying iron meets him and tears open the breast. He drops dead and the horses gallop away...

...We note the effect of the enemy's fire among the batteries and along the crest. We see the solid shot struck axle, or pole, or wheel, and the tough iron and heart of oak snap and fly like straws. The great oaks there by Woodruff's guns heave down their marry branches with a crash, as if the lightening smote them. The shells swoop down among the battery horses standing there. A half dozen start, they tumble, there legs stiffen, their vitals and blood smear the ground. And these shot and shells have no respect for men either. We see the poor follows hobbling back from the crest, or unable to do to, pale and weak, lying on the ground with mangled stump of an arm or leg, dropping their life-blood away; or with a check torn open, or a shoulder mashed ...

... Not ten yards away from us a shell burst among some small bushes, where sat three or four orderlies holding horses. Two of the men and one horse were killed. Only a few yards off a shell exploded over on open limber box in Cushing's battery, and at the same instant, another shell over a neighboring box. In both the boxes the ammunition blow up with an explosion that shook the ground, throwing fire and splinters and shells far into the air and all around, and destroying several men...

...We saw the missiles tear and plow the ground. All in the rear of the crest for a thousand yards, as well as among the batteries, was the field of their blind fury. Ambulances, passing down the Tanneytown Road, with wounded men, were struck. The hospitals near the road were riddled. The house which was General Meade's headquarters, was shot through several times, and a great many horses of officers and orderlies were lying dead around it... Mules with ammunition, pigs wallowing about, cows in pastures, whatever was animate or inanimate, in all this broad range, was no exception...[48]

Even in the middle of this massive bombardment by the Confederate artillery, the Union batteries gave back in kind; Haskell continues:

Our artillerymen upon the crest budged not an inch, nor intermitted, but, though caisson and limber were smashed, and guns dismantled, and men and horses killed, there amidst smoke and sweat, they gave back, without grudge, or loss of time in the sending, in kind whatever the enemy sent, globe, cone and belt, hollow or solid, an iron greeting to the rebellion, the compliments of the wrathful Republic.[49]

The firing of a concentration of so many guns from both sides was indeed a classic case of employing massed artillery fire very effectively, to disrupt and disorganize the enemy.

CONCLUSION

The famous Battle of Gettysburg, perhaps the bloodiest of the Civil War, ended on 3 Jul 1863. Both sides had suffered heavy losses. Owens estimates Meade's army as having suffered around 23,000 casualties and Lee between 20,000 to 25,000[50] (some other historians estimate Confederate losses at 28,000). For Lee, his losses at Gettysburg amounted to one-third of his Army of North Virginia.

Lee waited one whole day after the battle, before starting his retreat southward. Meade, however, did not attack him and missed this great opportunity to inflict the final crushing blow on the withdrawing Confederate forces. Joel Achenbach notes in his article, that Lincoln was furious with Meade for vacillating, and wrote out a letter (which he did not finally send); he wrote: 'I do not believe you appreciate the magnitude of the misfortune involved in Lee's escape. He was within your easy grasp, and to have closed upon him would, in connection with our other late successes, have ended the war'[51].

The gradual decline in the fortunes of the Confederacy started after this epic battle, fought on a grand scale, by two large opposing armies. Cole rightfully comments that: 'The Confederacy's high tide had come and passed'. Had Lee's Army of North Virginia won this battle, perhaps the history of United States may have taken a different turn.

There is no doubt that the artillery of both sides played a very decisive role during this battle. Ranged against 370 guns of this Union artillery, were 270 guns of the Confederacy, a total of 640 guns. This was indeed a very large mass of artillery pieces which unleashed its fire upon the relatively small battlefield. Although artillery provided yeoman service to their respective armies on all three days, their exploits on 3 July 1863 continue to remain etched in memory even today. Cole notes : 'On July 3 the gun crews of both armies stood erect at their vulnerable positions and performed their duties in the midst of raining iron *during the greatest cannonade yet unleashed in the Western Hemisphere*'[52] (emphasis by the author). The role of artillery in the Battle of Gettysburg has indeed been commended upon by several historians. In the words of Bradley M. Gottfried:

'The battle of Gettysburg was won for several reasons, but among the most important was the magnificent role the Federal artillery played in the engagement'[53]

Since the artillery was still in an evolutionary stage, the lessons learnt during this battle refined its employment during the later battles of the U.S. Civil War.

APPENDIX A

Artillery - Union Army of The Potomac

Ser No	Formation	Commander	Number of Batteries	Number of Guns	Remarks
Infantry Corps					
1.	1st Corps Artillery Brigade	Col. Charles S. Wainwright	Five	28	
2.	2nd Corps Artillery Brigade	Capt. John G. Hazard	Five	28	
3.	3rd Corps Artillery Brigade	Capt. George E. Randolph / Capt. A. Judson Clark	Five	30	
4.	5th Corps Artillery Brigade	Capt. Augustus P. Martin	Five	26	
5.	6th Corps Artillery Brigade	Col. Charles H. Tompkins	Eight	48	
6.	11th Corps Artillery Brigade	Maj. Thomas W. Osborn	Five	26	
7.	12th Corps Artillery Brigade	Lt. Edward D. Muhlenberg	Four	20	
Cavalry Corps Horse Artillery					
8.	1st Brigade	Capt. James M. Robertson	Five	28	
9.	2nd Brigade	Capt. John C. Tidball	Three	16	
Artillery Reserve (Commander-Brigadier General Robert O. Tyler)					
10.	1st Brigade (Regular)	Capt. Dunbar R. Ransom	Four	24	
11.	1st Volunteer Brigade	Lt. Col. Freeman Mc. Gilvery	Four	22	
12	2st Volunteer Brigade	Capt. Elijah D. Taft	Two	12	
13.	3rd Volunteer Brigade	Capt. James F. Huntington	Four	20	
14.	4th Volunteer Brigade	Capt. Robert H. Fitzhugh	Five	28	

Note : Extracted from Bradley M Cole, *Artillery of Gettysburg* pp. 249 - 258, which also gives in details the types of guns in each battery, as well as losses in personnel killed, wounded, taken prisoner.

APPENDIX B

Artillery - Confederate Army of North Virginia

Ser No	Formation	Commander	Number of Batteries	Number of Guns	Remarks
1ˢᵗ Corps					
1.	Mclaw's Division Artillery	Col. Henry Coulter Cabell	Four	16	These were organized in 2-gun sections
2.	Pickett's Division Artillery	Maj. James Dearing	Four	18	
3.	Hood's Division Artillery	Maj. Mathis W. Henry	Four	19	
Artillery Reserve (Col. James B. Walton / Col. Edward P. Alexander)					
4.	Alexander's Battalion	Col. Edward P. Alexander/Maj. Frank Hugar	Six	24	
5.	Washington (Louisiana) Artillery	Maj. Benjamin F. Eshleman	Four	10	
2ⁿᵈ Corps Artillery (Col. J. Thompson Brown)					
6.	Early's Division Artillery	Lt. Col. Hilary P. Jones	Four	16	
7.	Rodes's Division Artillery	Lt. Col. Thomas H. Carter	Four	16	
8.	Johnson's Division Artillery	Lt. Col. R. Snowden Andrews / Maj. James W. Latimer / Capt. Charles I. Raine	Four	16	
Artillery Reserve (Col. J. Thompson Brown)					
9.	1ˢᵗ Virginia Artillery Battalion	Capt. Wills J Dance	Five	20	
10.	Nelson's battalion	Lt. Col. William Nelson	Three	11	
3ʳᵈ Corps Artillery (Col R Lindsay Waller)					
11.	Anderson's Division Artillery (Sumter Battalion)	Maj. John Lane	Three	17	
12.	Heth's Division Artillery	Lt. Col. John Garnett	Four	15	
13	Pender's Division Artillery	Maj. William T. Poague	Four	16	
Artillery Reserve (Col R Lindsay Waller)					
14.	McIntosh's Battalion	Maj. D. G. McIntosh	Four	16	
15.	Pegram's Battalion	Maj. William J. Pegram Capt. E. B. Brunson	Five	20	
16	**Stuart's Division Horse Artillery**	Maj. Robert F. Beckhan	Six	21	
17.	**Imboden's Command**	-	Two	09	

APPENDIX C

Characteristics of Civil War Cannon Used at Gettysburg

TYPE OF CANNON	BORE DIA	TYPE	WEIGHT OF TUBE	RANGE AT 50 ELEVATION (Yards)	CS	US
Napoleon	4.62"	Smooth	1,227	1,619	98	142
6-pounder field gun	3.67"	Smooth	884	1,523	1	-
12 Pounder howitzer	4.62"	Smooth	788	1,072	33	2
24-Pounder howitzer	5.82"	Smooth	1,318	1,322	4	-
3-inch ordnance rifle	3.00"	Rifled	816	1,835	78	142
10-pounder Parrott	2.90"	Rifled	890	2,000	44	60
20 pounder	3,67"	Rifled	1,750	2,100	10	6
James rifle	3.80"	Rifled	918	1,700	-	4
Whitworth rifle	2.75"	Rifled	1,092	2,800	2	-
Blakely	3.40"	Rifled	800	1,850	2	-

Note:

1. Sourced from Bradley M Gottfried *The Artillery of Gettysburg,* Cumberland House, Nashville, 2008, p.259.

2. Although Blakely Rifle does not appear in the table given in his book, he mentions three Blakely Rifles were held by Washington Artillery Battery, at p.258

3.   CS- stands for Confederate States

      US- stands for United States

4.   There is a slight variation in ranges compared to the table given by Philip M Cole in his book *Civil War Artillery at Gettysburg, p.* 81.

APPENDIX D

Order of Battle – Opposing Forces

On the eve of the Battle of Gettysburg, the Order of Battle (ORBAT) of the opposing union and confederate forces is given below:

Union Army of the Potomac (Approximately 83000 personnel)
1ˢᵗ Corps (Maj. Gen. John F. Reynolds) : Three Divisions
    (a) First Division (Brigadier General James S. Wordsworth)
    (b) Second Division (Brigadier General John C. Robinson)
    (c) Third Division (Brigadier General Thomas A. Rowely)
2ⁿᵈ Corps (Maj. Gen. Winfield S. Hancock) : Three Divisions
    (a) First Division (Maj. Gen. John Curtis Caldwell)
    (b) Second Division (Brig Gen John Gibbon)
    (c) Third Division (Brigadier General Alexander Hays)
3ʳᵈ Corps (Maj. Gen. Daniel E. Sickles) : Two Divisions
    (a) First Division (Brigadier General J.H. Hobart Wald)
    (b) Second Division (Brigadier General Andrew A. Humphreys)
4ᵗʰ Corps (Maj. Gen. George Sykes) : Three Divisions
    First Division (Brigadier General Janes Barnes)
    Second Division (Brigadier General Romeyn B. Ayres)
    Third Division (Brigadier General Samuel W. Craneford)
5ᵗʰ Corps (Maj. Gen. John Sedgewick) : Three Divisions
    (a) First Division (Brigadier General Horatio G. Wright)
    (b) Second Division (Brigadier General Albion D. Howe)
    (c) Third Division (Brigadier General John Newton)
11ᵗʰ Corps (Brigadier General Oliver O. Howard) : Three Divisions
    (a) First Division (Brigadier General Francis C. Barlow)
    (b) Second Division (Brigadier General Adolph Von Steinwehr)
    (c) Third Division (Major General Carl Schurz)
12ᵗʰ Corps (Brigadier General Henry W. Slocum): Two Divisions
    (a) First Division (Brigadier General Alphons S. Williams)
    (b) Second Division (Brigadier General John W. Geary)
    Cavalry Corps (Major General Alfred Pleasanton)
The Artillery component of the Union Army of the Potomac is given at Table 2.1. The total number of guns have been assessed between 357 and 370; the table lists 370 guns.
Army of North Virginia (75,000 personnel)

1ˢᵗ Corps (Lieutenant General James Longstreet): Three Divisions
  (a) Mclaw's Division (Major General Lafayette Mclaw)
  (b) Picket's Division (Major General George E. Picket)
  (c) Hood's Division (Major General John B. Hood)
2ⁿᵈ Corps (Lieutenant General Richard S. Ewell) : Three Divisions
  (a) Early's Division (Major General Jubal A. Early)
  (b) Johnson's Division (Major General Edward Johnson)
  (c) Rode's Division (Major General R.R. Rodes)
3ʳᵈ Corps (Lieutenant General Ambrose P Hill) : Three Divisions
  (a) Anderson's Division (Major General Richard H. Anderson)
  (b) Heth's Division (Major General Henry Heth)
  (c) Pender's Division (Major General William D. Pender)
  Stuarts Cavalry Division (Major General J. E. B. Stuart)

The Artillery component of the Army of Northern Virginia is given in Table 2.2. Although the total number of guns has been assessed to be between 270 and 275 guns, Table 2.2 lists it as 270 guns.

NOTES

1. Philip M. Cole, *Civil War Artillery At Gettysburg*, Colecraft Industries, Orrtanna, 2002, p.11.
2. Bradley M. Gottfried, *The Artillery of Gettysburg*, Cumberland House Publishing Inc., Nashville, 2008, p.11.
3. W. Birbeck Wood and Brigadier General Sir James E Edmonds, *The Civil War in the United States*, Methuen & Co. Ltd, London, 1937, (Reprinted in 1960), p.1.
4. Ibid., p.1.
5. https://www.brittannica.com/event/American.civil.war accessed on 7 February 2018, p.14
6. Ibid., p.16.
7. Cole, *Civil War Artillery At Gettysburg*, p.17. Cole has covered in detail, the genesis and transition of the artillery of both armies in pp. 17 to 29.
8. Ibid., p.24
9. Ibid., p.22
10. Ibid, p.22.
11. Ibid., pp. 71 to 177, Chapters III, IV and V, Cole has given a detailed account of the artillery technology, guns, equipment and animals, as well as ammunition prevalent during the U.S Civil War.
12. Ibid., p. 130.
13. Jesse Bowman Young, *The Battle of Gettysburg*: A Comprehensive Narrative, has analyzed the various reasons which prompted Lieutenant General Lee to undertake the second invasion of Pennsylvania, in pp. 14 - 26.
14. Wood and Edmonds, *The Civil War in the United States*, p.46.
15. Young, *The Battle of Gettysburg*, pp. 156 - 157.
16. Mackubin Thomas Owens, *The Great Battle of Gettysburg*, National Review, USA p.5, accessed from http://www.nationalreview.com/article/352377/great-battle-gettysburg-macubin-thomas-owens, on 13 February 2018.
17. Ibid., p.7
18. Ibid., p.8
19. Ibid., p.9
20. Gottfried. *The Artillery of Gettysburg p.23.*
21. Ibid., p.28
22. Ibid., p.29.
23. Ibid., p.35.

24. Ibid., pp. 45-46, Gottfried quotes Capt. Robert Beecham of 2nd Wisconsin (Iron Brigade), who was at the receiving end of the Confederate artillery fire.
25. Ibid., p.78.
26. Frank, A. Haskell, *The Battle of Gettysburg,* Eyre and Spottiswoode, Norwich, 1959, pp. 16-17. Haskell served in 2nd Division of 2nd Corps of the Union Army of the Potomac, and has given a first hand account in this book.
27. Gottfried, *The Artillery of Gettysburg,* gives out in detail the deployment of the Federal and Confederate artillery down to battery level, in Chapter 3, pp. 79 - 92
28. Ibid., p.104.
29. Haskell, *The Battle of Gettysburg,* pp. 38 - 41.
30. Ibid., p 47.
31. Owens, National Review.com, p.17.
32. Joel Achenbach, Gettysburg: *The Battle and its aftermath,* Washington post, USA P.4, accessed from https:// www-washingtonpost.com/national/health-science/Gettysburg-the-battle-and –its aftermath/2013/04/26 accessed on 13 February 2018.
33. Gottfried, *The Arttillery of Gettysburg,* p 192.
34. Ibid, p.196, Gottfried quotes Aldrich from his book, *The History of Battery A, First Regiment Rhode Island Light Artillery* in the War to Preserve the Union
35. Ibid., p.196
36. Ibid., p.211.
37. Ibid., p.216.
38. Ibid., p.216
39. Ibid., P.216.
40. Ibid., p 232.
41. Ibid., pp. 232-233.
42. Ibid., p 12.
43. Ibid., p.12.
44. Cole, *Civil War Artillery At Gettysburg,* p.56. He has described in great detail, the organizational structures of the artillery of both armies in pp 31-s70.
45. Ibid., p.64.
46. Ibid., pp.66-7.
47. Ibid., p.271
48. Haskell, *The Battle of Gettysburg,* pp. 82-89
49. Ibid., p. 89
50. Owens, *National Review,* p18.

51. *Washington Post*, p.4.
52. Cole, *Civil War Artillery At Gettysburg*, p.16.
53. Gottfried, *The Artillery of Gettysburg*, p.246.

CHAPTER 3

Battle of Vimy Ridge

(9 to 12 April 1917)
First World War

*It is probable that with the exception of the Krakatoa
explosion of 1883, in all of history no human ears had ever been
assaulted by the intensity of sound produced by the artillery
barrage that launched the Battle of Vimy Ridge on April 9, 1917.*

*In the years that followed, the survivors would struggle
to describe that shattering moment when 983 artillery pieces and
150 machine guns barked in unison to launch the first British
victory in thirty-two months of frustrating warfare.*

PIERRE BERTON, MILITARY HISTORIAN,
IN HIS BOOK VIMY.

INTRODUCTION

The Battle of Vimy Ridge holds a special place in the collective
conscience of Canadians – and for very good reason too. This
battle, fought between 9 and 12 April 1917 during the First
World War, pitted the Canadians Corps against the German
Sixth Army in a bid to capture the Vimy escarpment, which
lies north – east of Arras. This was the first time that the four
Canadian divisions fought together as one entity to defeat the
Germans.

This battle was part of the wider Battle of Arras, wherein the
Canadian Corps operating in the northern flank as part of the
British 1st Army (of the British Expeditionary Force or the B.E.F)
captured the seven kilometre long well-fortified escarpment
held by the Germans. This ridge, which had seen two earlier
unsuccessful attempts by the French under Joffre in 1914 and
1915, was captured by the Canadians in just four days! The
artillery played a key role in the success of this attack.

In his book *Battleground Europe - Arras: Vimy Ridge*, Nigel Cave writes:

The artillery concentrations of the firepower of seven divisions, and eighteen artillery brigades, was of far greater density than had been available on the first day at Somme. On top of this were the big guns of eleven heavy artillery groups and the artillery of 1st Corps on the Canadian's left. This force provided Byng (The Corps Commander – author) with 377 heavy guns, over 550 eighteen-pounders and over 150 4.5-inch howitzers. At Vimy there was a heavy gun for every twenty yards of the 7000 yard front, and a field gun for every ten yards (emphasis by the author). On the Somme there had been a heavy gun for every sixty yards and a field gun to every twenty yards. The allocation for the operation was 42,500 tons of shells and a daily quota of 2465 tons.[1]

This great victory however came at a heavy cost. In the four days of bloody fighting, the Canadian Corps had 10,802 casualties, of which 3598 were killed.

THE WESTERN FRONT

SITUATION – WINTER OF 1916/1917

By the end of 1916, the war was well into its third year since its start in August 1914. After the initial German advance into Luxembourg, Belgium and France – *The Race to the Sea* – the situation had turned into a stalemate. In spite of the many battles fought in the preceding years, neither side had been able to achieve a decisive break through to end this impasse. The front line extended from the Belgian coast (near Ostend) and continued for over 1000 kilometres up to the boundary with Switzerland (See Map 5).

The B.E.F., which had deployed in August 1914, had been in continuous action for the past twenty-nine months. Starting with a deployment of four infantry divisions and four cavalry brigades it had grown into a large army. Initially under the command of Field Marshal Sir John French, it was now commanded by Field Marshal Sir Douglas Haig. During 1916, amongst other operations, the B.E.F. had fought two major battles – the Battle of Verdun and the Battle of Somme. The latter battle was fought by the combined forces of the French and British, in three phases between 1 July 1916 to 18

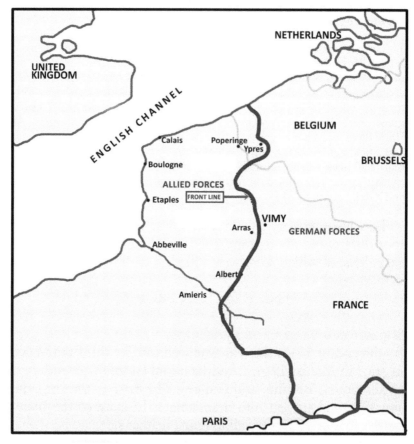

Map 5: The Western Front (April 1917)

November 1916 (141 days). Not only did the Allies fail to achieve the desired break-through, but they also suffered very heavy casualties. It is said that Somme was the costliest battle of the war.

As the exhausted Allied forces settled down to face the bitter winter of 1916, they contemplated the plans for the coming year. It was at the Chantilly Conference held on 16 November, that the seeds of the spring offensive of 1917 were sown. This offensive, whose plans were crystallized over the next few months, took the shape of the Battle of Arras which was launched on 9 April 1917, in which the Canadian Corps was destined to play a stellar role in the capture of Vimy Ridge.

THE CANADIAN CORPS

The relatively nascent Canadian Corps had interesting origins. In his book Vimy, Berton notes:

Almost every man who trudged the slopes of Vimy Ridge on the gloomy Easter Monday in April 1917 had been a civilian when the war broke out, and this included four of the five Canadian-born generals who helped to plan the attack... Canada in 1914 had scarcely any military tradition, no military aspirations, and little knowledge of war. Out of a population of eight million, she had barely three thousand permanent force soldiers, and these were under British command. If Canadians were to fight and win battles they would have to start from scratch with no background of experience – and also no pre-conceived ideas, which was not necessary a bad thing.[2]

With the declaration of war, the response of the population to the call to arms was overwhelming. Recruiting stations were literally overwhelmed by volunteers. The first regiment to be formed was Princess Patricia's Canadian Light Infantry Regiment, named after the only daughter of the then serving Governor General of Canada, Prince Arthur, the Duke of Connaught. Interestingly, this regiment was financed privately, and was the first Canadian unit to set foot in France on 24th December 1914 under the command of Colonel. F.D. Farquhar, D.S.O.[3] The recruitment proceeded at a fast pace; Tom Douglas notes in his book '*Valour At Vimy Ridge*': 'Back home, volunteers continued to pour into recruiting stations and, by late September, more than 30,000 hastily trained soldiers marched out of the Valcartier mobilization camp near Quebec City to board trains for the East Coast. On 1 October, officers and men stomped proudly up the gangplank of 33 ocean liners – including the *RMS Olympia*, sister ship of *RMS Titanic* – and set sail for England under the protection of British Royal Navy escort ships. It was the biggest convoy ever to cross the Atlantic'.[4]

After a two weeks sea voyage, this contingent docked at Plymouth on 14 October 1916. The Canadians were sent to the Salisbury plains to train during the rainy winter. Their training was affected not only by rains, but snow, mist, freezing temperature and a variety of sicknesses and ailments which plagued the men. Nevertheless, after a period of training of over four months these Canadian troops, now constituted as the 1st Canadian Division landed in France in March 1915 and were initially deployed near Armentieres along the Franco-Belgian border, only to be moved in April to join the British V Corps at the Ypres Salient. They received their baptism by fire on 22 April 1915, when the German Fourth Army struck at Ypres. In spite of putting up a stubborn defence, the Canadians suffered heavy losses.

In September 1915, the recently raised 2nd Canadian Division joined the 1st Canadian Division to form a Canadian Corps headquarter under Lieutenant General Edwin Alderson, a British army officer. The 2nd Canadian Division was blooded in battle in April 1916 in the action at St Eloi, suffering as many as 1,400 causalities. In May 1916 there was a change of command of the Canadian Corps, with Lieutenant General Sir Julian Byng taking over as the Corps commander. Around the same time, it was the turn of the 3rd Canadian Division to face the wrath of the Germans. The German XIII Corps attacked their positions at Mount Sorrel; they too suffered many losses included their divisional commander Major General Malcom Mercer who was killed in action. The Canadian Corps joined the Battle of Somme midway – in September 1916. In October the same year, the newly formed 4th Canadian Division too joined in the ill-fated Somme Campaign. In spite of the grim fight, the Canadians suffered comparatively less casualties. 'The Canadians suffered over 24,000 casualties on the Somme, just a small portion of nearly half million casualties that the British and Empire forces endured'.[5]

The Canadian Corps now comprised four infantry divisions, and had transformed into a battle-hardened formation. This corps was destined to play a major role in the spring offensive planned for April 1917, during which it captured the formidable Vimy Ridge escarpment as part of the Battle of Arras, in four days of intense combat.

THE BATTLE OF ARRAS

The Battle of Arras, fought by the B.E.F between 9 April 1917 and 17 May 1917, was a part of the larger spring offensive launched jointly by the British and French forces to regain the initiative after the failure at Somme the previous year. The attack in the Arras region was not the first choice of the British commander, Field Marshal Haig, who preferred to launch his armies to the north in order to recapture the Belgian coastline. He was however overruled, and the plan of the French Commander-in-Chief, General Robert Nivelle was accepted. In outline, the plan called for three offensives to be launched in a phased manner; the first two preliminary offensives were designed to draw in the German reserves, after which the main thrust would be launched in the south to roll up the German defence line in this area. These three offensives were to be launched as under:

1. The French *Groupe des Armies du Nord* to attack between the Oise and St. Quentin.
2. This would be followed by the B.E.F. attack to its north between Bapanne and Arras, astride to Scarpe River valley.
3. The main thrust, to be launched by the *Groupe des Armies de Reserve,* was to be directed between Reims and Valley-sur-Aisne, focussing on the Chemin des Dames heights that dominated the area. Looking for a break -through here, the French hoped to destroy the reserves drawn in by the two preliminary offensives (at Para 1& 2 above).[6]

Before this offensive could be launched, the Germans carried out a planned withdrawal of their forces in this sector to a newly created defence line in the rear, called the *Siegfried Stellung* (or the Siegfried Line) by the Germans, and the Hindenburg Line by the Allies. While pulling back, they destroyed everything of value in the wake of their withdrawal. This withdrawal was in consonance with their new defence doctrine and resulted in the shortening of their defence frontline by 25 miles, thereby freeing up some of their divisions. In view of this unexpected development, the Allied plans had to be modified to the extent that the French preliminary offensive, having lost its original relevance, was now reduced in scope to a 'diversionary' attack. The main offensive to the south remained unchanged as did the B.E.F. offensive in the Arras region.

Within the overall plan, Haig's plan for the B.E.F in the north was as follows:

1. The main attack to be launched by the British Third Army (XVIII, VI and VII Corps) along the Scarpe River valley, east of Arras.

2. Fifth Army, with its 1 Australian and New Zealand Army Corps (ANZAC), to attack along the open Southern flank towards Bullecourt.

3. First Army was assigned the limited task of the capture of Vimy Ridge in the northern flank.[7]

General Sir Henry Horne, commanding the First Army gave the task for the capture of this dominating escarpment to the newly formed Canadian Corps, with support of the 5th British Division of the XI Corps. In his book *Vimy*, Berton writes:

On January 19, 1917, Henry Horne the dapper commander of the British 1st Army, informed Julian Byng that in the coming spring offensive, the Canadian Corps would be responsible for capturing all of the four-mile (seven kilometre - author) crest of Vimy Ridge except for Pimple. The British 1st Corps, also in Horne's army, elements of which would be placed under Byng's command to strengthen the assault, would protect the Canadians' left flank. On the right, the British 3rd Army astride the River Scarpe would attack simultaneously on an eight - mile front. The exact date had not been set, but the time-table called for the job to be completed before April 1 (in the event however, the Vimy Ridge attack was pushed to 9 April 1917 - author). Byng and his staff had about two months to plan the operation and train the men.[8]

PLANNING AND PREPARATION

Lieutenant General Julian Byng planned to launch all four of his divisions simultaneously to assault the ridge (the detailed plan has been given later). However, he had learnt some very useful lessons from the failure at Somme the previous year, when the Allied Forces had suffered over 6,00,000 casualties (including over 24,000 Canadians). Byng realized that he needed to train and rehearse his troops, innovate his tactics and also have his logistics firmly in place. He was determined that every one down to the soldier, should know his role in the attack, and train and rehearse accordingly. He spent the next two months doing precisely that.

He summoned his divisional commanders and senior staff officers to a place called Camblain l'Abbe, and outlined to them the task of the corps. He also re-organised the deployment of his divisions on ground by placing them in seniority from right to left (or south to north in this case). Thus the 1ˢᵗ Canadian Division moved to the right flank, on its left was positioned the 2ⁿᵈ Division, followed by the 3ʳᵈ and 4ᵗʰ Divisions, with the latter occupying the left flank of the corps.

TRAINING

Under Byng's direct supervision, the Canadians trained and rehearsed vigorously for the task at hand. In February 1917 the British General Staff issued a pamphlet titled *'Instructions for the training of platoons for offensive action'*, enunciating the re-organisation of platoons and their tactics in field. The new organisation added a section of bombers (hand-grenade throwers) as well as Light Machine Gun sections. Byng's instructions were clear – that every person must not only know his own task /role to the minutest detail, but also that of the person one rank above him.

Commenting upon the intense training carried out by Byng's Canadian Corps, Alexander Turner writes:

In training his men, Byng developed the tactical doctrine for small units by issuing platoons with specific objectives. This gave them focus and allowed them to rehearse. Full-scale drills were conducted in rear areas with tape representing trenches and officers with flags displaying the progress of the creeping barrage. Currie (GOC 1ˢᵗ Canadian Division – author) was even more vehement about this process and drilled his division to the point of tedium. Every single man in the attack was made to file past the scale models of their objectives. Byng encouraged every officer and senior non-commissioned officer to visit the vast plasticine model of Vimy Ridge near First Army Headquarters. Nobody was under any illusion that the affair would be bloodless. Every soldier was made to learn the job of the man alongside him and more importantly, above him. 45,000 maps were issued so that platoon seargents and section commanders had them as well.[9]

The plasticine model of Vimy Ridge was indeed a replica of the ridge; not only did it have all the physical topographical details of the feature, but also showed the location of the German trenches, strong points, pill boxes and so on. It helped to familiarise the troops with the objective they were to attack. Such were the preparations for this battle, that one officer recorded: 'For two months I have had the plan of the battle before me in as much detail as if it were the plan of a house which an architect proposed to build; the disposition of every man in the corps is settled and the moment of his movement arranged'.[10]

LOGISTICS
Considering the magnitude of the planned offensive, the logistics planning was a major challenge for the Corps administrative staff led by the Chief of Staff, Brigadier – General Percy Pellexfen de Blaquire Radcliffe, as well as the Chief Administrative officer and Logistician, Brigadier – General George Farmer. The following statistics give an idea of the magnitude of the effort involved:

(a) The corps was supplied by eight trains a day, each carrying 370 tons of stores; these included ammunition, engineering stores, general supplies as well as animal fodder.

(b) These stores had to be unloaded and moved by road or light rail tramway to the required areas.

(c) Over 50,000 horses and mules had to be supplied on a daily basis.

(d) The daily requirement of water of the Corps was 6, 00,000 gallons which had necessitated the construction of 72 Kilometres of pipeline, six purpose-built reservoirs and 24 pumping stations. In addition, a 2,25,500-litre reservoir was constructed 12 meters underground.

(e) As a sample of requirements for the actual attack, Brigadier-General Farmer indented for 24 million rounds of small arms ammunition, 4,50,000 grenades and 1,005,000 rounds of 18-pounder gun ammunition.[11]

The months preceding the attack were spent improving

roads, building a 20 - mile rail tramway system, water-pipline construction, building water-reservoirs etc. to support this colossal logistics effort. In order to ensure stable communications within the corps, a staggering 1,440 kilometres of cable was laid; such cables which were within five miles of the frontline had to be dug to a depth of seven feet.[12]

ARTILLERY

Other than the marshalling of the guns and ammunition, the artillery preparation hinged on the planning of a 'Creeping Barrage' in support of the advancing infantry, as well as ensuring effective counter-battery fire to suppress the enemy artillery fire, so that they could not interfere with the advance of the assaulting troops.

CREEPING BARRAGE

Although first tried in the battle of Loos in 1915 and later, in Somme, the concept of the 'creeping barrage' was now refined in order to provide maximum protection to the advancing infantry as they advanced to their objectives. Tim Cook notes in his article *The Gunners At Vimy*:

Previously, the artillery bombardment laid a terrific weight of shell on enemy strong points, and then jumped to next position. This helped smash defences and defenders, but not all of them. When the barrage jumped off to the next objective, the defenders rose from their dugouts and shot down the infantry still struggling through no-man's land. Learning from these failures, gunners began to fire a creeping barrage, or wall of fire, that slowly moved over the enemy lines in shorter leaps. The infantry were to stay close to the wall of shrapnel and, in the words of instructions, "lean into the barrage" for protection. The barrage would usually rest on an enemy position for a few minutes, and then leap forward 100 yards .

The infantry tried to follow the barrage closely, aware that if they were slowed down by enemy strong points, they would be left defenceless in no-man's land as the barrage moved away. The creeping barrage was a vast improvement on previous tactics, yet it was difficult to have several hundred guns fire in unison on the same target and then move forward at the same pace along different terrain across the front. As well, communication was so rudimentary that once a barrage started, it could not be called off or brought back to deal with obstinate defenders. There was little flexibility.[13]

To minimize such problems, troops were made to practice movement on ground with 'dummy' barrages being simulated, and with the 100 – yard lines being indicated by white tape laid on ground. Such practices gave confidence to the infantry that this moving ball of fire would provide them safety during the attack.

COUNTER BOMBARDMENT (CB)

In the Battle of Vimy Ridge, 'counter-battery' operations paid a key role in neutralizing the German artillery batteries. At the beginning of the Great War, the methods of locating guns were still in the nascent stage. It was left to Lieutenant- Colonel Andrew G.L. McNaughton to refine the procedures to near perfection. In the preparatory phases of artillery bombardment (20 March to 9 April 1917), Byng had placed Counter-Battery fire as his top priority, followed by destruction of firing positions, destruction of wire entanglements, and interdiction of re-supply and repair parties in that order. Alexander Turner writes that : 'To place counter-battery fire at the top of his priorities was one of Byng's most significant displays of prescience. It was understood that enemy artillery posed a great threat to attacking infantry, but the difficulty had always been in locating it'.[14]

Byng appointed McNaughton as the Counter -Battery Officer on 27th January 1917, and the latter spent the next couple of months in working on techniques in acquiring accurate intelligence of enemy gun locations.

McNaughton created a specialist staff of officers and personnel of a science back-ground, and got down to refining the newly discovered methods of locating guns viz. sound-ranging and flash spotting. While sound - ranging involved the recording of the vibrations of passing shells by numerous oscillographs deployed in the area, flash - spotting involved the triangulation of flashes of gun fire. These methods which are taken for granted today, were in the very nascent stages then. McNaughton and his staff worked hard to sophisticate these procedures to the extent, that they were able to locate the guns to an accuracy of 10 metres.

Such readings were cross-referenced, where-ever possible, by confirmatory over-flights by 16 Squadron. In addition, McNaughton was able to get enemy battery locations from tethered observation balloons, as well as from Patrols/Raiding parties who brought back maps, aerial photographs and other documents. Information from these sources was co-related to the findings of their sound - ranging/flash - spotting troops. In order to bring in greater accuracy in 'gun shooting' on to these hostile batteries, McNaughton also brought in corrections for barrel-wear and muzzle velocity of individual guns, as well as corrections for wind and weather. Pierre Berton in his book *Vimy* notes that it was this Canadian's pioneering work that resulted in calibrating each gun individually (to cater for its muzzle velocity due to barrel wear), as well as to adjust the range tables to correct for weather.[15] Dedicated artillery, mostly from the heavy artillery groups, was assigned for Counter-Battery fire during all the phases of battle.

By 9 April 1917, the guns had been sited, ammunition had been dumped and the very detailed Fire Plan Tables for Creeping Barrages across the fronts of all four Canadian Divisions, as well as the Counter-Battery Fire Tables had been prepared. The artillery was now ready to support the attack on Vimy Ridge, and the gunners waited for the dawn of Easter Monday (9 April 1917), which would witness the greatest artillery barrage in history.

TOPOGRAPHY

The importance of Vimy Ridge lay in its location and commanding height vis-à-vis the area around it. The ridge lay between the Souchez River in the north and Scarpe River to the south, north-east of Arras in northern France, to the west of the vast Douai Plain. It was essentially an escarpment a little over 7 Kilometres long, which gave an unhindered view of the countryside around it. It had gentle slopes towards the western side, and a steeper drop towards the east. Its highest point was Hill 145, a feature which rose 470 feet above the surrounding plains; a little further to its north was another high bump called the Pimple; (both these were to play a key role in the Battle of Vimy Ridge).

As the Vimy escarpment sloped downwards towards the south, lay the La Folie Farm, and the abandoned villages of Les Tilleuis and Thelus. Towards the eastern side there were some forests and the villages of Givenchy-en-Gohelle, Vimy, Petit-Vimy and Farbus. The Lens-Arras road ran through thus region (See Map 6).

The Germans had built strong defences along this ridge on the forward slopes as well as the top. There were strong fortifications, tunnels, barbed wire, trenches and so on. From the top of the ridge, the Germans had a clear view of the area under Allies. The Ridge was the 'lynch pin' of the German defences in the area, the loss of which would expose the German held territory in the Douai Plain to the Allies. Conversely, any Allied attack from the west would be under direct observation of the German troops deployed on top and along the forward slopes of this commanding feature. Two earlier attempts by the French to capture this Ridge had failed.

GERMAN DEFENCES

German Sixth Army

The area of Vimy Ridge was within the theatre of responsibility of the German Sixth Army, commanded by Colonel-General Freiheir von Falkenshausen, which had fought tenaciously at Somme the previous year. Under him were four *Gruppes* – deployed north to south were *Gruppe Loos, Souchez, Vimy and Arras*. These *Gruppes* were centred around Corps headquarters which were organised and resourced depending upon the operational requirement. Such as arrangement gave great flexibility in organizational structuring of higher formations.

Amongst these four *Gruppen*, two *(Souchez* and *Vimy)* were involved in the defence of Vimy Ridge. Although most of Vimy Ridge came under the *Gruppe Vimy* (based on the 1st Bavarian Reserve Corps commanded by General of Infantry Karl Ritter von Fassbinder), the northern extremity of this ridge was defended by units of *Gruppe Souchez,* which was led by General of Infantry Georg Karl Wichura (based upon the VIIIth Reserve Corps).

DEPLOYMENT IN AREA VIMY RIDGE

The area of responsibility of *Gruppen Souchez* and *Vimy* overlapped in the area of Givenchy. While the former (consisting of three divisions) was responsible to north of this town, the latter was south of it till the River Scarpe. (See Map 6) *Gruppe Souchez* consisted of 16th Bavarian, 56th Bavarian and 80th Bavarian Reserve Divisions, while *Gruppe Vimy* comprised 1st Bavarian Reserve, 14th Bavarian, 18th Bavarian (held in reserve) and 79th Prussian Reserve infantry Divisions. In the Battle of Vimy Ridge, it was the elements of 16th Bavarian Infantry Division (*Gruppe Souchez*), 79th Prussian Reserve Division and 1st Bavarian Reserve Infantry Division (both of *Gruppe Vimy*) which saw action.

The northern portion of the Ridge was held by 16 Bavarian Infantry Division (14th and 11th Bavarian Infantry Regiments); in the Centre was the 79th Prussian Reserve Infantry Division (261st, 262nd and 263rd Prussian Reserve Infantry Regiments); while further south was the 1st Bavarian Reserve Infantry Division, (3rd and 1st Bavarian Reserve Infantry Regiments).[16]

While comparing troop levels, it needs to be noted however, that the German division (at 11, 650 men) was numerically inferior to the Canadian division (by over 40 percent). In his article *Vimy Ridge: A Canadian Reassessment*, Andrew Godefroy notes:

At approximately 19,772 all ranks the Canadian division by comparison dwarfed its German competitor. But whereas the Canadian divisions consisted of three infantry brigades, German divisions contained only a single infantry brigade along with a pioneer battalion, cavalry squadron and a field artillery regiment. Apart from the lone pioneer battalion, the German infantry brigade contained three regiments of 2,789 officers and men each (including headquarters) formed into three battalions of approximately 910 officers and men each; each of these battalions in turn were divided into four companies plus a machine gun company. By comparison, Canadian infantry brigades (including headquarters) consisted of approximately 5,200 officers and men with the four infantry battalions each totaling approximately 1240 all ranks. At every tactical level, the Germans were

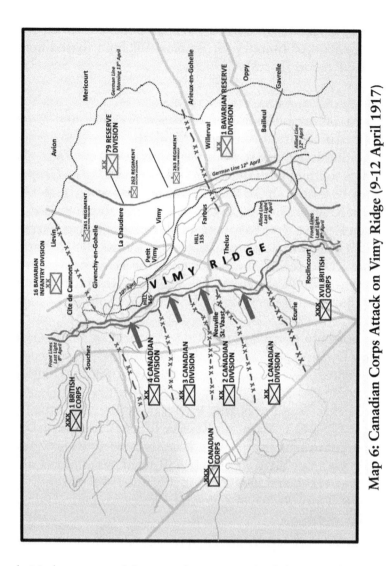

Map 6: Canadian Corps Attack on Vimy Ridge (9-12 April 1917)

decisively outmanned; however they were on the defensive and made every effort to compensate for the lack of personnel with fire power.[17]

German Defence Doctrine

As mentioned earlier, *in February 1917* the Germans had conducted a well-planned withdrawal to the Hindenburg Line with a view to shorten their frontline. They also formulated a new defence doctrine called *Eingreifentaktik;* In brief, this enunciated the establishment of a series of elastic defence zones. The 'forward zone' or *Vorwartszone* consisted of well manned series of trenches and outposts which channelized the attacking enemy to the next zone, called the *Widerstand* or the 'resistance line'.This line consisted of concrete strongpoints, designed to cover a 360-degree arc; these defences were generally sited out of the view of the enemy or on reverse-slopes. Once channelized into the open spaces between these strongpoints, the enemy would be subjected heavy machine gun and artillery fire, before being counter- attacked by highly trained shock troops - the *Sturmbattaillone*. The last line was that of the uncommitted reserves located well to the rear and out of artillery range.[18] Unfortunately Vimy Ridge, with its restricted depth precluded the employment of this new defence doctrine; the defences were therefore of the more conventional nature of dug-outs, trenches and machine gun posts in echelons.

Thus it was that the German regiments deployed at Vimy Ridge were holding a frontage of approximately 1,000 meters each. These regimental defended sectors had their battalions holding defences echeloned one behind the other - front to rear - in the classic German *Stellung* defence system. Turner notes that:

Each regimental sector was responsible for manning its own depth back to the rear areas. This was achieved by rotating the three battalions through one of three duties. One battalion held the frontline positions - normally at least two parallel fire trenches known as I Stellung. The second battalion was situated in like manner on the support line (or II Stellung) to the immediate rear. Distances varied, but generally it was about one kilometre or more behind. The third battalion was placed 'at rest' up to six kilometres to the rear and beyond the range of most enemy artillery. In the event of attack, the reserve battalion was earmarked for counter-attack or manning of the third line (III Stellung) reserve positions nearest their billets. The term 'at rest' is placed in inverted commas because usually it was anything but that. At Vimy Ridge, defences were thickened by the addition of another support trench system between I and II Stellung, dubbed the Zwischenstellung - 'intermediate position; Therefore, the II Stellung to the east of the ridge became the regimental reserve line manned by resting battalions, and the III Stellung (known to the British as the Oppy-Mericourt Line) in the middle of the Douai plain was set aside for reserve divisions under Sixth Army control.[19]

The reverse slopes also had a system of dug-outs called the *Hangstellung*. Each battalion was also deployed in an echeloned configuration, i.e. two companies forward and two behind. Going into the third year of war, the German companies were woefully undermanned. Organised to an establishment of 264 men, in effect each company was staffed by around 150 men at most. This deficiency of manpower was offset by a well designed trench system, dug-outs, concrete strong points, barbed wire entanglements and well sited machine gun posts. Pierre Berton, in his book *Vimy*, writes that: 'Beyond the crater line - in places no more than a few dozen yards away- three parallel rows of German trenches zig - zagged along the lower slopes of the ridge, protected by forty-foot rolls of heavy steel wire with razor-sharp barbs and machine-gun nests and concrete pillboxes'.[20]

The German machine guns were great force multipliers. Vimy defences had a mix of 1908-pattern heavy Maxim machine guns, as well as the lighter Maxim 08/15 light machine guns, the former, with a cyclic rate of up to 500 rounds a minute and an effective range of 1000 meters, could literally decimate an infantry attack. The six 7.6 cm infantry mortars supplemented the fire of the machine guns.

Each division had three batteries of 7.7 cm field guns and three batteries of the heavier 10.5 cm field howitzers- Each battery had four artillery pieces - In addition there was additional large calibre artillery at the Corps and Army Group level, which was made available as required.

CANADIAN PLAN OF ATTACK

After almost four months of planning, preparation and intensive training the Allied Forces were ready to launch the Arras offensive. The date set for the launch of this offensive was 9 April 1917. As part of the British First Army (of the B.E.F.), the Canadian Corps was tasked to capture Vimy Ridge. This was the first time that this corps was being employed as a composite force, under the command of Lieutenant General Sir Julian Byng.

Byng's plan envisaged the simultaneous attack by the four Canadian divisions, assaulting astride one another on a 7000 yards front up the slopes of Vimy Ridge, with the view to capture most of the objective on the first day itself. The Canadian divisions were poised for the attack in their serial order, i.e. 1st Canadian Division in the south, then 2nd and 3rd Canadian Divisions, and finally 4th Canadian Division in the north (See Map 6). Since the southern portion of the ridge was wider than the northern part, 1st and 2nd Canadian Divisions had deeper objectives to capture as compared to the 3rd & 4th Canadian Divisions. In consonance with the overall plans of the Arras offensive, Byng had divided his objectives into four distinct coloured objective lines - the Black, Red, Blue and Brown lines. The Black Line depicted the forward German defences, while the Red Line denoted the main defences on top of the crest of the Ridge. These objectives were assigned to all four divisions. In addition, the southern divisions (1st and 2ndCanadian Divisions) had to advance further to capture the Blue Line (Village of Thelus) and the Brown Line (The German second line in the south – east of the ridge).

The outline tasking was:

(a) 1st Canadian Division – Up to the Commandant's
(Major General   House (Brown line)
Sir Arthur Currie)

(b) 2nd Canadian Division – To include village Thelus
(Major General Henry   and Boulet Wood (Blue
Burstall)   Line) and Boise de la Ville
                          (Brown Line)

(c) 3rd Canadian Division– Le Folie Farm and Ecole
(Major General Louis   Commune (Red Line)
Lipsett)

(d) 4th Canadian Division – Area of Hill 145 and Pimple
(Major General David Watson) (Red Line)

Byng also kept an uncommitted reserve comprising 15th and 95th Infantry Brigades of 5th British Division, and 9th Infantry Brigade of the 3rd Canadian Division. The reserve was tasked to be prepared for the following three contingencies:-

(a) Relief of troops in forward positions
(b) To assist in the capture of Pimple, if 4th Canadian

Division was unable to do so.

(c) To be prepared to carry out exploitation of the operations.

The coloured objective lines also helped in the preparation and execution of the artillery fire-plan timetable. The artillery barrage would 'pause' at these lines to enable the infantry to consolidate (before the next phase), and also for the artillery to re-arm and re-lay the guns. The infantry would advance in the wake of a 'creeping' artillery barrage of field guns, which was timed to advance in increments of 100 yards (90 metres). At the same time, the medium and heavy guns would fire the standard barrages well ahead of the advancing infantry and onto the known German depth positions. The infantry was to attack in waves, and leap frog over one another as the advance progressed.

So confident was Byng of the success of his plan that he hoped to capture bulk of the Vimy Ridge (except the Pimple) by the afternoon of the 9 April. This was indeed a very tight time schedule for an operation of this magnitude. Military historian Pierre Berton offers the following comments on the aspect of the time-table of the attack:

… the Canadians planned to attack on 9 April and they intended to take the ridge not in a matter of days or weeks, but in a matter of hours. The plan was simple. For the first time (and, as it turned out, the last) all four Canadian divisions would surge forward simultaneously to seize the crest by lunch hour under the curtain of the greatest artillery bombardment of the war.

They would do it in a series of carefully timed stages, the objective of each stage, marked on a map by a coloured line. At each stage the forward troops would consolidate, reporting their arrival to low-flying aircraft, while fresh troops leap-frogged through to the next objective.

The times allowed for these forward bounds were remarkably short. The troops had exactly thirty – five minutes to pass through Von Falkenstein's forward defensive belt, seven hundred yards deep. This, the planners marked on the map as the Black Line. They were given forty minutes to dig in before the barrage lifted and the next wave moved through.

The 3rd and 4th Division on the left of the line had the shortest distance to travel. They were expected to be over the top of the ridge and into the woods at the bottom of the rear slope past the Germans' second defence line – the

Red Line on the Planners' maps – in twenty minutes. It was a tall order. For here was a vast and carefully constructed trench barrier, supported by more parallel trenches, wire entanglements, concrete forts, and machine – gun nests. To reach it, one division – the 4th – would have to leap across Hill 145, enduring flanking fire from the Pimple, which was not scheduled to be taken until the following day.

In brief, by 0705 hours Monday morning, just one hour and thirty – five minutes after the opening of the barrage at dawn, the two divisions on the left were expected to be dug in on the far side of Vimy Ridge.

The 1st and 2nd Divisions on the right had much further to go. For them there were four reporting lines – Black, Red, Blue and Brown. Fresh troops would jump through the forward battalions consolidating on the Red Line to advance over the ridge, seizing the villages of Thelus and Farbus, both strongly fortified by the Germans. A British Brigade, attached to the 2nd Division, would thicken that final advance. The last objective, marked as the Brown Line on the maps, ran along the eastern base of the ridge. The troops of Currie's 1st and Burstall's 2nd Division were expected to be there, digging in, at exactly 0118 hours that afternoon.

In short, the Canadians were given less than eight hours to capture all of Vimy Ridge except Pimple. All things considered, the French might be pardoned for scoffing.[21]

The Order of Battle (ORBAT) of both sides is given in Appendix E and F.

THE ATTACK ON VIMY RIDGE

As mentioned earlier, the Canadian Corps had arrived in the Arras Theatre in November 1916; by late January they had been assigned the task of capturing Vimy Ridge. After months of planning, preparation, training and rehearsals the Canadians were now ready for launch. Although earlier planned for 8 April, the attack had been postponed to 9 April at the behest of the French. On the intervening night of 8 / 9 April the troops moved into the tunnels and subways, under the *No Man's Land*, awaiting the dawn when they would be hurled into the assault.

Pierre Berton writes : 'By this time, the entire Canadian Corps was in position, twenty-three battalions in the forward line, thirteen more waiting directly behind, and another nine along with three British battalions in reserve, waiting to leap-frog through more than thirty thousand men stretched out over nearly four miles of front...'[22] the attack was to be launched in waves. Each battalion would assault with two companies in the first wave and two companies following in the second wave.

The time of launch was 0530 hours on 9 April 1917, the Easter Monday. The day of reckoning for the Canadian Corps had arrived. As dawn broke and minutes ticked by, the men waited tensely for the battle to begin. To quote Berton again:

Three minutes to go. A barrage of gas shells landed in the German rear, killing hundreds of horses...

Two minutes, Now came the whispered order to fix bayonets. The sound of the loose locking rings, rippling all along the miles of trenches, was like a humming of a thousand quivering bees.

Silence, thirty thousand men held their breath, tensing their cramped muscles for the moment that some had been awaiting since November.

One more minute ticked by, and then a single gun fired. One second elapsed, and then the world exploded as the greatest artillery barrage in the history of warfare burst upon the unsuspecting Germans and the Battle of Vimy Ridge began.[23]

At exactly 0530 hours, 983 guns and mortars opened fire simultaneously lighting up the entire frontline. While the field guns fired the Creeping Barrage in support of the assaulting infantry, the medium and heavy guns and howitzers pounded the Germany batteries in the rear to suppress their fire. The leading wave of the four Canadians divisions moved out of their positions in the tunnels, subways and trenches and began their advance towards Vimy Ridge, looming ominously in front of them.

Due to the asymmetrical nature of the objective, the four Canadian divisions had varying distances to cover to reach their final objectives; 1st Canadian Division in the south had the longest march, while the 4th Canadian Division in the north had the shortest. However, the highest features such as Hill 145 and Pimple lay in the north. The attack plan of each division varied depending upon the distance, frontage and type of terrain.

1ST CANADIAN DIVISION

The 1st Canadian Division, commanded by Major General Sir Arthur Currie, was the southernmost division of the Canadian Corps. It had the longest distance to traverse to its final objective of Farbus Wood - 3560 meters; the terrain was however, relatively plain. On its south was the 51st Highland Division of XV11 Corps of the British Third Army. On its north was the 2nd Canadian Division.

The division commenced its assault at 0530 hrs with two brigades, the 2nd Canadian Brigade on the right and 3rd Canadian Brigade on the left. The attacking battalions, moving behind the deadly artillery Creeping Barrage, made steady success. Everything went as per the rehearsed plan and they reach the first objective - the Black Line - by 0605 hours. After a very brief pause, to enable the barrage to shift further ahead, the next wave resumed the advance and within half an hour the Red Line too had been breached. While the forward two brigades now began to dig in and consolidate, Currie ordered his reserve 1st Canadian Brigade to move forward. Passing through the Red Line, the battalions assaulted down the slopes and captured the Blue Line by 1130 hours. The artillery barrage now moved to their final depth objective of Farbus Wood, and the Canadians raced further down the sleep eastern slopes of the ridge and reached the Brown Line by 1330 hours. The battle was over for the 1st Canadian Division. In an article in *Vimy Ridge: A Canadian Reassessment*, Andrew Iarocci writes: 'Vimy was a great operational success for 1st Canadian Division. By the evening of 9 April the three infantry brigades advanced 3,500 meters into enemy territory, capturing more than 1,200 prisoners, seven artillery pieces, forty machine guns, twenty mortars and 900 rifles.'[24] It is noteworthy that Private William Milne of 16th Battalion (Canadian Scottish) was awarded the Victoria Cross posthumously for destroying two Germans machine guns.

2ND CANADIAN DIVISION

Major General Henry Burstall's 2nd Canadian Division was operating to the north of the 1st Canadian Division. His plan was to lead the initial assault with two brigades, 4th Brigade on the right and 5th Brigade on the left. Both brigades were to advance on a front of two battalions each, who were tasked to capture the first objective of the Black Line. Upon reaching this, the reserve battalions were to leap-frog through towards to Red Line. Thereafter, the reserve 6th Brigade was to move up and capture the next two objectives - the Blue and Brown lines. The total distance was about two miles.

The assault of the leading waves proceeded as per plan and in about 45 minutes (by 0614 hours) the Black line had been reached. The going had not been easy as there was murderous fire from the German machine guns. During the advance of 18th Battalion of the 4th Brigade, Lance – Sergeant Ellis Clifton was involved in a daring attack on an enemy machine gun post, earning a posthumous Victoria Cross. Berton writes: 'During the advance Clifton had performed an act of conspicuous gallantry, hurling himself at a machine gun that was mowing down his men, charging directly at its crew, clubbing some with his rifle and slashing at others with his bayonet.'[25]

It was now the turn of the two depth battalions (one each of both the brigades) to move forward to capture the next objective of the Red Line, which lay approximately 550 metres ahead. Passing through the forward troops, they began their assault at 0645 hours. Advancing steadily behind the moving artillery barrage, these waves soon reached the Red Line at around 0715 hours.

For the next phase, i.e, the capture of the Blue Line, Burstall ordered his 6th Brigade to move through the forward troops of 4th Brigade, and the 13th British Brigade (now under his command) to attack through the 5th Brigade in the north and capture Hill 135 and the area of Bois de Bonval. According to its planned schedule, at 0935 hours the artillery barrage began to creep ahead. The British and Canadian troops pushed forward. Although they encountered much resistance from the Germans, they continued to make slow, but steady, progress.

Soon the villages of Thelus, Les Tilleuis, Hill 135 and Bois de Bonval were in their hands. The Blue Line had been breached between 1050 and 1110 hours.

The Brown Line was now only a few hundred metres ahead. As the artillery barrage commenced its move towards the line, the infantry began its movement at 1300 hours, the troops of the 6th Brigade on the right and the British 13th Brigade on the left. The assaults were successful and the Canadians and the British had captured Bois de la Ville and Bois du Goulot respectively; the final Brown Line had been reached by approximately 1415 hours - in just under 10 hours since the attack had been launched earlier that morning. The 6th Canadian Brigade now exploited up to the deserted town of Farbus, capturing three German officers. Over the next couple of days the Germans made many unsuccessful attempts to counter-attack Canadian positions.

The division did however pay a heavy price for this spectacular victory. David Campbell in his article encapsulating the operations of 2nd Canadian Division, in the book *Vimy Ridge: A Canadian Reassessment* notes: 'The human cost was substantial; the division suffered approximately 2,547 causalities, all ranks (including 381 casualties from the 13th British Brigade). Of these, twenty – seven officers and 597 other ranks were killed.'[26]

3ᴿᴰ CANADIAN DIVISION

To the north of 2nd Canadian Division, was the 3rd Canadian Division, commanded by Major – General Louis Lipsett, who was the only British regular officer commanding a division in the Canadian Corps. On paper at least, the task of this division appeared to be the easiest; firstly, the total distance to be covered was less than the 1st and 2nd Division to its right, and secondly, it did not have to capture any high features like Pimple or Hill 145 which lay in the path of 4th Canadian Division as its left. However, due to its close proximately to the divisional boundary, Hill 145 had the capability to disrupt the advancing infantry of the 3rd Canadian Division, which indeed played out with devastating effect later that day.

The division's depth objectives lay just 1200 metres from the front line, and it had only two lines to capture – the Black and Red Line (unlike four lines of the two southern divisions. Lipsett planned to launch his assault with two brigades over a frontage of 1500 meters, 7th Brigade on the left and 8th Brigade as the right. His third brigade, the 9th was not available to him as it had been earmarked as part the Corps Reserve.

As the artillery barrage opened up at 0530 hours, the leading waves of the two brigades launched their attack. Such was their determined assault, that within approximately half an hour they had reached the first objective of the Black Line, having overcome the three sets of German forward defence lines. The first to report arrival was 2 Canadian Mounted Regiment (2 CMR) of 8th Brigade at 0600 hrs. Within minutes, 7th Brigade too reported their arrival. The first objective had been captured. After a brief pause, the advance was resumed. 8th Brigade reported the capture of La Folie Farm at 0650 hours, and an hour later, at 0750 hours, the final objective of the Red Line had been reached.

On their left, 7th Brigade too had made steady progress forwards their final objective of the Red Line. However, they soon ran into an unexpected opposition – accurate fire from Hill 145 in the north. Somehow, 4th Canadian Division had not been able to capture this hill as per its scheduled time table, and the German machine gunners and snipers played merry hell into the troops of the 7th Brigade. Berton notes that 'During the past hour the Black Watch Regiment had lost fifty dead and wounded from the sniping on Hill 145.'[27] The Germans also attempted to counter-attack the Canadian forward positions, but the latter continued to hold on, though very tenuously, to their defences. It was late at night, around 2230 hours, that news came of the capture of Hill 145, much to the relief of 7th Brigade. In this action, the 3rd Canadian suffered over 2000 casualties.

4TH CANADIAN DIVISION

The 4th Canadian Division, commanded by Major General David Watson, was the youngest of the Canadian divisions, having been formed in the spring of 1916, i.e., barely one year prior. It had also been weakened by the disastrous raid launched on 1st March to reconnoitre the area of Hill 145, in which it had suffered close to 700 casualties. It was now operating in the northern flank of the corps. Although it had the least distance to travel, it would have to contend with two of the strongest German positions on Vimy Ridge, namely Hill 145 and Pimple. Like its neighbouring 3rd Canadian division, this division too had only the Black and Red Lines to capture. Watson also planned, (like the other divisions), to advance with two brigades, 11th on the right and 12th on the left. His 10th Brigade had been held back for the subsequent attack on Pimple.

In consonance with the rest of the corps, 4th Canadian Division also commenced its movement at 0530 hours. But nothing seemed to go right from the start. The division met with stiff resistance from the Germans, and its advance soon got stalled. One reason perhaps was that at the behest of the commanding officer of the 87th Battalion (Grenadier Guards) Major Harry Shaw, one of the German trench lines (of the second defence line) was left untouched by the artillery barrage. Shaw had reasoned that his men could quickly rush this trench line which was approximately 100 meters from the front line, and thereafter use it for protection against fire from the top of the ridge. This turned out to be a grave mis-calculation. The German machine gun nests operating from these trenches played havoc on to the advancing Canadian troops of the 87th Battalion. Berton has commented: 'Whatever his reason, Shaw's request was granted, with devastating results. In the first six minutes, the Grenadier Guards (87th) lost half their number. Of eleven officers, ten were wounded - five mortally. The fire from the undamaged trench slowed the advance; the troops, unable to maintain the time-table, lost the protection of the barrage, which leaped over the German positions. Nor did they ever regain it.'[28] This is further elucidated by Andrew Godefroy in his article chronicling the operations of 4th Canadian Division in the book Vimy – *A Canadian Reassessment*; he writes:

The 87th Battalion fared ever worse in its initial assault. The enemy's 1st

Battalion, 261ˢᵗ Regiment, under command of Major Zickner, shook off the initial bombardment and emerged from dug-outs to stop the Canadians struggling towards them. Of the eleven Canadian officers and one seargent commanding the four companies in the initial advance, only one officer and the seargent remained in action after the first few minutes. The history of the German Army in Arras suggests that perhaps as few as two machine guns from 5ᵗʰ Company, 261ˢᵗ Infantry Regiment were involved in the annihilation of the 87ᵗʰ Battalion's entire right flank... The centre of the 87ᵗʰ was also quickly smashed.[29]

A sort of a stalemate had temporary developed in the centre of the 11ᵗʰ Brigade due to this fiasco. Other battalions too were making very slow progress. Very accurate fire from the Pimple and Hill 145 was hampering the movement of the Canadians. Further move, Hill 145 was also disrupting the advancing troops of the 3ʳᵈ Canadian division in the south. It was therefore imperative to capture this fortified German position at the earliest. In the northern flank, the battalions of the 12ᵗʰ infantry Brigade were faring no better. The only noteworthy act was of Major Thane McDowell (of the 38ᵗʰ Battalion) who not only bombed out two machine gun nests, but also effected the capture of two German officers and seventy – seven soldiers. He was decorated with Victoria Cross for this act of gallantry.

With the divisional assault having stalled, Major –General Watson assigned the task of capturing Hill 145 to the 85ᵗʰ Battalion (also known as the Nova Scotia Highlanders). This young battalion, which had not yet fought any battle, was about to receive its 'baptism by fire'! Zero hour was 1845 hours; the troops were to assault behind a creeping barrage of twelve minutes. However, at the appointed hour there was no artillery barrage. After waiting in vain for a few minutes, the C and D companies assaulted without artillery cover. They were met by a hail of machine gun fire as well as artillery bombardment. Unfazed, the plucky Canadians carried on gamely, and soon the top of the very troublesome Hill 145 was in their hands.

It was now the turn of the 10ᵗʰ Brigade to join action. In the afternoon of 10ᵗʰ April two battalions of this brigade were tasked to capture the German positions on the eastern slopes of Hill 145, which they managed within one hour. In this action,

Private John Pattison of the 50th Battalion was awarded the Victoria Cross for rushing and destroying a German Machine Gun nest. Though he survived this action, he was killed in another action seven weeks later.

Now only the Pimple remained. Having rested on the 11 April, the 10th Brigade was now ordered to capture Pimple on 12 April. Despite meeting stiff resistance from the re-inforced defences at Pimple, it took only two hours for the Canadians to capture it. The final objective had fallen on the fourth day of fighting!

Without doubt, the 4th Canadian Division had fought the toughest action in the Battle of Vimy Ridge

ARTILLERY OPERATIONS

Artillery played a dominant role in the Canadian victory at Vimy Ridge. Indeed, in the preceding years, with the introduction of heavier calibre guns and howitzers (6-inch, 8-inch, and 9.2 inch guns) as well as changes in doctrinal thinking (creeping barrages and counter – bombardment) artillery had emerged as a battle – winning factor. At Vimy Ridge, the artillery was employed in multiple tasks – pre-attack bombardment to destroy or soften the defences, 'shooting in' the infantry during the actual assault, and counter-bombardment (CB) fire to supress the enemy guns from interfering with own attacks. Artillery fire was deadly, causing death and destruction in its wake. In his article *The Gunners at Vimy*, Tim Cook writes about the effects of artillery fire thus:

But the artillery was the true killer, causing an estimated sixty percent of all wounds. The crash of high explosives, whirling shrapnel and shell splinters proved early in the conflict that artillery would decide the fate of empires.

Artillery fire wrecked havoc on those caught in the open. Shrapnel shells exploded downwards in a shotgun-like blast, spraying the front with hundreds of lead balls. High explosive shells exploded like dynamite, killing through the force of the blast that could collapse lungs and kill a man without leaving a mark. The explosive charge that shattered the shell casing also created jagged shell splinters. The irregular wounds caused by artillery fire were deadly; a victim was three times likely to die from a shell fragment wound to the chest as from a bullet wound to the same region.[30]

The three officers who played a key role in the employment of artillery at Vimy Ridge were Major-General Edward Morrison (the GOC RA at First Army Headquarters), Brigadier-General R.H. Massie (GOC Heavy Artillery) and Lieutenant Colonel Andrew McNaughton (the Counter Bombardment Officer). Each Canadian infantry division had two artillery brigades, each composed of three batteries of 18-pdr guns, and one battery of 4.5 - in howitzer. At six guns per battery, there were 48 artillery pieces per division. The divisional artillery resources were supplemented by mortars as well as the heavy artillery groups available at the Army Group level. For the battle of Vimy Ridge, the bulk of this artillery was made available to the Canadian Corps. In his book *Vimy Ridge 1917,* Alexander Turner notes: '...Byng's foremost means of protecting his infantry was the artillery at his disposal. This fact was not lost on General Sir Henry Horne either and he put the weight of his First Army's artillery behind the Canadians. He gave Byng all three of his heavy artillery groups, four extra divisional artillery groups and (less obvious but most significant of all) the overwhelming share of his ammunition allocation. *There was an artillery piece to every 10 metre of Corps frontage – a greater concentration than seen at the Somme the previous year*[31] (emphasis by the author) (See Table 3.1).

This was indeed a very formidable force of artillery which was destined to play a very decisive role in the Battle of Vimy Ridge.

The artillery plan was divided into four phases, excluding the Preparatory Phase. The plan was to be put into action three weeks prior to the commencement of the actual attack, i.e., on 20 March 1917.

PREPARATORY PHASE
This period was one of planning, preparation, coordination of artillery effort and marshalling of resources. It encompassed the logistics of moving the artillery to the deployment areas, digging gun pits, dumping of ammunition, fire-planning,

TABLE: 3.1 DISTRIBUTION OF ARTILLERY AT VIMY RIDGE

Division	Approx Frontage	Generic FA Bdes	Attached FA Bdes	2in. Trench Mortars	9.45in. Trench Mortars	Div. Heavy Art. Group	9.2in Howitzer Batteries	8in Howitzer Batteries	6in. Howitzer Batteries	60-pdr. Gun Batteries	6in. Mark VII Gun. Batteries	Remarks
1st	2,000m	2 (8)	4 (16)	18	5	11th	1	1	3	Nil	Nil	No of Field Artillery Batteries is in brackets
2nd	1,400m	2 (8)	5 (20)	18	5	77th	1	2	2	Nil	Nil	No of Field Artillery Batteries is in brackets
						64th	1	2	2	Nil	Nil	
3rd	1,300m	2 (8)	2 (8)	36	6	70th	Nil	Nil	4	Nil	Nil	No of Field Artillery Batteries is in brackets
						13th	1	1	3	Nil	Nil	
4th	2,00m	2 (8)	5 (20)	24	4	53rd	1	Nil	3	Nil	Nil	No of Field Artillery Batteries is in brackets
						1st (can)	1	Nil	4	Nil	Nil	
						51st	Nil	2	3	Nil	Nil	
C/Bty Group 1	18-pdr	24	48	9	4	N/A	2	1	1	2	-	Also 1x4 5in Howitzer Bty
C/Bty Group 2	4.5in	8	16				Nil	Nil	Nil	4	1	Also 1x4 5in Howitzer Bty
C/Bty Group 3	18-Pdr	160	320				Nil	1	1	3	-	Also 1x4 5in Howitzer Bty
Total Batteries	4.5in.	46	92				8	10	26	9	2	See Notes for explanation of odd
Total Guns				96	24		36	36	104	54	8	

Notes: 1. All Field Artillery Batteries had six pieces, as old 60-pdr, Batteries. 6in Mark VII Gun. 6.8 and 9.2in, Howitzer Batteries all had four apiece. 2in. Trench Mortar Batteries had eight barrels; 9.45in. Batteries.

2. In some instances, the 'Total Guns' figures do not confirm to the set number of guns per battery. Some batteries were over established strength whilst others were suffering shortage. An obvious example of this is the 9.45in. Trench Mortar. Each battery was established for four mortars but three of our divisions were fielding extra.

3. Sourced from Peter Dennis, *Vimy Ridge 1917: Byng's Canadians Triumph at Arras. p 32*

preparing the counter-bombardment plan and fine-tuning the creeping barrages in each of the divisional sectors.

Finding deployment areas for almost 1000 artillery pieces was a very challenging task. These needed to be located out of visual observation of the German positions, and yet to be able to fire at their optimum range. There was also the need for deployment of massive quantities of ammunition for this artillery enumeration. Nigel Cave writes in his book *Vimy Ridge* that: 'The allocation for this operation was 42,500 tons of shells with a daily quota of 2465 tons'[32]. The movement and stock –piling of such a quantity was a logistician's nightmare. There was also a requirement of positioning ammunitions lorries in the near vicinity for replenishment. Lieutenant Colonel McNaughton was busy throughout this period, acquiring intelligence of the German artillery batteries deployment behind the Vimy Ridge, based upon which he then prepared the detailed Counter-Bombardment Plan. He was given a dedicated allocation of artillery guns for this purpose. During this period, artillery officers also were busy preparing detailed Fire Plan Tables for their creeping barrages. By 20 March 1917 all artillery preparations were in place.

PHASE I (20 MARCH 1917)

Phase 1 of the artillery plan was conducted over two weeks from 20 March 1917 to 2 April 1917. This was basically designed to soften up the German defences over a sustained duration of 14 days. Byng, however, decided to employ only half his available artillery, with a view to conserve his ammunition (which would be required in the attack phase) as well as to preserve barrel wear and tear. Byng gave the following priorities for this Phase – counter-battery fire, destruction of firing positions, destruction of barbed wire entanglements, and interdiction of re-supply and repair parties.[33]

From 20 March to 2 April 1917, the German positions were subjected to incessant pounding by the Allied massed artillery. In his article *The Gunner At Vimy,* Tim Cook Writes:

The first guns that opened up on 20 March targeted enemy dug-outs, trenches and known strong points that had been identified through aerial and ground intelligence. The incessant pounding by the guns, trench mortars, and indirect machine gun fire (not controlled by the gunners) was to prevent the repair of trenches. An extensive Canadian raiding program snatched dozens of prisoners, most of whom were willing to pass along information as they were interrogated. Throughout this first phase of the artillery battle, more batteries arrived at the front, were situated in their gun pits and joined in the methodical, punishing bombardment.[34]

Cook further notes that in this Phase more than 2,00,000 shells of 18 - pounders were fired, as well as another 1,43,000 of the longer calibre of medium and heavy guns.

Phase 2 (2 April 1917)

On 2 April 1917, one week prior to the actual attack, the artillery plan moved into its second phase. This seven-day incessant pounding of German positions by all available artillery was designed to soften up the defences. Such was its intensity that it broke windows in Douai, 20 kilometres away. The Germans later referred to this as the 'Week of Suffering' or 'The Symphony of Hell'. The ammunition scales for this phase, at 1,050 per gun and 600 per gun for the 18-pounders and 9.2 inch howitzers respectively, reflect the ferocity of the artillery bombardment. In this short period the 18-pounders fired an astounding 3,36,000 rounds, or roughly ten rounds per yard of the front! Turner writes that:

The shelling was conducted round the clock, giving the hapless Germans no respite from the incarceration of their airless dugouts. During the one hour a day that firing ceased to allow 16 Squadron to conduct battle damage assessments, the Vickers machine guns would send thousands of rounds arcing on to the junctions and entrances of communication trenches to deter relief, ration parties and repair details. The already – shattered villages of Thelus, Les Tillieus, Farbus, Givenchy-en-Gohelle, Vimy, Petit Vimy and Willerval were levelled to rubble. Hitherto spared German concrete strong points were smashed by massive, moaning howitzer shells whose detonation knocked the wind out of men nearly a kilometre away from impact.[35]

This artillery bombardment continued relentlessly right through the week causing immense physical and psychological damage to the Germans. The Counter-Bombardment teams were also very active in targeting known German gun positions. Tim Cook describes this artillery onslaught in his article: 'German trenches were pounded hour after hour, day after day. Even in dark there was no escape. Byng ordered his gunners to fire all night to interrupt reliefs and working parties and to keep the enemy in a "state of alarm" and "deny him rest." The Germans went to ground in deep dugouts that offered good protection, but the psychological strain was terrible.'[36]

To enforce this point, he quotes a German account:

What the eye sees through the clouds of smoke is a sea of masses of earth thrown up and clouds of smoke rolling along... among all of these are spitting fuzes, slow burning gas shells, exploding trench mortars, and the white vapour appears to consume everything until it obliterates the whole spectacle of dancing madness in impenetrable fog. How long did this nightmare last? The sense of time seems intensified so that every second is divided in to one hundred moments of fear.[37]

While it was a 'Week of Suffering' for the Germans, it was also a period when the endurance of the Allied gunners was tested to the limit. They toiled day and night unloading ammunition from the lorries, preparing the ammunition, loading the guns, re-laying the trails and so on. But they did not give up.

PHASE 3 (9 APRIL 1917)

After three weeks of intense pounding and weakening of German defences, the stage was set for the attack on Vimy Ridge. This was also the commencement of Phase 3 of Artillery Operations. Initially planned for 8 April the attack had been postponed by 24 hours to 9 April. It was Easter Monday.

As dawn broke there was a kind of ominous silence amongst the leading infantry waves waiting to be launched – the weeks of waiting were finally over. Back in the gun positions the guns were loaded and readied for the artillery fire plan scheduled to commence at 0530 hours. As minutes ticked towards H hour, the gun crews were ready, with watches synchronized and firing lanyards in firing position. At exactly 0530 hours, a signal gun located in the centre of the firing line fired a single round. As if on cue, 983 guns opened fire simultaneously. The countryside reverberated with the intensity of this sound.

This was, till then, the largest concentration of artillery fire in history. This was a moment which would forever remain etched in the memory of all those who were witness to this roll of thunder. One soldier, J.A Bain – a Canadian Signaler – is quoted thus:

The din was terrific – deafening –indeed it is hard to find suitable words to describe the awful uproar made by thousands [sic] of our guns and the shells passing through the air, bursting on and over the enemy's trenches ahead of us. The rattle of machine guns, the detonation of hand grenades and bombs, and the enemy's counter – barrage which although not very formidable, was bursting on our old front line, all joining in one vast volume of noise.[38]

Similarly, a German eyewitness (who was at the receiving end of this barrage, Lieutenant Bittlan has described it thus:

As if on command a barrage spat from large and small calibre mouths, building to an unsurpassed frenzy of fire. The impact of each salvo is indistinguishable from the next... Nerves are stretched to breaking point, drinking in this image, the beautiful terrifying painting. A pulsating beat in the left breast... the heart is like lead; it beats in the throat and stops breathing. Blood surges into the mouth, sense fades away.[39]

The impact of this mass of shells on the Vimy Ridge was deadly; and it was a sight that the frontline Canadian soldiers would never forget. Turner notes that,:

The entire length of the ridge just 100 yards to their front became of boiling, angry, tearing mass of explosions – each penetrating the gloom like lightening. Clods of chalk and timber were raining down. To their flanks, the machine guns barked into life, the damp air reducing their report to laboured slapping sound. They were barely audible above the din of the barrage, which many described as a tangible "ceiling of sound."[40]

As the greatest artillery barrage in history exploded over Vimy Ridge, it first rained its vast array of shells from guns of a variety of calibres upon the German first defence line for three minutes, and then, as per plan started moving forward at the rate 100 yards (91 metres) every three minutes. As they had practiced for weeks, the infantry pressed forward in the wake of this artillery fire towards their assigned objectives. One infantry soldier described it thus: 'The infantry advance in long waves, the first wave keeping forty yards behind the barrage or as near as comfortable. When the barrage lifts the waves of men jump forward at a given distance, keeping close to the barrage until it lifts again, when the same tactics are repeated. The concentrated drumfire of artillery and machine guns keeps the enemy in his dugouts. When the barrage lifts he hasn't time to come out of his subterranean galleries to work his machine-guns before our infantry are on top of him.'[41]

In conjunction with the Creeping Barrage, the Counter Battery Fire Table was also executed, in which the heavy calibre guns rained their shells upon the mass of German battery positions in the rear of Vimy Ridge. Alexander Turner notes that: 'McNaughton's counter-battery plan was initiated – gun positions were being hit with a mix of high explosive and gas shells. His precise calculations paid dividends; all but two of *Gruppe Vimy's* 69 Artillery batteries had been plotted accurately and were shelled that morning. As soon as it was light enough, 16 Squadron was in the air over the German rear areas, prioritizing counter-battery fires as the German guns attempted to react. This was hazardous duty. A sky thick with passing shells buffeted the little planes. Pilots recall the hum and vibration of a near miss. 'Friendly' shells brought down three aircraft that day.'[42]

PHASE 4 (12 APRIL)
The final phase entailed the movement of guns forward to their new defences on the ridge. German counter-attacks were expected, and it was imperative to have the guns in their new positions, to increase their range. This forward movement proved to be quite a challenge due to the slushy roads and craters. The heavy snow of 9 April had greatly deteriorated the condition of the roads, hampering the movement of guns and horses. Parties of engineers, pioneers as well as infantry worked in tandem using 'fascines' to layer the muddy and slushy roads. It was with great difficulty that the guns were moved forward to their new positions, from where they continued to provide effective fire support for further operations.

CONCLUSION

The victory at Vimy Ridge continues to hold a special place in Canadian military history. In its first operation as a composite entity in the form of the Canadian Corps, the four Canadian divisions fought courageously to evict the Germans from the formidable Vimy Ridge. This was a stupendous achievement after months of stalemate in the Western Front. Though it came at a loss of 10,602 casualties, this success was a defining movement for the Canadian Corps. In this battle, four Canadians were awarded the Victoria Cross for valour – Captain Thain Mcdonald, Lance- Seargent Ellis Sifton, Private William Milne and Private John Pattison.

The Canadian Corps together with the British Corps to its south, had captured more ground, prisoners and artillery pieces than any previous British offensive of the war. This stupendous victory was achieved due to a variety of factors such as '... technical and tactical innovations, *very powerful artillery preparation* (italics by the author), sound and meticulous planning and thorough preparation.'[43] The artillery indeed played a very crucial role not only during the actual four days of battle, but also in the massive preparatory bombardment conducted over the preceding seven days to pulverize the German defences. The *Canadian Encyclopedia* notes:

The week before the assault, more than a million shells were fired at German forces manning the ridge itself, and waiting in reserve in the villages behind it. The intense bombardment destroyed enemy trenches, gun emplacements, communication lines, transportation cross roads, even whole villages.

According to the *Official History of the Canadian Army in the First World War*,... a crushing bombardment fell on German positions. One Canadian observer records that the shells poured over heads like water from a hose, thousands and thousands a day - the enemy named this period the *Week of Suffering*.[44]

The greatest barrage in history (till that date) which was fired on 9 April 1917 to signal the start of the attack of the Canadian Corps on Vimy Ridge, is remembered till today. Pierre Berton quotes an infantry soldier who participated in this now famous assault:

> 5.30 came and a great light lit the place, a light made up of innumerable flickering tongues which appeared from the void and extended as far to the south as the eye could see, a light which rippled and lit the clouds in that moment of silence before the crash and thunder of the battle smote the senses. Then the Ridge in front was wreathed in flame as the shells burst, confining the Germans to their dugouts while our men advanced to the assault.[45]

While commemorating the emphatic victory of the Canadian Corps, we must also acknowledge the contribution of the British and Indian troops who fought alongside the Canadians. While the role of the British Heavy and Field artillery is well-known, the part played by the Indian gunners has not received adequate recognition. Pierre Berton, in his well-researched book Vimy makes a passing remark of Sikh gunners, while narrating how the badly injured Corporal Gus Sivertz (2 Canadian Mounted Rifles) made his way back to the medical dressing station.

He (Sivertz) was in the Army vernacular, one of the 'walking wounded'. Back he walked to his own artillery lines, where the turbanned Sikhs of the Lahore heavy artillery were manning the big guns. They had already moved forward to lengthen the range into the German back areas. Sivertz, now completely punch drunk, oblivious to his surroundings, walked directly into their muzzles. He dimly heard an officer give the order to fire. Four gigantic shells, screamed not more than a foot above his head.

The website of Sikh Heritage Museum of Canada, Mississauga, records:

> In September 1914, the Punjab Lahore Division arrived in France as the first of the colonial forces to defend the Crown. In late 1915, Divisional Infantry embarked for Mesopotamia (Iraq) while the artillery remained in France. Initially attached to the Third Canadian Division, the Lahore Division's Artillery was subsequently attached to the Fourth Canadian Division in April 1916. This artillery saw action at the battle of Somme and then at Vimy. Confronted with a heavy defended position (Vimy author) which had resisted earlier British and French attacks, the Canadian assault began as one officer wrote with, 'the most wonderful artillery barrage known in the history of the world...

When we remember the valour and sacrifice to achieve this victory, we should also celebrate the ties that bound men from different races and religions to unite under one flag in the common cause of freedom.

A painting at this Museum shows Sikh soldiers of the Divisional Ammunition Column along with British gunners firing a 'creeping barrage' in support of advancing Canadian infantry on the assault at Vimy Ridge on Easter Monday morning in 1917.[47]

In spite of this decisive victory at Vimy Ridge, it did not contribute strategically to the future outcome of the war; even the Battle of Arras ground to a halt in May. The Great War continued for another year and a half till the final surrender on 11 November 1918.

Considering its iconic status, it was only befitting that the Canadian War Memorial to those countrymen who died in the Great War should come up on Vimy Ridge. Known as the Vimy Memorial To The Missing, it is located on the highest feature as the ridge, Hill 145, which was captured with great cost by the 4th Canadian Division on 13 April 1917. There is a very impressive twin-pillar monument on top of this hill, sculpted by Canadian sculptor Walter Symour Allward. These 120 feet high pillars signify the English and French speaking parts of Canada. Between the pillars is a 30 ton shrouded figure representing the spirit of Canada honouring 11,285 Canadians who died in France, but do not have a grave. Their names are inscribed in the monument. The base reads:

'To the valour of their countryman in the Great War and in memory of their sixty thousand dead, this monument is raised by the people of Canada.'

Inscribed on the base are the names of 11,285 Canadian soldiers who were listed as missing or presumed dead in France, i.e., who do not have a known grave. This Memorial stands in a 250 acre park, whose land was gifted by the French to Canada. The Memorial was unveiled by King Edward VIII of Great Britain on 26 July 1936 in the presence of President Albert Lebrun of France. It was restored over three years beginning 2004, and rededicated by Queen Elizabeth II on 9 April 2007, on the occasion of the 90th Anniversary of this great battle.

APPENDIX E
Order of Battle - British Army

The Canadian Corps - Lt. Gen. Hon Sir Julian Byng

Corps troops

Canadian Cavalry Brigade – Brig. Gen. J.E.B. Seely
    Royal Canadian Dragoons (Detached to Third Army)
    Fort Garry Horse (Detached to Third Army)
    Canadian Light Horse
Artillery – Brig. Gen. E. W. B. Morrison
    Royal Canadian Horse Artillery Brigade
    1st Brigade, Canadian Garrison Artillery
    2nd Brigade, Canadian Garrison Artillery
    3rd Brigade, Canadian Garrison Artillery
Engineers – Brig. Gen. E.W.B Morrison
    Corps Survey Section
    1st Tramways Company
    2nd Tramways Company
    1st, 2nd, 3rd, 4th Field Engineer Companies
    67th Canadian Pioneer Battalion
    123rd Canadian Pioneer Battalion
    1st, 2nd, 3rd, 4th Canadian Entrenchment Battalions
    Machine guns – Col. R. Brutinel
    1st Motor Machine – Gun Brigade
1st Division - Maj. Gen. A.W. Currie
    1st Brigade Canadian Field Artillery
    2nd Brigade Canadian Field Artillery
    1st Division Ammunition Column
    1st Division Signal Company
    1st Canadian Infantry Brigade – Brig. Gen .W.A. Griesbach
    2nd Canadian Infantry Brigade – Brig.Gen. F. O. W. Loomis
    3rd Canadian Infantry Brigade – Brig. Gen. G. S. Tuxford
2nd Division – Maj. Gen. H.E. Burstall
    5th Brigade Canadian Field Artillery
    6th Brigade Canadian Field Artillery
    2nd Brigade Canadian Engineers
    2nd Division Ammunition Column
    2nd Division Signal Company
    12 Company, D Battalion, Heavy Machine-Gun Corps
    (8xMk II Tanks)
    4th Canadian, Infantry Brigade – Brig. Gen. R. Rennie
    5th Canadian Infantry Brigade-Brig. Gen. A. H. Macdonnell
    6th Canadian Infantry Brigade -Brig.Gen. H.B.D Ketchen

3rd **Division** – Maj. Gen. L.J. Lipsett
    9th Brigade Canadian Field Artillery
    10th Brigade Canadian Field Artillery
    3rd Brigade Canadian Engineers
    3rd Division Ammunition Column
    3rd Division Signal Company
    7th Canadian Infantry Brigade – Brig. Gen. A. C. Macdonnel
    8th Canadian Infantry Brigade – Brig. Gen. J. H. Elmsley
        9th Canadian Infantry Brigade (earmarked as corps reserve)
4th **Division** – Maj.Gen. D. Watson
    3rd Brigade Canadian Field Artillery
    4th Brigade Canadian Field Artillery
    4th Brigade Canadian Engineers
    4th Division Ammunition Column
    4th Division Signal Company
    10th Canadian Infantry Brigade – Brig. Gen. E. Hilliam
    11th Canadian Infantry Brigade – Brig. Gen. V.W. Odlum
    12th Canadian Infantry Brigade – Brig. Gen. J. H. MacBrian
Attached from I Corps
5th **Division** – Maj. Gen. R.B. Stephen
    1st/6th Hussars
    15th Brigade Royal Field Artillery (Attached to 2nd Division)
    27th Brigade Royal Field Artillery (Attached to 2nd Division)
    59th Field Company Royal Engineers
    491st Field Company Royal Engineers
    527th Field Company Royal Engineers
    205th Machine-Gun Company (Attached to 4th Division)
    5th Division Ammunition Column
    5th Division Signal Company
    13th Infantry Brigade- Brig. Gen. L. O.W. Jones (Attached to 2nd Division)
    95th Infantry Brigade – N/K
    1st Battalion, Devonshire Regiment
    1st Battalion, East Survey Regiment
    1st Battalion, Duke of Cornwall's Light Infantry
    12th Battalion, The Gloucestershire Regiment
    95th Machine-Gun Company
    15th Infantry Brigade – Brig. Gen. M. N. Turner
Attached from First Army
Heavy Artillery
2nd (Canadian) Heavy Artillery Group, Canadian Garrison

Artillery (Counter-Battery Group 1)

50th Heavy Artillery Group, Royal Garrison Artillery(Counter-Battery Group 2)

76th Heavy Artillery Group, Royal Garrison Artillery(Counter-Battery Group 3)

11th Heavy Artillery Group, Royal Garrison Artillery(Attached to 1st Division)

77th Heavy Artillery Group, Royal Garrison Artillery (Attached to 1st Division)

64th Heavy Artillery Group, Royal Garrison Artillery(Attached to 2nd Division)

70th Heavy Artillery Group, Royal Garrison Artillery(Attached to 2nd Division)

13th Heavy Artillery Group, Royal Garrison Artillery (Attached to 3rd Division)

53rd Heavy Artillery Group, Royal Garrison Artillery(Attached to 3rd Division)

51st Heavy Artillery Group, Royal Garrison Artillery(Attached to 4th Division)

1st (Canadaian) Heavy Artillery Group, Royal Garrison Artillery(Attached to 4th Division)

Field Artillery

31st Division Field Artillery Group (Two Royal Field Artillery brigades)

63rd Division Field Artillery Group(Two Royal Field Artillery brigades)

Reserve (Lahore) Field Artillery Group (Two Royal Field Artillery brigades)

5th Brigade, Royal Horse Artillery

8th Brigade, Canadian Field Artillery

18th Brigade, Royal Horse Artillery

26th Brigade, Royal Horse Artillery

28th Brigade, Royal Horse Artillery

76th Brigade, Royal Horse Artillery

93rd Brigade, Royal horse Artillery

242nd Brigade, Royal Horse Artillery

Tunnelling Engineers

172nd Tunnelling Company Royal Engineers

176th Tunnelling Company Royal Engineers

182nd Tunnelling Company Royal Engineers

185th Tunnelling Company Royal Engineers (Approx 500 men each)

1 Corps, 24ᵗʰ Division – Bois-en-Hache, 12 April 1917
    73ʳᵈ Infantry Brigade – Brig.Gen.W.J Dugan

APPENDIX F
Order of Battle - German Army

1st **Bavarian Reserve Corps** (*Gruppe Vimy*)- General of Infantry Karl Von Fasbender

Corps troops

Artillery

> 9th Field Artillery Regiment
>
> 25th Reserve Field Artillery Regiment
>
> 66th Reserve Field Artillery Regiment
>
> 69th Field Artillery Regiment
>
> Three Batteries of Kriegsmarine 30 cm Naval guns

79th Reserve Infantry Division – General of Infantry von Bacmeister

> 63rd Reserve Field Artillery Regiment
>
> Pioneer Batttalion
>
> Cavalry Squadron
>
> Filed Replenishment Depot
>
> Specialist Machine-gun Battalion
>
> 261st Reserve Infantry Regiment – Oberst von Goerne
>
> 262nd Reserve Infantry Regiment– Major Frehierr von Rotenhan
>
> 263rd Reserve Infantry Regiment – Ober stlieutnant von Behr, Reinforced on 9 April by :
>
> 1st Battalion, 118th Reserve Infantry Regiment, 56th Infantry Division
>
> 3rd Battalion, 34th Reserve Infantry Regiment, 80th Infantry Division
>
> 1st Bavarian Reserve Infantry Division Generalmajor Freiherr von Bechmann
>
> 3rd Reserve Field Artillery Regiment
>
> Pioneer Battalion
>
> Cavalry Squadron
>
> Field Replenishment Depot
>
> Specialist Machine-Gun Battalion
>
> 3rd Bavarian Reserve Infantry Regiment-Major Maier, Regiment reinforced on 9 April by:
>
> 1st Battalion, 225th Infantry Regiment, 17th Division

Note: 1st Bavarian of Reserve Infantry Regiment (Oberstlieutnant von Fuger), 2nd Bavarian Reserve Infantry Regiment (Oberstlieutnant von Brunner) fought the 51st Division of XVII corps in the Third Army area of operations to the south of

Vimy Ridge. They were not involved in the actions described.

14th Bavarian Infantry Division-General Ritter von Rauchenberger
Though part of *Gruppe Vimy*, it took no part in the battle for
Vimy Ridge. It was posted on the northern side of the river
Scarpe and fought the 34th and 9th Divisions of XVII Corps.

8th Reserve Corps (*Gruppe Souchez*) = General of Infantry Wichura

16th Bavarian Infantry Division – Generalmajor Mohl

Field Artillery Regiment (Title N/K)

Pioneer Battalion

Cavalry Squadron

Field Replenishment Depot

Specialist Machine-Gun Battalion

11th Infantry Regiment – Major Ritter von Braun

1st Battalion, 2nd Battalion, 3rd Battalion

Regiment reinforced on 10 and 11 April by:

1st Battalion, 14th Bavarian Infantry Regiment (16th Bavarian
Infantry Division)

1st Battalion, 21st Bavarian Infantry Regiment (16th Bavarian
Infantry Division)

3rd Battalion, 5th Guards Infantry Regiment (4th Guards Division)

1st Battalion, 93rd Reserve Infantry Regiment (4th Guards Division)

Note: With the exception of reinforcing battalions specified above,
16th Division's 14th and 21st Bavarian Infantry Regiments remained uncommitted to battle; 56th and 80th Divisions forming the remainder of *Gruppe Souchez* also only played a reinforcing role.

NOTES

1. Nigel Cove, *Vimy Ridge*, Pen & Sword Books Ltd, Barnslay, Canada, 2013, p.120.
2. Pierre Berton, *Vimy*, Pen & Sword Books Ltd, Barnslay, Canada, 2003, pp. 25-6
3. Tom Douglas, *Valour at Vimy Ridge*, Altitude Publishing Canada Ltd, Canmore, Alberta, 2007, p.16
4. Ibid., p.17
5. Geoffrey Hayes, Andrew Iarocci, Mike Bechthold, (Editors), *Vimy Ridge: A Canadian Reassessment*, Wilfrid Laurier University Press, Waterloo, Ontario, Canada, 2014, p.9
6. Alexander Turner, *Vimy Ridge 1917: Byng's Canadians Triumph at Arras*, Osprey Publishing, Oxford, UK, 2010, pp. 8-9.
7. Ibid., pp. 12-13
8. Pierre Berton, *Vimy*, p.92.
9. Alexander Turner, *Vimy Ridge* 1917, p.39
10. Pierre Berton, *Vimy*, p.163.
11. Alexander Turner, *Vimy Ridge* 1917, p.33
12. Ibid., p.39
13. Tim Cook, in his article *Gunners At Vimy*, published in *Vimy Ridge: A Canadian Reassessment*, pp. 108-9
14. Alexander Turner, *Vimy Ridge* 1917, p.38.
15. Pierre Berton, *Vimy*, p.168.
16. Andrew Godefroy, in his article *The German Army At Vimy Ridge*, published in *Vimy Ridge: A Canadian Reassessment*, p.229.
17. Ibid., p.227.
18. Alexander Turner, *Vimy Ridge* 1917, describes the new German Doctrine in p.29.
19. Ibid, p.21.
20. Pierre Berton, *Vimy*, p.74.
21. Ibid., pp. 178-9.
22. Ibid., p. 209.
23. Ibid, p. 212
24. Andrew Iarocci, in his article *The 1st Canadian Division* published in *Vimy Ridge: A Canadian Reassessment*, p.166.
25. Pierre Berton, *Vimy*, p.223
26. David Campbell, in his article *The 2nd Canadian Division*, p.185
27. Pierre Berton, *Vimy*, p.257.

28. Ibid., p.262.
29. Andrew Godefroy, in his article *4th Canadian Division,* published in *Vimy Ridge: A Canadian Reassessment,* p.219
30. Tim Cook, in his article *The Gunners At Vimy Ridge,* p.106.
31. Alexander Turner, *Vimy Ridge 1917,* p.36.
32. Nigel Cave, *Vimy Ridge,* p.120
33. Alexander Turner, *Vimy Ridge 1917,* p.36.
34. Tim Cook, in his article *The Gunners at Vimy Ridge,*p.113.
35. Alexander Turner, *Vimy Ridge 1917,* p.48.
36. Tim Cook, in his article *The Gunners At Vimy Ridge,* pp 114.
37. Ibid., p.115.
38. Ibid., p.116.
39. Alexander Turner, *Vimy Ridge 1917,* pp. 53-4
40. Ibid., p.53.
41. Tim Cook, in his article *The Gunners At Vimy Ridge,* p.109.
42. Alexander Turner, *Vimy Ridge 1917,* p.54.
43. *The Battle of Vimy Ridge:* Fast facts, accessed from http://www/veterans.gc.co/eng/remembrance/memorials/overseas/first.world.war/vimy/battle p.1
44. *Battle of Vimy Ridge* accessed from http://www.the canadian encylopedia-ca/en/article/vimy.ridge/p.5.
45. Pierre Berton, *Vimy,* p.13.
46. Shmc.ca/battle-of-vimy-ridge.

CHAPTER-4

Battle of Bir Hacheim (Point 171)

(27 May 1942)

Second World War

I also vividly recall the dust and fury of the Battle of Bir Hacheim, replete as it was, with numerous acts of valour and courage.

GENERAL P. P. KUMARAMANGALAM

DSO, MBE, (Retd),
Former Chief of Army Staff,
who commanded 7 Field Battery in this battle.[1]

INTRODUCTION

The Battle of Bir Hacheim (Point 171) will go down in the annals of military history as one of the finest examples of an artillery battle, where the gunners of 2 Indian Field Regiment (later re-designated as 2 Field Regiment [SP]), as part of the 3 Indian Motor Brigade, firing over their gun's 'open sights' in the direct-firing role, knocked out 56 enemy tanks (although some other estimates vary between 46 and 54). On Wednesday, the 27 of May 1942, in the Libyan desert in North Africa, the gun crews of the 25 Pounder Guns of the regiment literally fought to 'the last man last round', till over-run by the might of General (later Field Marshal) Erwin Rommel's *Panzerarmee Afrika*.

This battle has been immortalized by artist Walter Langhammer's painting depicting a Sikh gun detachment of 7 Indian Field Battery engaging the German and Italian tanks (see book cover). This painting now adorns the walls of the Regimental Mess. Major General Francis de Guingand, the Chief of Staff to General Sir Claude Auchinleck, Commander-in-Chief of the Eighth Army, called it 'the fateful day'.[2]

After the battle General Auchinleck sent the following message to the brigade commander: 'I wish to tell you how proud I am of 3rd Indian Motor Brigade. Your courage and sacrifice on that day (27 May 1942 - author) did much, I feel, to break the force of the enemy'.[3] Sir Winston Churchill, the British Prime Minister made the following statement in the House of Commons on 2 June 1942: 'The full brunt of the enemy's initial advance to the East of Bir Hacheim was taken by 3rd Indian Motor Brigade Group, which was overborne by sheer weight of metal, but not until after it had inflicted heavy casualties on the enemy and seriously impeded its advance'.[4] Out of a total of 80 tanks which were destroyed or put out of action, 56 had been destroyed by 2 Indian Field Regiment.[5] The Regiment had been baptized in fire during intense combat within two years of its raising, in what was clearly a 'gunner's battle'.

RAISING OF 2 INDIAN FIELD REGIMENT

As a result of the British decision to 'Indianise' the artillery of the Indian Army, the first field artillery unit to be raised was 'A' Field Brigade on 15 January 1935. (To commemorate this event, 15 January was celebrated as Gunners Day, till it was changed to 28 September in 1988 - Author) A few years later, it was decided to increase the number of 'Indianised' Artillery Regiments, as a result of which the second regiment, the 'B' Field Brigade was raised in Bangalore on 15 May 1940. The initial raising of this regiment was with only two batteries, i.e. 3 and 4 Indian Field Batteries. Strangely, the regiment had a mix of 18 Pounder guns and 4.5 inch howitzers. The nucleus of officers (including the Commanding Officer, Lieutenant Colonel Guy Horsfield), Viceroy's Commissioned Officers (VCOs) and men came from 'A' Field Brigade. In April 1941 'A' and 'B' Field Brigades were re-designated as 1 Indian Field Regiment and 2 Indian Field Regiment respectively. In September 1940 (within four months of its raising) , the regiment moved to Jhansi, and later in May 1941 to Trimulghery (near Secunderabad). Meanwhile, the third battery (7 Indian Field Battery) was raised here on 1 July

1941 under Major Parmasiva Prabhakara Kumaramangalam, with 25 Pounder guns. Kumaramangalam, known simply as 'K', was educated in Eton and was the second Indian artillery officer (after Prem Singh Gyani) to be commissioned from the Royal Military Academy (RMA), Woolwich. He had initially joined 'A' Field Brigade and was later transferred to 'B' Field Brigade in May 1940. 'K' was destined to play a stellar role in the famous Battle of Bir Hacheim earning the D.S.O, and later to be the Chief of Army Staff of the Indian Army from 1966 to 1969.

At Trimulgherry the regiment received 25 Pounder guns (to replace the 4.5 inch howitzers and 18 pounder guns). It now had its full complement of three (eight-gun batteries), each divided into four-gun troops. These batteries were:

3 Indian Field Battery (Madrassis)
4 Indian Field Battery (Marathas)
7 Indian Field Battery (Sikhs)

THE REGIMENT MOVES TO NORTH AFRICAN THEATRE

The regiment continued to conduct intensive training, knowing that it was only a matter of time before it was moved overseas to join the Allied war effort. It was declared 'fit for war' in September 1941, and in the end of October it received orders to join the 6 Indian Division in the Middle East Command. By 1 November 1941, the Regiment (less 3 Indian Field Battery which was left behind) arrived in Bombay (now renamed as Mumbai) for embarkation on two ships, SS JALAVIHAR and SS EL-MEDINA. By 4 November all the guns, vehicles, trailers and other equipment had been loaded on the JALAVIHAR. The embarkation of personnel on SS EL-MEDINA was completed on 5 November. The two ships sailed for Basra on 6 November; while the former reached the port on 11 November, the latter docked on 17 November.

On 20 November 1941, 4 Indian Field Battery was detached and ordered to move to Deir-El-Zor. Moving via Amara, Kot Kul, Baghdad, Habaniya and Abu-Kemal, it arrived at its destination on 1 December, where it come under command 3 Indian Motor Brigade. Meanwhile, 2 Indian Field Regiment (less 3 and 4 batteries - the former still in India) which had moved from Basra to Sara Pul Zuhab, received orders on 2 February 1942 to join the 9th Army. It left its location at 0700 hrs in the morning of 6 February arriving in Baghdad at 1600 hrs the same evening. Here, fresh instructions were issued to it to move to Haifa in Palestine. It left the next morning, and moving via Rutbah it reached Mafraq in Palestine, where once again new orders were issued, this time to move to Khatabat (near Cairo) in Egypt. It commenced its move on 12 February and arrived at its new location on 16 February. Meanwhile, 4 Indian Field Battery which had already moved here with 3 Indian Motor Brigade rejoined the Regiment at Khatabat. For the next three months the Regiment remained in Khatabat and did intensive training alongside the cavalry regiments of the Brigade, viz. 2 Lancers, 11 Cavalry (PAVO) and 18 Cavalry. An Anti-tank Battery was raised here by the Regiment in March, with manpower received from other infantry units of the Indian Army and class composition of Punjabi Mussalmans. It was equipped with 2 Pounder guns. Captain (temporary Major) P.J. Burt of the Royal Artillery was attached from 3 Indian Motor Brigade to command it. On 16 April, 3 Indian Field Battery (which had been left behind in India) arrived from Basra to rejoin the unit. The Regiment now had its full complement of three field batteries and an attached anti-tank battery.

During its stay in Khatabat, the guns of the regiment underwent calibration, anti-tank shooting and practice firing at Almaza ranges. Vigorous training was carried out; such as night movement in 'square' formation, advance by day and night, signal exercises etc. Keeping its likely future role in mind, the 3 Indian Motor Brigade practiced operations in a 'box' formation – a lesson learnt in the open desert terrain of North Africa. On 13 April 1942, the Commander-in-Chief of the 8th Army, General Sir Claude Auchinleck inspected 3 Indian Motor Brigade while it was deployed in a 'box formation' during a training exercise. After a series of Brigade level exercises (or 'schemes' as they were also called), 2 Indian

Field Regiment was now ready for combat.

Soon enough, on 11 May orders were received by the Regiment to be prepared to move in 48 hours. It left Khatabat on 13 May, and passing through Daba, reached the area of Garawla on the Mediterranean Coast. On the 15, while the regiment (less one battery was located in Garawla, 3 Indian Battery was deployed a few miles away at Fuka. Between 16 and 22 May, the regiment remained deployed along the coastline in support of 3 Indian Motor Brigade, whose task was to defend against any sea or air landings by the enemy between Mersa Matruh and Buglah.

On 23 May the brigade was placed under command the 7th Army and ordered to move to Sidi Rezegh, (18 miles west of Sidi Barrani) in Cyrenaica (Libya). The move was conducted in two columns, viz. Brigade HQ and the cavalry regiments (Column 1), and 2 Indian Field Regiment (Column 2). Moving through Sollum, the regimental column joined up with the brigade at Sidi Rezegh, where it was also replenished by the Field Army Maintenance Centre (FAMC). The brigade was now tasked to be a reserve to the XXX Corps. However, the next morning it was ordered to move and occupy a defensive 'box' around a Point 171, a small hump in the featureless desert terrain, which was located approximately five kilometres south-west of Bir Hacheim garrison (an abandoned fort held by the Free French Brigade).

SITUATION IN NORTH AFRICA – MAY 1942

The battle for North Africa was fought between June 1940 and May 1943, the ultimate aim being the control of Suez Canal through which passed the oil, and other raw materials from Asia. The control of the Northern Africa was also essential for the control of the Mediterranean Sea. This vast expanse of barren desert land was termed as 'tactician's paradise and a logistician's hell' by German Lieutenant General Johann Von Ravenstein. A brief recapitulation of events prior to May 1942 is necessary.

Italy had entered the Second World War on the side of

Germany on 10 June 1940. The Italian 10th Army under Marshal Graziani attacked the British Forces under General Archibald Wavell on 8 September, and pushed them all the way up to Sidi Barrani, where they halted due to extended 'lines of communication' and dug down in fortified camps. Wavell, who had by then been re-inforced by the arrival of troops from British and other Commonwealth countries (India, Australia, South Africa, New Zealand), launched a counter strike called Operation Compass on 9 December 1940, under Lieutenant General Richard O'Conner (Western Desert Force). The Italians were routed and the British forces reached as far as El Aghella. On a request from Mussolini, Germany dispatched a Panzer Division under Major General Erwin Rommel, while the Italians also sent some re-enforcements, including their elite Aricte Armoured Division. This force was the nucleus of what later became the famed Afrika Korps. Germany later sent two more Panzer Divisions and one Motorized Division.

In March 1941 General Rommel launched his attack on the Allies from El Aghella and pushed the Allied forces all the way back, in the process capturing Sollum and the important Halfaya Pass. Meanwhile the Australian 9th Infantry Division fell back to the Tobruk Fort and held on tenaciously, surrounded on all sides on the land, and receiving its supplies by sea.

Wavell then launched two ill-fated offensives against the Afrika Korps to regain the Halfaya Pass and the area beyond; Operation Brevity and Operation Battleaxe on 15 May and 15 June respectively. In both these battles, the Germans used their 88 mm anti-aircraft guns in the direct firing anti-tank role and played havoc on the British armour. By one account Wavell lost as many as 91 of his new tanks[6]. On 21 June, he was replaced by General Sir Claude Auchinleck as Commander of XIII Corps. Meanwhile with arrival of XXX Corps, the Western Desert Force was re-designated as the Eighth Army under General George Cunningham. When Germany launched its invasion of Soviet Union on 22 June 1941 (Operation Barbarossa), much of the air effort of the Luftwaffe was diverted to the Eastern Front and Afrika Korps was placed on a lower priority. Later that year, Auchinleck launched Operation Crusader on 18 Nov

1941 to evict the Axis forces and by January 1942 they had once again reached El Aghella, relieving the garrison at Tobruk on the way.

Rommel used December 1941 and January 1942 to recoup his losses, while he planned his next move. On 25 January, Rommel once again launched an offensive against the British, and drove them back 300 miles, where they established their defenses along the line Gazala – Bir Hacheim. This line was held by creating a string of strong points in the form of defensive 'Box' positions. From North to South, they were held by the South African Division, Australian Division and the Free French Brigade. (See Map 7). The period between February and May 1942 was spent by both the sides formulating their offensive plans. Rommel launched his final assault on the night of 26/27 May against this defence line, with a view to bypass it from the south and head towards the Tobruk from the rear .

THE BATTLE OF BIR HACHEIM (POINT 171)

26 MAY 1942

As mentioned earlier, 3 Indian Motor Brigade had arrived in the area of Point 171 (five kilometres south-west of Bir Hacheim) in the late afternoon of 26 May 1942. Its commander was Brigadier A.E. Filose (an ex-Commandant of 18 Cavalry). Its ORBAT was as under:

> 2nd Royal Lancers (Gardner's Horse): CO – Lieutenant Colonel G.W. Bomford
>
> 11th PAVO Cavalry (Frontier Force): CO-Lieutenant Colonel P. R. Tatham
>
> 18th King Edward VII's Own Cavalry : CO -Lieutenant Colonel H.O.W. Fowler, D.S.O.
>
> 2 Indian Field Regiment : CO-Lt Colonel Guy Horsfield.
>
> 2 Indian Anti-Tank Battery : Major P.J. Burt.
>
> 31st Field Squadron, Royal Indian Engineers.

The cavalry regiments had only recently been re-organized into a motor- regiment establishment. Each regiment had one anti-tank squadron and two carrier squadrons. The anti-tank squadron had four troops each consisting of four 2-Pounders

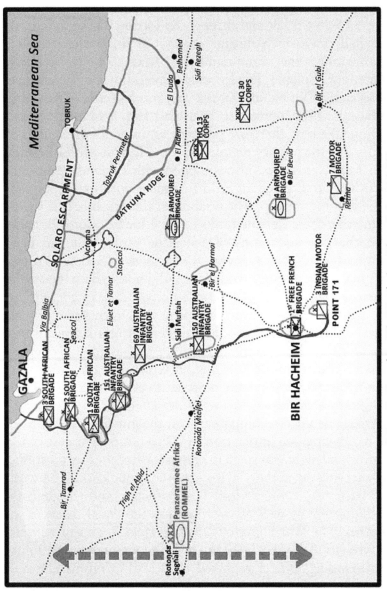

Map 7: Gazala - Bir Hacheim Line (May 1942)

carried on modified 3 tonners called '*portee*' lorries (total 16 guns). The other two squadrons had three carrier troops (five T-16 tracked carriers each) and one support troop consisting of one 15 cwt truck and three 3 ton lorries. These squadrons also had one 3-inch mortar each.[7] On this rather peculiar organization, the Commanding Officer of 18 Cavalry, Lieutenant Colonel Fowler commented in the Regimental Newsletter: 'Our equipment is a very mixed kettle of fish - and one seems at the moment to be neither fish, fowl nor good red herring. Training therefore presents a number of difficulties'.[8]

Just like the cavalry regiments, the 3 Indian Motor Brigade Anti-Tank Battery was also equipped with 2 Pounder guns. On the other hand, 2 Indian Field Regiment with its 25 pounder guns, had the most potent weapon in the brigade. It is worth noting that there were *no* tanks in the 3 Indian Motor Brigade. Even the two squadrons of Valentine tanks that had been promised by Major General R. Messervy, General Officer Commanding 7 Armoured Division did not arrive to boost the defensive potential of the motorised brigade, leaving it without any armour support. Even the cavalry regiments had not yet received their full authorization of their anti-tank guns. It was this '*tank-less*' brigade which faced the onslaught of the mighty Afrika Korps the next morning, in which the gun crews of 2 Indian Field Regiment were destined to etch their heroic stand in military history.

After a detailed reconnaissance of the gun area, the guns of the regiment came into action by 1700 hours. The rest of the evening and night was spent in preparation of the gun positions, viz. carrying out survey, laying cable communications between the batteries, Observation Post officers and Regimental Headquarters as well as coordinating the 'local defences' of the area. The War Diary of 2 Indian Field Regiment records: 'Moved to BIR HACHEIM, arriving at about 1500 hrs. Commanding Officer reported to Brigade Commander and proceeded on reconnaissance with him at once. Guns came into action at 1700 hrs. Digging operations were started at once and continued well into the night'.[9]

The deployment of the brigade was in the well-rehearsed

circular 'Box' defensive position, which was pivoted around the Point 171 feature. 18 Cavalry was deployed facing the west, 2nd Royal Lancers occupied the southern perimeter while the 11 PAVO Cavalry held the line running from the north to north-east. Each of these defence lines was about 2000 meters long. The cavalry units were all deployed in the 'dismounted' role. The War Diary of 11 PAVO Cavalry records: 'North face of the Box ran one mile east and west through Trig Point 171 (PAVO Cavalry) area, 18th Cavalry faced west and 2nd Royal Lancers faced south. Positions dug and camouflaged.'[10] The short gap in the rear between 11 PAVO Cavalry and 2nd Royal Lancers was occupied by 31 Field Company R.I.A. In the centre of the box were the three batteries of the 2 Indian Field Regiment; one battery each was deployed in support of the cavalry regiments. The War Diary of the 2 Indian Field Regiment records: '3 and 7 Field Batteries primarily in the anti-tank role in support of 2nd Royal Lancers and 18 Cavalry. 4 Field Battery in normal role in support of 11 Cavalry'.[11] The 2 Indian Anti-Tank Battery under Major Burt was deployed to cover the rear of the brigade 'Box'. The deployment of 3 Indian Motor Brigade is shown in Map 8.

As mentioned earlier, about five kilometres to the north west was the 1st Free French Brigade holding the Bir Hacheim Box, to the south east was the 7 Motor Brigade, while further east was the 29 Infantry Brigade Box at Bir-el-Gibi.

Throughout the night of 26/27 May 1942, the 3 Indian Motor Brigade continued with the preparations and coordination of the defences in the Point 171 Box. A few patrols were sent out in the near vicinity. Even while these activities were going on, unknown to them, Rommel's forces had commenced their movement towards the Gazala - Bir Hacheim defence line.

Later at night, some indication of the enemy's movement came from a South African unit. Major General Gurcharan Sandhu writes in his book *The Indian Armour*:

The first intimation the brigade had of the enemy's approach was from a South African armoured car regiment which was falling back in front of German armour south-east of Mekili... Patrols were sent out by regiments to cover their front, and the brigade HQ told them to expect contact early

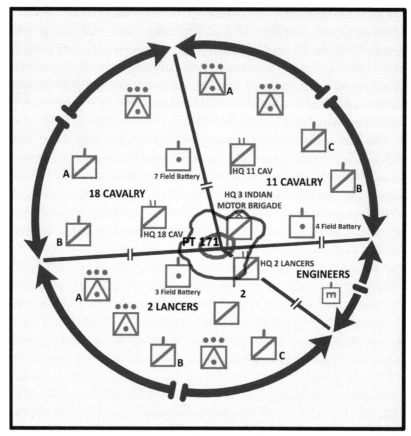

**Map 8: 3 Indian Motor Brigade Defensive Position Around Point
171 (As on 26 May 1942)**

morning... At 10 p.m. enemy aircraft dropped para flares over the brigade's
location; these were apparently meant to help armoured columns keep
direction by night. Tank noises were heard through the night and at 2.30
a.m. *very light pistols* were seen. These were usually used by the enemy
units in harbour to help stragglers.[12]

In his other book *I Serve*, Major General Sandhu quotes
from the 18 Cavalry records: 'At 10 p.m. aircraft were heard
overhead and suddenly three strings of parachute flares
appeared suspended in the air above us. We all realized that the
flares were direction markers for the advancing columns. One
of our gunner patrols returned after midnight and reported the
sound of heavy mechanized forces on the move to the north-

west of us".[13]

The gunner patrol mentioned above was that of 2 Indian Field Regiment led by Captain R.C. (Bob) Frisby, the Observation Post (OP) Officer of 'D' troop, 7 Indian Field Battery. Along with a carrier based escort form 18 Cavalry, Frisby was ordered to move ahead of the defences, establish a Listening Post and report any enemy movements. The activities of Frisby's patrol are documented in the book on the history of 2 Field Regiment titled *Har Maidan Fateh*:

The Listening Post proceeded east for about six miles where it deployed. It was a bright, quiet and a very clear night. It appeared that as if nothing was happening. However the Sikh Havildar accompanying the officer suddenly lay down with one ear to the ground and listened for a few minutes. He then got up and said, at the same time pointing with his hand in a south-easterly direction, "tracked vehicles are moving out there". Bob Frisby could not hear anything but decided to investigate. They all got back into the carrier and moved slowly towards the direction that the Havildar had shown. After a mile or two, the rumbling of the tank tracks could be distinctly heard, and what could be seen was an artificial light swinging in the air. It turned out to be a guiding light on the top of a pole fastened onto the leading vehicle of the column. They got as near as possible and identified that it was a column of mixed German vehicles (tracked and wheeled) moving on a night march in the direction of own defences. Bob Frisby thereafter contacted SUNRAY (the code word for his Battery Commander) on the 22 Wireless Set and gave him a report of what he had seen and what was going on, and what he thought it was. The Battery Commander Major P.P. Kumaramangalam contacted Headquarters 3 Indian Motor Brigade but was told that the observation made by his OP Officer was incorrect, and it could actually be the South African armoured cars pulling back, as no enemy was reported in the area. The same was relayed to Bob Frisby.

This made Captain Frisby mount another close reconnaissance. As they got closer, they found a gap in the German column. They popped into it and joined the column and rode along with them and made a note of the various points like 'Tin Hats' were of German pattern, the formation sign on the tank was *Palm Tree* etc. Soon they found a gap and left the column towards the direction of own defences. Bob Frisby mentions that their breaking of columns was noticed by the enemy personnel. There was much shouting and firing of small arms but nobody followed them. At a safe distance Bob Frisby stopped his carrier and gave his full report on wireless. Time was running out and he was asked to return to the OP. They got back to the OP about a half to three quarters of an hour before dawn (they did not have any rest or sleep for over 24 hours). This act of valour on part of Captain

R. C. Frisby is recorded in the Royal Artillery Regimental History account of the 1939/45 Battles, in the colonial section under the heading *Indian Artillery: The Account of the Battle of Bir Hacheim on 27 May 1942*, and that Captain R. C. Frisby R A during the night previous to the battle had, from a listening post sent back throughout the night, a number of reports of the German Army's advance towards Bir Hacheim.

It was later found out that 7 Armoured Division's intelligence section had also been listening into Captain Frisby's transmissions of the night 26/27 May and tried to get their headquarters interested but without any success.[14]

27 MAY 1942

27 May 1942 was destined to be the 'moment of truth' for the hapless 3 Indian Motor Brigade, which had moved in the previous afternoon and had only one night to prepare its defences. Armed with the 2 Pounder anti-tank guns (of the armoured regiments) and the artillery 25-pounder guns, it was going to face the full fury of Field Marshal Rommel's *Panzerarmee Afrika* in what was clearly an unequal match. The assault of the German and Italian armour started at the crack of dawn, and in a matter of hours it was all over (See Map 9). The Indian cavalry units and 2 Indian Field Regiment fought bravely but stood no chance against this overwhelmingly strong force. The accounts of the cavalry units clearly show how their positions were overrun by this mighty onslaught in a matter of hours.

In his book *The Indian Armour,* Major General Gurcharan Sandhu describes how 18 Cavalry fought this action:

On 27 May at first light, 18th Cavalry reported an enemy harbour with 80 tanks and 600 vehicles in it, located about four kilometres west of the regiment. Colonel Fowler, the commanding officer, had personally reconnoitered it. 2nd Lancers reported another large concentration of tanks and vehicles about the same distance from 'Lone Tree Hill'. Brigadier Filose went to the hill for a personal reconnaissance. 'C' Squadron 2nd Lancers reported that a large column consisting of tanks and soft vehicles had passed the brigade's eastern flank and advanced north. In fact the entire Afrika Korps had harboured for the night to the west, south-east and south of the brigade's defences. The 21st Panzer Division lay to the west of 18th Cavalry, the Italian Ariete (armoured) Division was concentrated to the southwest of the 2nd Lancers perimeter. The 15th Panzer Division was behind 'Black Ridge', and the 90th Light Division had bypassed the brigade from the east. Confronting the whole armoured might of the *Panzerarmee Afrika* plus

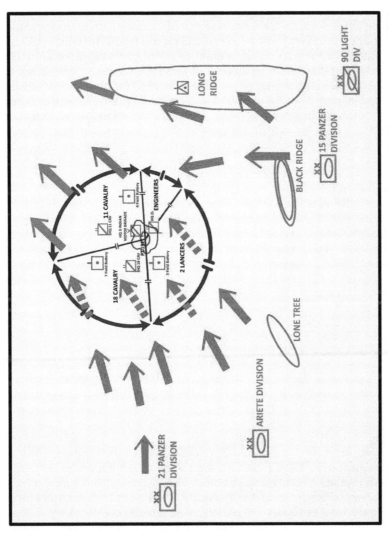

Map 9: Battle of Point 171 (27 May 1942) Attack by Rommel's *Panzerarmee Afrika*

an Italian armoured division was the 3rd Indian Motor Brigade with not a single tank, with less than two score anti-tank guns which could do little damage to the Panzers except at very close range; *it was supported by only one Indian field regiment equipped with 25-pounder guns and about to see its first action* (emphasis by the author). Its defences were without any mines or wire obstacles; the defences were incomplete and uncoordinated and it was hopelessly outnumbered. Yet the Indian Motor Brigade and its motor cavalry regiments decided to stand and fight.

The first shot was fired by the Brigade; 2ⁿᵈ Field Regiment opened fire on enemy laagers and the Germans replied with counter-battery fire (emphasis by the author). Enemy soft vehicles dispersed in a hurry. At about 6-45 a.m. 21 Panzer Division sent its light tanks to reconnoitere the defences of 18ᵗʰ Cavalry and determine the location of anti-tank weapons. Light tanks of the Ariete Division advanced to 'Lone Tree Hill' for observation and for reconnoitering the defences of 2ⁿᵈ Lancers. The Cavalry anti-tank gunners, however, held their fire. At 7 a.m. 15ᵗʰ Panzer Division started to bypass Point 171 from the east. It advanced in three columns. The right column passed behind 'Black Ridge' and advanced through the Brigade Anti-tank Battery holding 'Long Ridge'. The battery was overrun after it had done some damage to the enemy. The centre column went through the valley and the dispersed vehicles of the brigade. Some vehicles were destroyed but most escaped damage. The left column passed between 'Black Ridge' and the 2ⁿᵈ Lancers who could not engage even the enemy's soft vehicles because 'C' Squadron holding this flank had no anti-tank guns, and were even without their allotted machine guns. Some of the German medium tanks turned west and attacked 'C' Squadron (2ⁿᵈ Lancers) holding the south-eastern corner of the defences. *They made for the guns of the 3ʳᵈ Indian Field Battery which engaged them over open sights. The tanks withdrew towards 'Black Ridge' with the prisoners they had taken from the 2ⁿᵈ Lancers* (emphasis by the author). A Dafedar tried to stop a tank by jamming a crowbar between its tracks. He was spotted by the tank gunner and shot. Two VCOs collected some men and vehicles from the valley and escaped.

The 21ˢᵗ Panzer Division, with the Ariete Division in support, launched the main assault with 200 to 300 tanks in three waves followed by the motorized infantry of the Ariete Division. The Panzers advanced slowly and deliberately towards 'B' Squadron of 18ᵗʰ Cavalry and No.1 anti-tank troop of the 2ⁿᵈ Lancers. As the Panzers closed in, the Anti-tank troops of 'C' Squadron 18ᵗʰ Cavalry and 'A' Squadron 2ⁿᵈ Lancers engaged them at very close range. 15 to 20 Panzers were knocked out but others continued to advance until both anti-tank troops were overrun. *Now a duel started between the left troop of the 7ᵗʰ Field Battery and the Panzers. Another 16 tanks were in flames before the guns were also overrun* (emphasis by the author). An anti-tank troop of the PAVO Cavalry had been moved in depth to the 18ᵗʰ Cavalry defences when the attack started. It carried out a parade ground withdrawal in front of the advancing Panzers, stopping to engage and then withdrawing to the next position. The carriers of the 18ᵗʰ Cavalry, on their way to join their regiment from brigade HQ, met the Panzers head on. The carriers launched a gallant but hopeless charge on the tanks; they kept advancing until all were hit and set of fire. Two other waves of Panzers followed the leading tanks until both the 18ᵗʰ Cavalry and the PAVO Cavalry defences were completely dominated by enemy tanks milling around and firing at everything within sight.

Captain David Wauton and Lieutenant Goldingham, both 18th Cavalry, lay close to a 2-pounder gun pretending to be dead. As soon as a tank had passed, they would man the gun and engage the tank from the rear. They knocked out 3 tanks in this manner and killed a tank commander and a motor cyclist. They were eventually spotted engaging a self-propelled gun and were forced to surrender. Both were awarded the Military Cross. With the regimental defences totally dominated by the Panzers, the regimental HQ 18th Cavalry decided to withdraw.

By about 8-15 a.m. the two Panzer Divisions had overrun the defences of the motor brigade except a small portion of the 2nd Lancers defences and the brigade HQ. The Germans had left the Italian Ariete Division to mop up. Italian tanks now advanced towards the centre of the southern face of the perimeter, followed by another wave of tanks and lorried infantry. No.2 Anti-tank troop 2nd Lancers held its fire until the leading tanks were at 400m. *A furious duel followed, joined in by the 3rd Field Battery firing over open sights. Ten tanks were knocked out and the attack beaten off* (emphasis by the author); enemy tanks had turned away when only 75 metres from the defences. This was, however, a short-lived triumph. The enemy was already holding 'Lone Tree Hill' on the southern flank. The 18th Cavalry and the PAVO Cavalry having been overrun, the northern flank was also open. Enemy tanks and armoured cars had reached the area of regimental HQ 2nd Lancers from the north. At this time orders were received from Brigade HQ to withdraw and rendezvous six kilometres north of Point 171.

Survivors from brigade HQ and 2nd Lancers got away in three parties. One party with approximately 100 vehicles led by Brig. Filose, included Colonel Bomford and three officers 2nd Lancers. It managed to dodge several enemy columns and reached the rendezvous. It waited there until 10-30 a.m. and then made for El-Gubi. The Italians had not taken much notice of small pockets left in the 2nd Lancers defences; these were collected by their officers and VCOs. Under Captain Reynolds these men in several carriers reached Tobruk and from there rejoined the regiment. Risaldar Lakhan Singh with 40 men from 2nd Lancers and some from the PAVO Cavalry, reached the 7th Armoured Division. A few individuals also escaped and got back.

The 2nd Indian Field Regiment had fought its very first action most gallantly. Apart from carrying out its normal field role, almost every individual gunner had been under attack from the Panzers. The crew stood to their guns and engaged the enemy over open sights. They can claim a fair share of up to 80 tanks which the enemy lost at Point 171. General Tuker, who visited the battle field in December 1942, counted 50 hulls scattered about and the enemy must have salvaged some of the casualties. Major Kumaramangalam and Lieutenant. P.B. Clarke, reconnaissance troop leader 18th Cavalry, returned to the battle field a few days later to salvage the 2ⁿᵈ Field regiment's guns. The gunners returned to Buq Buq with 16 of their guns. Major Kumaramangalam was awarded the Distinguished Service Order for his conduct in the battle (emphasis by the author).[15]

In another book *I Serve,* Major General Gurcharan Sandhu further recounts the activities in the 18 Cavalry area thus:

At about 7 a.m. both 'A' and 'B' Squadrons reported that enemy were commencing their attack. The 15ᵗʰ Panzer Division circled round the south of the 2ⁿᵈ Lancers and went through the rear of the defensive position, killing Major Burt and knocking out his battery. The Panzers, thereafter, headed North East for the 7ᵗʰ Armoured Division. The 21ˢᵗ Panzer Division, with the Ariete Division in tow, in all about two to three hundred tanks, moved slowly forward in three or four waves, coming in through 'B' squadron, and its junction with the 2ⁿᵈ Royal Lancers. *The Panzers headed primarily for the guns. A tank versus gun battle began, our supporting Battery under Major 'K' (Kumaramangalam) firing over open sights. The left troop, with 16 tanks to its credit, was overrun* (emphasis by the author). Instead of enemy infantry following their tanks, more enemy tanks appeared. There were tanks everywhere – some stationary, some knocked out and some advancing, with their machine guns firing in every direction.

Our 2-pounder guns had waited for the enemy to come close and then opened fire. Some tanks were hit and damaged but others soon got behind them and began to machine gun their crews from the rear. Hopelessly outranged and outnumbered, our little 2-pounders were soon knocked out. A section of PAVO anti-tank guns *portee*, part of the troop sent to our help, were seen moving slowly back in front of the German tanks, engaging them as laid down in Range Practices, until blown up. Orders to withdraw came from Brigade HQ when regimental HQ was under heavy machine gun fire. The Colonel ordered away Peter Clarke, the Reconnaissance and Liaison Troop and the RDM (Asghar Ali), all that could be got out.

RDM Asghar Ali with some of the regimental carriers tried to force his way without success. RHQ was overrun by tanks and forced to surrender. Our defences were now completely overrun and the Brigade smashed. We had, however, destroyed at least 60 tanks of which 23 lay in front of, or in the position held by the 18ᵗʰ Cavalry.[16]

The 11 PAVO Cavalry's actions on that fateful day, are also documented by Colonel M.Y. Effendi in his book *Punjab Cavalry:* 'The Regimental War Diary entry for 27 May is very terse and not very descriptive, but under the surface seethes the anger and frustration of the diarist:

27 May – 0600 Hrs   Second   Lieutenant   J.F.W.   Howes

	arrives with carriers. Carriers drove on to the Regiment position and dismounted their guns and returned to where the soft vehicles were positioned.
0800 Hrs	Message received form Brigade that position was surrounded by tanks...
0815 Hrs	Light artillery bombardment commenced.
0845 Hrs	GERMAN & ITALIAN tanks having broken through south face of Box arrived on our position and overran it.
0900 Hrs	Resistance having ceased, Tanks rolled on towards BIR HACHEIM. Enemy left small force of tanks and armoured cars to deal with any further resistance.
0945 Hrs	Enemy infantry arrived on position and took those remaining there, prisoners; Some 215 I.O.R.s and the following officers: Lieutenant Colonel P.R. Tatham Captain H.M. el Effendi Captain C.L.F. Du Vivier Captain D.S Carmichael Second Lieutenant J.F.W. Howes Major A.A.J. Danvers[17]

Colonel Effendi further quotes from the War Diary:

The Germans initially probed the 3 Motor Brigade positions with their light tanks (Panzer Mark 2s). 15 Panzer Division began to by-pass the

'Box' going to the east in three columns, overrunning the 2 Royal Lancer positions. Some medium tanks (Panzer Mark 3s) turned and moved in, to destroy the south- eastern portion of the regiment's defences. *The 3 Indian Field Battery located in the area engaged the 15 Panzer's tanks over open sights, and the tanks took cover behind the 'Black Ridge'* (emphasis by the author).

The main thrust of the German attack was delivered by 21 Panzer Division, with the Italian Ariete Division following close behind, with motorized infantry. The 18 Cavalry and 2 Royal Lancers anti-tank troops were destroyed, but not until over 18 Axis tanks were left in flames. *The Germans eventually ran into a troop of 7 Field Battery, and another sixteen tanks were destroyed before the gallant Indian gunners were overrun* (emphasis by the author). A troop of PAVO Cavalry anti-tank guns had been placed in depth of the 18 Cavalry defences, and it carried out a 'parade ground withdrawal' to an alternative position, and re-engaged the enemy armour. A gallant charge by the carriers ended in the destruction of all the vehicles. Two further waves of the German and Italian tanks finished off both the 18 KEO Cavalry and the 11 PAVO Cavalry. By 0815 hours it was all over, and from both units eighteen officers and 670 other ranks were made prisoners. From 18 Cavalry, three Indian, and from PAVO Cavalry two Indian officers were part of the bag; Captain (later Lieutenant General and foreign minister of Pakistan), Sahabzada Yaqub Khan was among the first three.

The Axis released all the Indian VCOs and other ranks along with the respective medical officers, and retained only seventeen officers. Sahabzada Yaqub Khan recalls the problems the Axis troops had in providing water for the prisoners. Soon thirst started driving the men mad, and distributing the meagre supply provided in cans became a problem. He remembers seeing a vehicle carrying a senior officer stop and talk to the officer commanding the detachment guarding the prisoners, Sahabzada Yaqub Khan thinks it could have been Rommel himself. However, the British officers spoke to the senior-most German officer and it was arranged that the officers would be retained and the men released. The latter were marched off to the Free French box at Bir Hacheim, where they were made to lie under the vehicles as there was no shade available. When the French had to move they found the thirst-maddened Indian troops had been drinking the rusty water from the cooling system. While they had lain under the vehicles, they had opened the spigots and helped themselves to the almost poisonous water. The Official History's comment on the 3 Indian Motor Brigade action was; 'an audacious and forlorn affair from the very start'.[18]

THE ARTILLERY BATTLE

(This part has been largely derived from the book 'Har Maidan Fateh : History of 2 Field Regiment (SP), Point 171 and Letse'- Author)

27 May 1942 was destined to be the `day of reckoning' for 2 Indian Field Regiment, which had been raised barely two years earlier. Having moved to this position only the evening before, they had not fully coordinated their defences. In his article *2 Indian Field Regiment and the Battle of Bir Hacheim - Point 171*, Lieutenant General P.K. Singh writes, 'The defences at Point 171 were incomplete, without mines, uncoordinated and without any tanks deployed in the Brigade Box area, but were ready to face the might of Rommel's forces which had 15 Panzer Division, the Italian Ariete Division and 90 Light Division. Needless to say the defenders were hopelessly outnumbered but determined to give a fight, and ended up creating history'.[19]

The batteries of 2 Indian Field Regiment were located within the defended areas of the affiliated Cavalry Regiments, viz. 7 Indian Field Battery with 18 Cavalry in the west of the 'Box', 3 Indian Field Battery with 2nd Royal Lancers in the south, and 4 Indian Field Battery was located with 11 PAVO Cavalry facing north and north-east. While 3 and 7 Field Batteries were deployed in the anti-tank role, 4 Field Battery was deployed in the conventional role of providing indirect artillery fire support to the OP officers. The command structure of the regiment was:

CO	:	Lieutenant Colonel Guy Horsfield
2IC	:	Major M. G. Colchester
BC 3 Field Battery	:	Major A.B. Howard
BC 4 Field Battery	:	Major G.S.Brook
BC 7 Field Battery	:	Major P.P. Kumaramangalam

INITIAL ENGAGEMENTS

Just before the start of this epic battle there was an interesting incident. The Brigade Commander of 3 Indian Motor Brigade,

Brigadier A.A. Filose came to the OP position of 7 Field Battery early morning, and admonished Captain Frisby for what he termed as 'exaggerated reporting' earlier that night. He was then informed that it was not three enemy columns as reported earlier, but two more had been reported since then making it a total of five! The brigadier's only comment was 'Oh my God' before he took off. Thereafter Lieutenant Colonel Horsfield went around the gun position and also visited all the OP positions; he was accompanied by his battery commanders. He told them to be ready and await his orders to commence firing.

Soon, the German and Italian divisions commenced their advance towards the 'Box' held by 3 Indian Motor Brigade. Lieutenant Colonel Horsfield, who was at that time at the OP position occupied by Captain A.S. Naravane, ('F' Troop commander), gave his orders to commence firing. Captain Naravane thus has the distinction of ordering the firing of the regiment's opening salvo against the advancing enemy. He has vividly recalled the initial moments of the Regiment coming into combat.:[20]

At about this time Colonel Horsfield came up to the OP and approved the location on the forward slope of the sand dune, as it gave a good field of view, yet was not highlighted on the skyline. Shortly thereafter the brigade commander also came to OP and after seeing the situation sent a cavalry officer to go forward and have a closer look. When this officer came within 500 yards of the vehicles as I have mentioned earlier, he was fired upon. There being no doubt in his mind as he had also identified a few enemy tanks, this cavalry officer intimated to the Brigade Commander that these were infact enemy troops. I was here upon ordered by my CO to engage the enemy. I fired a few ranging rounds and then opened fire with rounds of gunfire. I had laid out in front of me such a concentration of vehicles that I could switch right or left eight degree and up and down a thousand yards and not fail to do damage. It was a dream target that few other gunners could have dreamt of; I was then ordered by the CO to engage the enemy with the whole regiment. The rounds of gun fire could not but cause damage to tanks and vehicles. We saw men jumping out of their vehicles which had caught fire. By then the visibility had improved so much that enemy tanks were able to move forward for action. Four enemy armoured cars advanced to within a thousand yards of our line of OPs and opened fire towards the position. Cavalry regiments opened fire with their 2-Pounder anti-tank guns which were quite ineffective at that range against the enemy armoured cars. They only gave away the layout of our anti-tank defences.

By then the enemy had finalized his plan of attack and the enemy tanks started advancing toward our position on a broad front. They came wave after wave. Our OPs engaged them with rounds of gunfire forcing them to close their turrets. Enemy guns started shelling our OP area as well as the gun areas. My CO who was still at my OP drew my attention to an enemy gun on my left flank and ordered me to engage it. I did it effectively and the gun stopped firing. The gun was an anti-aircraft 88 mm which also was deployed by the Germans effectively in the field and anti-tank role as well. The CO then pointed to another similar gun on the right flank which I engaged with rounds of gun fire. Whilst I was busy engaging it, my CO moved to another OP. Meanwhile the enemy tanks continued the advance toward our position. When they were about 1500 yards away I spoke to Lloyd Thomas and gave the picture on my front. The tanks continued to advance though they were being shelled by our guns. They were shelling our forward positions in which the OPs were sited. Just when that tanks were within 200 yards from my position Lloyd Thomas rang me up again and said the gun positions were being heavily shelled. When I informed him that the tanks were only 200 yards from my OP he said 'in that case good – bye and good luck'. That was the last time I spoke to him till I met him after the war. He repeated these words again when we met at Deolali during reunion of 1985. My vehicle was hit by a shell and went up in smoke however the wireless set and the operator were in a slit trench and escaped unscathed.

The first wave of tanks went past the OP position and so did the second wave. By now the Free French from Bir Hacheim fort also started shelling our position with air burst high explosive shells as they saw the enemy tanks in the midst of our position. The tanks did not seem to have seen our OP as they had their turrets closed to protect themselves from the air burst shells. By now the leading enemy tanks had passed our OP line and the fire of the guns from Bir Hacheim fort also moved to our rear. Next came armoured cars. Their turrets were open with a person standing and looking out. I felt that as my vehicle was already destroyed the best course was for us to hide in the slit trench and wait for an opportunity to make a bid on foot towards our guns that were still firing. As the line was cut and the remote control was not functioning we had no way of knowing what was the position in the gun area. After some time an enemy armoured car came straight for our slit trench with his light machine gun directly pointing in the direction of our trench. It halted a short distance away from our trench and an officer pointing his revolver in our direction beckoned us to get out. Obviously we had been spotted and any hope of getting away had gone for the present. I and my OP assistant had no option but to surrender as the enemy's supporting infantry also came up. We were searched and directed to move towards the rear to a collecting point for prisoners of war. We got no opportunity to give a slip and make a getaway. Thus began our start of the journey to Italy and later to Germany. But we could still hear our guns firing.

Major General Naravane later goes on to record the actions

at the 'gun end', which he pieced together after hearing the accounts of other captured regimental officers at the prisoner of war camp:[21]

When my orders for going to rounds of gunfire were received at the gun position after only a few ranging rounds, and when I called for a large number of rounds of gunfire from the whole regiment several degree left and right as well as up and down hundreds of yards at a time, there was some skepticism in the minds not only of my battery commander but also of the Numbers 1 of the guns; they wondered whether they were hearing the orders correctly, till at the first opportunity I told the GPO that the whole of the Africa Korps was spread out in front of me! In fact the battery commander had come personally to see for himself and agreed that I was right. The other batteries also then started engaging targets on their front. Soon the first wave of the tanks were visible advancing towards our guns with their guns engaging our gun position with high explosive shells. All the troops including the young recruits serviced the guns unflinchingly, inspite of some casualties amongst officers, NCOs and gun numbers. It was indeed a remarkable 'baptism by fire' of the personnel of the regiment. When tanks came within range of engagement by the solid shot and armour piercing sabot rounds, our 25-pounder guns were used to great effect, and a number of tanks were seen 'blowing up' all across the front. As Fox Troop was on the extreme left of the line of guns, the left flank was completely open. Soon they saw some enemy tanks advancing towards them from that direction and firing at our guns. They promptly engaged the enemy and a number of tanks were hit. These tanks then swung east to try and pass behind the guns, but suffered several casualties before they got out of the range of our guns.

After this there was a period of comparative quiet in the vicinity of 4 Indian Field Battery gun area although heavy firing from the right was observed. German bombers too came over and dropped few bombs. At about this time a German fighter came down near the 4 Indian Field Battery Wagon lines. The pilot, a very arrogant young man, told Lieutenant Roger Thomas that it would be better for the gunners if they surrendered. On this Lieutenant Roger Thomas asked the pilot in his broken German if he had ever been to India. He said, 'No, but why do you ask?' Thomas replied, 'because that's where you are going now' and he sent him off in a truck with two signallers to the regimental HQ. The pilot was not seen again. The guns of 'A' Troop commanded by Lieutenant D Miller and 'B' Troop commanded by Lieutenant (later Major General) Kalyan Singh opened fire. The other observation posts did likewise inflicting casualties on the enemy vehicles. With the first salvos of 25-pounder guns from the regiment, the whole of the enemy's tank formation seemed to close their tank lids as if operated by one man. Germans replied with counter battery fire, while the enemy's soft vehicles dispersed in a hurry. At about 0645 hours 21 Panzer Division set its light tanks to reconnoitre the defences of the 18 Cavalry and determine the location of anti-tank weapons. Light tanks of the Ariete Division advanced to 'Lone Tree Hill' for observation and for reconnoitering the defences of 2nd Lancers. At about 0700 hrs 15 Panzer Division started to bypass Point 171 from the east.

The battery-wise actions are narrated below.

7 INDIAN FIELD BATTERY

7 Indian Field Battery, commanded by Major (later General P.P. Kumaramangalam), was deployed in the north-west portion of the 'Box' in support of 18 Cavalry. It bore the brunt of the 21 Panzer Division's assault. The Sikh battery fought bravely, knocking out many German tanks. Throughout this gun - versus - tank engagement, Major Kumaramangalam was at the gun-positions guiding the gun crews of his 25-Pounder guns. This gallant action was later recreated in a painting by German artist Langhammer (see cover of book). 18 Cavalry historical accounts also describe very glowingly the fight given by this battery, which fought till the last man.

As soon as he saw the advancing enemy tanks on the skyline, Lieutenant Corcoran (the Command Post Officer of 'C' Troop, 7 Battery) gave the orders 'Tank Alert', preparing his guns for the duel which was to follow. Lieutenant General M.S. Shergill an armoured corps officer who rose to be the Director General of Mechanized Forces (DGMF) of the Indian Army, put this heroic action in perspective. In his article *To Honour A Past,* he writes that:

7 Field Battery bore the brunt of the Panzer attack. This was a Sikh battery. They were standing by their guns in the same manner as their forefathers did in the six battles against the British (Mudki, Ferozshah, Aliwal, Sobraon, Chillianwala & Gujarat (*during the Anglo-Sikh wars –* author). Then, the artillery of the Sikh army had been trained by General Claude Auguste Court who was educated at Ecole Polytechnique, Paris and General Paulo Martolome Avitable, a Neapolitan...). Standing behind the battery with complete sangfroid was a tall, slim, handsome Major P.P. Kumaramangalam. The Panzers were to be engaged at 'open sight'. The German tanks were now a thousand metres away.

...The first wave of tanks swept past the OP position and so too the second. The Free French from Bir Hacheim started to shell the tanks in vain; The Afrika Korps was on a roll. Their objective was Tobruk to the north and nothing was going to stop them, least of all the 'pea shooters' and the field guns'.

Lieutenant Corcoran (the Command Post Officer of 'C' Troop – author) observed that his Sikh gun layer was killed; he pushed his body off into the gun pit and took on his duties. He too was killed. His body was later found lying on top of his gun crew, the last to perish. The dead were all covered and buried in a gun pit in a communal grave. Havildar Modan Singh, the Gun Number One, similarly met his death sitting on the gun controls. Havildar Tara Singh was critically wounded in like fashion. *The last German tank this troop destroyed had been stopped a mere 10 metres from their guns* (emphasis by the Author).[22]

During the next few hours the gun crews exhibited many such acts of conspicuous gallantry. 'C' troop literally fought to the last round and was virtually decimated. They knocked out 16 German tanks. A few move were hit by D Troop. Lieutenant General Shergill further notes that : The Free French Brigade were observing this unequal contest from nearby Bir Hacheim, with awe and admiration. It was only two days ago that this Indian brigade had moved in its vicinity, which they called the *Anglo-Hindu Brigade.* They fully comprehended and realized the sacrifice that this brigade was undergoing… With fortitude unequalled, the gunners stood by their guns without flinching, whilst Rommel's might sliced through them. The Free French could very clearly observe the Panzers go past this battery with the Sikh gunners still manning their guns, if alive.[23]

While 21 Panzer Division and the Italian Ariete Division had attacked the 'Box' from the west (18 Cavalry position) and south-west (2nd Royal Lancers), the 15 Panzer Division and 90 Light Division attempted to go around the defences from the south and head towards the north from the rear of the brigade. These columns were initially engaged by indirect firing of the artillery guns, causing some disruption, but soon the enemy tanks were upon 18 Cavalry and 2nd Royal Lancers. The units fought gamely what was virtually an unequal battle; their 2-pounder 'pea-shooters' were no match for the Panzers. Soon it was the turn of the more lethal 25-pounder guns of 7, and 3 and 4 Indian Field Batteries to engage them with open sights.

In this book *I Serve*, Major General Gurcharan Singh Sandhu has also extolled the action of these gunners: 'The 21st Panzer Division, with the Ariete Division in tow, in all about two or three hundred tanks, moved slowly forward in three or four waves, coming in through B Squadron, and its junction with the 2ⁿᵈ Royal Lancers. The Panzers headed primarily for the guns. A tank - versus - gun battle began, our supporting 7 Indian Field Battery under Major K (Kumaramangalam) firing over open sights. The left troop (C Troop) with 16 Tanks to its credit was overrun'.[24]

3 INDIAN FIELD BATTERY

Having received the Fire Orders from the CO, the OP officers of other batteries too had called for fire from their guns to engage the enemy. In the initial stages, guns of 'A' and 'B' troops of 3 Indian Field Battery also engaged the advancing enemy columns by indirect fire. While the GPO of 'A' Troop was Lieutenant D Miller, 'B' Troop guns were being directed by Lieutenant (later Major General) Kalyan Singh. Soon the enemy tanks had advanced into the 2ⁿᵈ Royal Lancer's position. The gun crews quickly reverted to the anti-tank role and engaged the assaulting tanks. Just like with the 7 Indian Field Battery to their north, this battery was also involved in a *gun-versus-tank* duel. They fired at the German tanks with 'Armour Piercing' (AP) shots at a range of barely 300 metres causing much damage. Jamadar Lakshmanan (later killed in combat) and Subedar Alogiriswamy displayed conspicuous gallantry in steadying the gun detachments by their cool and courageous behavior, in the face of this onslaught. 'A' and 'B' Troops knocked out seven and five enemy tanks respectively of the first wave. There were many acts of valour in the midst of this 'close quarter combat'. Lance Naik Jesudas and Naik Jaganathan disabled many tanks before being grievously wounded. The battery history records that Jesudas, a young nineteen year old gunner from Nellore, continued to lay and fire his gun till they were over-run by the enemy; in this 'direct shooting' he knocked out a few tanks earning an IDSM (Indian Distinguished Service Medal) for his gallantry. When the GPO of 'A' Troop got wounded Battery Havildar Major (later Subedar Major) Lakshmi Narasu took over his duties and fearlessly guided his gun crews to continue engaging the armour, which was all over the gun area.

4 INDIAN FIELD BATTERY

As the battle was still raging in the 18 Cavalry and 2nd Royal Lancers defended areas, the enemy armour which had attacked the 'Box' from the south and gone around to the rear, attacked the 11 PAVO Cavalry area. 4 Indian Field Battery, deployed in support of the regiment immediately swung into action. As Major General Naravane (OP officer of 4 Battery) recalls: 'As 'F' Troop was on the extreme left of the line of guns, the left flank was completely open. Soon they saw enemy tanks advancing towards them from that direction and firing at our guns. They promptly engaged the enemy and a number at tanks were hit. The tanks then swung east to try and pass behind the guns, and they suffered several casualties before they got out of the range of our guns. By now most of the ammunition except for some smoke rounds had been expended. The casualties had been heavy, and a number of officers and men of the OPs and signal personnel reeling in telephone cables were taken prisoner'.[25]

In the midst of this anti-tank engagement, 4 Battery was shelled by the German Artillery units which had outflanked the brigade defences, and was engaging them from the rear. The battery had to turn their guns 180 depress to conduct 'counter-battery' fire on these enemy guns.

While 'E' Troop was engaging the German tanks from 'open sights', the officiating Gun Position Officer Lieutenant Ronald MacDonald Lumsden, received a machine gun burst on his knee. The plucky officer was later killed, when the vehicle he was being evacuated in got a direct hit form an artillery shell. Neither his body nor his grave was found during a subsequent search. 'F' troop too continued to engage the enemy tank by direct fire till it was overwhelmed. Havildar Ghulam Ali and Lance Naik Damodar Yadav, need special mention for their gallant acts of continuing to engage the enemy tanks till they were both grievously wounded. Their acts gave literal meaning to phrase - 'fighting to the last man last round'.

The battle of the 'Point 171 Box' was over in a matter of three hours. Though poorly equipped, 3 Indian Motor Brigade had stood its ground, with the gun crews of 2 Indian Field

Regiment playing a stellar role in knocking out 56 enemy tanks. Major General Naravane (who was among the first OP officers to be taken as a POW) states that: 'To go back to the early stage of my capture and our being moved around in the Brigade Box area, I paid particular attention to the number of tanks that had been knocked out and I made a note of the numbers that I saw. On passing 'C' Troop gun position, I was very pleased and proud to see that they had knocked out nine tanks, all very close and in front of their gun positions; this suggested to me that it must have been two tanks per gun and one sub-section must have excelled itself by knocking out three tanks. The grand total of the number of tanks that were knocked out by the 2 Indian Field Regiment, and I personally counted them, was fifty six tanks in the Brigade Box Area. I did not bother for wheeled vehicles as they appeared to be so many scattered around'.[26]

The 3 Indian Motor Brigade had been literally overwhelmed by the mass of German and Italian armour. It had been an unequal battle right through, but the brigade stood and fought. In the end, 18 officers and 670 VCOs and ORs from the Cavalry Regiments were captured; these included two commanding officers (11 and 18 Cavalry), and the adjutants of all three cavalry units. 2 Indian Field Regiment suffered three officers killed, 19 officers were listed as missing/ taken POW (some of whom were wounded), and over 200 ORs killed/ wounded/missing. The 'casualties list' of 3 Indian Motor Brigade is given at Table 4.2. The remnants of the brigade made it back to Buq Buq where they reorganized themselves; most cavalry regiments were now essentially on a 'two squadron' basis. Even 2 Indian Field Regiment was reorganized into two batteries, viz, 3 and 7 Indian Field batteries. Later, 4 Indian Field Battery was re-formed with some men transferred from the 3/5 Maratha Light Infantry Battalion. Although initially only seven guns had been taken out of the 'Box', a few days later Major Kumaramangalam along with the Recce Troop Leader of 18 Cavalry Lieutenant P.B. Clarke returned to the battlefield and managed to salvage nine more guns. Thus 2 Indian Field Regiment was able to re-equip itself as five gun batteries. Major Kumaramangalam, the battery commander of 7 Indian Field Battery was awarded the Distinguished Service Order (DSO) for his gallantry in the field. Ironically he was later captured on 24 June while leading a 'JOCK' column. He escaped from the Italian POW camp in October 1943, only to be re-captured by the Germans a few months later. He remained in captivity till the end of the war. He rose to be the Chief of Army Staff of the Indian Army, a post he held from 8 June 1966 till 7 June 1969. His last official engagement outside of Delhi was to visit 2 Field Regiment (SP) on 26/27 May 1969 at Ambala, as part of the Bir Hacheim Day Celebrations. On this occasion he also presented his DSO to the regiment, dedicating it 'To the brave gunners of 7 Indian Field Battery'. This author was present at this function. The DSO was later sent to the Regiment of Artillery Museum at the Artillery Centre, Nasik Road, where it continues to occupy a pride of place.

CONCLUSION

As can been seen from the above account, the Battle of Bir Hacheim (Point 171) was essentially a 'gunner's battle. Major General Gurcharan Sandhu writes in his book. 'The 2nd Indian Field Regiment had fought its very first action most gallantly. Apart from carrying its normal field artillery role, almost every individual gunner had been under attack from the Panzers. The stood to their guns and engaged the enemy over open sights. They can claim a fair share of up to 80 tanks which the enemy lost at Point 171.[27] As ascertained by independent sources (and recorded in the book *Har Maidan Fateh*), the gunners had knocked out 56 tanks in a single action lasting just a few hours – a rare feat by any standard !

The history of 2nd Royal Lancers records:

A word of praise must be given to the gunners of 2nd Indian Field Regiment. This was their first action and they had only arrived just before dark on the 26 May. Owing to the large gaps in our anti-tank defence they were forced to take on this role at an early stage of the action, as well as their normal field artillery tasks. They stood and fought it out to with utmost coolness, and yet were able to get 16 Guns back to Buq Buq where the brigade re-formed. Several of these were collected by a party led by Major Kumaramangalam nearly a week after the action.[28]

Quite interestingly, one of the officers of 18 Cavalry who was captured was Admiral Sir Walter Cowan, KCB, DCO, MVO, Royal Navy (Retired), aged 71 years! Born in 1871, he had seen action in the First World War and had since retired in 1931 after a very distinguished service. At the outbreak of the Second World War the Admiral requested to be re-drafted for active service. He was given a temporary rank of Commander and was appointed as Naval Liaison Officer of the Special Services Squadron at Tobruk; upon its disbandment he decided to remain with 18 cavalry. His capture at point 171 is recorded thus:

With the regimental defences totally dominated by the Panzers, regimental HQ 18 Cavalry directed to withdraw. Among the last left behind was Admiral Sir Walter Cowan ... The Admiral now stood in the middle of the Panzers engaging passing tanks with his revolver. As he himself narrated his experience later: "A wave of tanks and armoured cars advanced against our position. An Italian armoured car stopped 40 yards in front of me. I drew my revolver and fired until it was empty. The Italians ran behind their armoured car. Their crew-leader, a captain then shouted at me to surrender, but I did nothing. The captain then fired at me with a machine gun and missed. Again he shouted at me to surrender but I stood there with my empty revolver. He again fired with his

machine guns and missed although I was still standing up. I did not take cover.[29]

In his book *I Serve*, Major General Gurcharan Sandhu notes that: 'The Admiral, at RHQ, refusing all cover stood in the open engaging passing tanks with his revolver until, out of ammunition, he was bodily carried off';[30]

Barely two years (to the month) since its raising, 2 Indian Field Regiment had covered itself with glory in the barren desert of North Africa. They paid a very heavy price indeed for this gallant action, suffering many killed, wounded or taken as POW. The decorations awarded included two DSOs, two MCs, two IOMs, four IDSMs and seven Mention-in-Dispatches – a total of 17. Their names and given at Table 4.1. Later the regiment was also awarded the Honour Title 'Point 171' (During the re-designation of the regiment in 1946, the men of 3 Indian Field Battery were transferred initially to 14 Field Regiment and the following year to 7 Field Regiment. Based on this, the latter regiment too put up an independent case for an Honour Title, and was awarded the Honour Title 'GAZALA' – author)

TABLE 4.1 : GALLANTRY AWARD WINNERS

DISTINGUISHED SERVICE ORDER (DSO)
1. Major M.G. Colchester.
2. Major P.P. Kumaramangalam.
MILITARY CROSS (MC)
3. Captain APHB Fowl
4.Captain D. Rouse
INDIAN ORDER OF MERIT (IOM)
5. Havildar Major Jaganathan
6. Havildar Major Modan Singh
INDIAN DISTINGUISHED SERVICE MEDAL (IDSM)
7. Havildar Major (later Subedar Major) Laxmi Narasu
8. Havildar Major Darshan Singh
9. Naik Kehar Singh
10. Lance Naik Jesudass
MENTIONED-IN-DISPATCHES
11. Subedar Major Karan Singh
12. Subedar Raja Ram Sawant
13. Subedar Prem Singh
14. Jemadar Nalliah Gounder
15. Havildar Major Ram Singh
16. Havildar Ram Parshad
17. Lance Naik Sulakhan Singh

Note : 1. Extracted from *Har Maidan Fateh,* by Colonel Anjan Mukherjee, pp.174-5.
2. Major P.P. Kumaramangalam, rose to the rank of General and served as Chief of Army Staff (COAS) of the Indian Army from 8 June 1966 to 7 June 1969.

It is interesting to note that many of 2 Indian Field Regiment's officers who fought in The Battle of Bir Hacheim (Point 171) went on to have distinguished careers. Amongst these, Major P. P. Kumaramangalam and Lieutenant Tikka Khan (both of whom were part of the Sikh 7 Field Battery) rose to the rank of General to command the armies of India and Pakistan respectively. 2 Field Regiment (SP) thus holds the distinction of being the only regiment in the world to have produced two Army Chiefs of two different countries. Captain A.S. Naravane and Lieutenant Kalyan Singh rose to the rank of Major General (to become Director of Artillery and Military Secretary of the Indian Army respectively).

TABLE 4.2 : LIST OF CASUALTIES - 27 MAY 42

Cat	Killed	Missing	Wounded
2 R.L			
Officers	-	Maj A. D. Macnamara	
		T/Capt. J.F. Hall @	
		Lt. W. Vincent @	
Other Ranks	8	109	5
18 Cav			
Officers	2/Lt. H. R. MacDonald	Lt. Col. H.O.W. Fowler @	-
		T/Capt. J.G. McGowan @	
		T/Capt. J.Meares @	
		Lt. D.H. Wauton @	
		2/Lt. M.J.D. Goldingham @	
		2/Lt. KanwarAbhey Singh @	
		2/Lt S.M. Yaqub Khan @	
		Admiral Sir Walter Cowan KCB	
		DSO MVO RN (Attd) @	
		Capt. S. Ghose, IMS (Attd)@	
Other Ranks	1	15	1
11 Cav			
Officers	-	Lt. Col. P.R. Tatham @	Capt. W.B.D. Prosser
		T/Capt. C.L.E. DuVivier @	
		A/Capt. H.M.El Effendi @	
		Lt. D.S. Carmichael @	
		2/Lt. J.F.N, Howes @	
Other Ranks	2	22	4
2 Fd Regt Ind Arty			
Officers	Lt. R.M. Lumsden	T/Maj. G.S. Brooks @	
	2/Lt. E.T. Ormerod	T/Maj. A.B. Howard @	
	2/Lt. D.E.J. Corcoran	T/Maj. P. J. Burt	
		T/Capt. L.P. Driver @	
		T/Capt. J.H. Wyatt	
		T/Capt. F.A. Calverley @@	
		T/Capt. R.C. Frisby @	
		Capt. P.G. Heathcoat-Amory	
		T/Capt. A.S. Naravane @	
		Lt. D.A.H. Thomas @	
		Lt. R.G. Williams @	
		Lt. Tikka Khan @	
		Lt. Kalyan Singh @	
		2/Lt. E.N. Chambers @	
		2/Lt. A. Murray @	
		2/Lt. D.K. Knight @	
		2/Lt. G.P. Knowles @	
		2/Lt. P. Montague @	
		2/Lt. C.J. Miller @	
Other Rank	29	187	17

@ Believed P.O.W,
@@ Wounded and belived P.O.W.
Source : War Diary of 3 Indian Motor Brigade (entry dated 27 May 1942)
Note : These are the final figures, after hundreds of V.C.O.s and other ranks were released.

NOTES

1. Col. Anjan Mukherjee, *Har Maidan Fateh: History of 2 Field Regiment (SP) Point 171 and Letse,* p.(i) (General P.P. Kumaramangalam in his Preface to the book).
2. News item in the *Daily Telegraph dated, 27th May 1982.*
3. Lt. Gen. M.S. Shergill, *To Honour A Past,* USI Journal, Vol. CXXXV, No. 560, April-June 2006, New Delhi, p. 312.
4. Statement by Sir Winston Churchill, Prime Minister of Great Britain, in the House of Commons; HC Deb 2 June 1942 vol. 380 cc 528-34.
5. Col. Anjan Mukherjee, *Har Maidan Fateh, pp.35and 44;* Lt. Gen. MS Shergill, *To Honour A Past,*USI Journal, New Delhi, April – June2005 p.311.
6. Zabecki, David T, *World War II:North Africa Campaign,* accessed from *www.historynet.com/world-war-ii-northafrica-campaign-htm.*
7. Maj. Gen. Gurcharan Singh Sandhu, *I Serve : The Eighteenth Cavalry,* p.139.
8. Ibid., p.139 where the author quotes 18 Cavalry commanding officer Lt. Col. H.O.W Fowler.
9. *War Diary* of 2 Indian Field Regiment; entry dated 26th May 1942.
10. Col. M.Y. Effendi, *Punjab Cavalry: Evolution. Role, Organization and Tactical Doctrine 11 Cavalry (Frontier Force) 1849-1971,* p.91, quotes this entry from the regimental War Diary.
11. *War Diary* of 2 Indian Field Regiment; entry dated 26th May 1942.
12. Maj. Gen. Gurcharan Singh Sandhu, *Indian Armour,* p.95.
13. Maj. Gen. Gurcharan Singh Sandhu, *I Serve,* p.143.
14. Col. Anjan Mukherjee, *Har Maidan Fateh,* pp.19-20.
15. Maj. Gen. Gurcharan Singh Sandhu, *Indian Armour,* pp.95-7.
16. Maj. Gen. Gurcharan Singh Sandhu, *I Serve,* pp.143-44.
17. Col. MY Effendi, *Punjab Cavalry,* p.92.
18. Ibid, p.93.
19. Lt. Gen. P.K. Singh, *2 Indian Field Regiment And The Battle Of Bir Hacheim – Point 171,* Salute Magazine, April – , 2019.
20. Col. Anjan Mukherjee, *Har Maidan Fateh,* quotes a first hand count by Major General (then Captain) A.S. Naravane, who was the O.P. Officer of 'F' Troop, pp. 23-6.
21. Ibid., pp.26-7.

22. Lt. Gen. MS Shergill, *'To Honour A Past'*, pp.309-10.
23. Ibid., p.310.
24. Maj. Gen. Gurcharan Singh Sandhu, *I Serve*, p.144.
25. Col. Anjan Mukhejee, *Har Maidan Fateh*, pp.21-2.
26. Ibid., p.35.
27. Maj. Gen. Gurcharan Singh Sandhu, *Indian Armour*, p.97.
28. History of the 2nd Royal Lancers, p.157.
29. Maj. Gen. Gurcharan Singh Sandhu, *Indian Armour*, p.96.
30. Maj. Gen. Gurcharan Singh Sandhu, *I Serve*, p.14.

CHAPTER 5

Battle of Chhamb

(3 December - 17 December 1971)

Indo - Pakistan War of 1971

The Guns, Thank God, The Guns.

RUDYARD KIPLING

But for the artillery support we may not have successfully sustained the initial onslaught of the enemy on our FDLs for more than 72 hours.

COLONEL MAHESH CHADHA

(ADC to GOC 10 Infantry Division during the War)

INTRODUCTION

The area of Chhamb - Jaurian - Akhnur has been the focus of attention of Pakistani military planners in all the wars fought with India since 1947. It is perhaps the only sector which has been subjected to large - scale Pakistani attacks in the 1947 - 48 Operations, the 1965 War (where its offensive reached just a few kilometres short of Akhnur), and during the 1971 Indo - Pakistan War when it once again made a bold and audacious attack in this area. However, unlike its grand success in 1965, this time the Pakistani's were stopped at the line of the Manawar Tawi River, and were unable to achieve their military objectives.

The Battle of Chhamb is considered to be perhaps the toughest and bloodiest battle fought at the divisional level during the 1971 Indo-Pakistan War. Prime Minister Indira Gandhi termed it as the 'toughest'. This was Pakistan's biggest land offensive of the war, for which it had mustered a very large force level. To illustrate this point, it is pertinent to note that the quantum of artillery employed by Pakistan to support this offensive against Chhamb was more than she had to defend itself in the entire East Pakistan ! The available Pakistani force amassed for this attack was centred around their 23 Infantry Division and consisted of five infantry brigades (out of which one was employed in the Hill Sector of the Indian 10 Infantry Division), an armoured brigade with a total of three armoured regiments and an independent squadron, and over ten artillery regiments. In addition it had been given dedicated air support of the Pakistani Air Force, which was coordinated by a PAF officer of the rank of Air Commodore. The eventual objective of this formidable force was Akhnur.

Facing this Pakistani force was the Indian 10 Infantry Division, whose task had been changed as many as four times, the last change of plan was literally at the eleventh hour, i.e. the night of 1 December 1971. The division was now ordered to put its well- rehearsed offensive plan 'on hold' and adopt a defensive posture by 4 December. It was however to be prepared to launch the offensive with a 48 hour notice, if required. This 'duality of aim' thrust upon the division had a bearing on its defensive posture. In the event, when Pakistan attacked on the night of 3/4 December1971, 10 Infantry Division was still in the process of re-adjustments, and thus commenced the battle from this initially unbalanced state. In spite of numerous handicaps the Division fought stoically, inflicting very heavy casualties on the Pakistani forces and put paid to their attempts to capture Akhnur.

The artillery of both sides played a decisive role in this intensely fought battle; maximum casualties on either side were caused by artillery fire.

STRATEGIC SIGNIFICANCE AND TOPOGRAPHY OF THE CHHAMB SECTOR

STRATEGIC IMPORTANCE OF THE CHHAMB SECTOR

The importance of this sector lies in its geo-strategic location and favorable topography (see Maps 10 and 11). While Map 10 elucidates the importance of the Chhamb – Jaurian Sector to the Pakistanis, Map 11 depicts the area extending from the Cease Fire Line (CFL)/ International Border (IB) in the West up

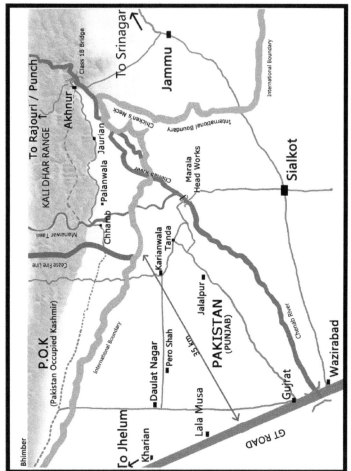

Map 10: Strategic Importance of Chhamb Sector

Note : Map has been sourced from *BATTLEGROUND CHHAMB : The Indo-Pakistan War of 1971* by Major General A.J.S. Sandhu, p.40

to Akhnur in the east.

It can be seen in Map 10 that the area towards the west of the Manawar Tawi River is in the form of a bulge (or salient), thereby providing the Indians a firm base from which to launch an offensive into Pakistan in multiple directions, i.e. towards the West, South-West or South. This map clearly shows the vulnerability of Pakistan's heartland Punjab province to any Indian offensive from the Chhamb Sector. The Grand Trunk Road is the closest to the Indian border in this area, as are their military garrison towns of Kharian, Lala Musa and Gujrat - all of whom are within 'striking distance'. Even closer is the

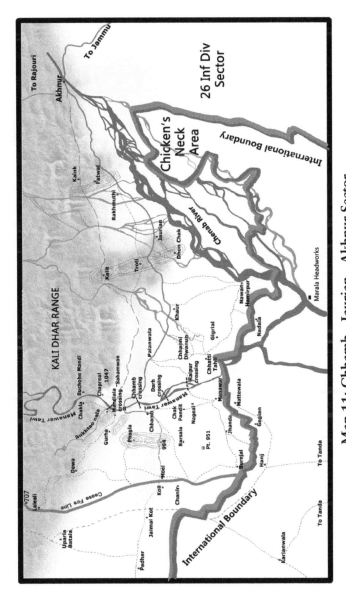

Map 11: Chhamb - Jaurian - Akhnur Sector

Note: Map has been sourced from BATTLEGROUND CHHAMB: The Indo-Pakistan War of 1971 by Major General A.J.S. Sandhu, p.47

Marala Headworks which feeds the canal system; its capture would cut off the water supply to Punjab which is the granary of Pakistan. The Hamoodur Rehman Commission sums up the importance of this Indian threat:

It is an open terrain which lies between the foothills and the Chenab river and provides a direct approach to the area of Lala Musa - Gujrat, ...any advance in this area by the enemy would pose a serious threat to the main lines of communication between Rawalpindi and Lahore. The Indians could also have combined with such a move, another major threat through the Sialkot – Shakargarh - Narowal area, linking up of somewhere near the Wazirabad bridge. They could also launch attacks from their territory on both sides of Chenab to converge on Marala Headworks, which is from the defence point of view of great strategic importance to Pakistan, as the Marala-Ravi link in Sialkot and the Lahore-Kasur sectors are all fed from these headworks.[1]

In 1971 there were no intervening water obstacles between the G.T. Road and the IB, accentuating the Pakistani vulnerability. The Pakistanis called this area the 'Manawar Gap', and realized the best way to thwart any possible Indian attack was to launch one of its own. Their military planners realized that a Pakistani offensive into this salient, would in one stroke, pre-empt any Indian designs in this sector; this indeed is what also happened in the 1971 war.

TOPOGRAPHY
Another factor favouring a Pakistani offensive in this sector was the topography (or terrain) and the proximity of the Indian township of Akhnur with the bridge on the Chenab river, which they felt were attainable objectives by suitably grouped military force (see Map 11). In fact, just six years earlier the Pakistanis had sliced though Chhamb - Jaurian area and reached just a few kilometres short of Akhnur.

As can been seen in Map 11, the Chhamb sector can be divided into the Hill Sector and Plains Sector. The Hill Sector comprised the southern reaches of the Kalidhar range, which gradually peter out into the plains of the south. The Plains Sector is bounded by the Kalidhar Hills in the north, the CFL in the west, and the International Boundary / Chenab River in the south. The area is shaped in the form of a funnel, which progressively becomes narrower as one moves eastwards; the broad end of this funnel is the CFL in the west while the tip is the township Akhnur in the east. At the time of the war, there was only a 'Class 18' Girder Bridge over the Chenab River at Akhnur. This was a very lucrative military target, as not only was this the life-line of logistic supplies to 10 Infantry Division deployed in the Chhamb sector, but the road leading northwards towards the Naoshera, Rajauri and Punch Sectors (25 Infantry Division) also passed over this bridge.

The Chhamb-Jaurian-Akhnur 'funnel' was the only place in Jammu and Kashmir where tanks could be employed by both sides. Any Pakistani offensive towards Akhnur through the Chhamb Sector had the advantage of deriving natural flank - protection from the Kalidhar Hills in the north and the mighty Chenab River in the south. In 1971, there were only two natural 'defence lines' between the CFL and Akhnur, one was the Manawar Tawi River which was seven to   nine kilometres from the CFL, and the other was the Tamka Tilla – Kalit – Troti - Dhon Chak ridgeline, which was a further 18 to 20 kilometres to the east.

The Manawar Tawi River effectively cut the divisional sector into two unequal parts. Although any water obstacle in front of a defended sector greatly increases its defence potential, in this case it was in its rear, thereby creating attendant problems for the defender. This river was a partial tank obstacle with one concrete bridge over it. There were four fords on this river which could be used as crossing places in dry seasons; north to south these were the Mandiala, Chhamb, Darh and Raipur Crossings.

In 1971 there were only two roads connecting Akhnur with Chhamb:

(a) Southern Axis. Road Akhnur – Jaurian – Palanwala - Mandiala Bridge - Chhamb. This was the only 'Class 9' road (though in a poor state of repair) in the sector, which supported the logistic chain of 10 Infantry Division.

(b) Northern Axis. Road Akhnur – Kaink – Kachreal - Mandiala Bridge / Mandiala Crossing. This was a one way, un-metalled kutcha road which supported only light traffic.

While the Hill Sector provided dominating heights, which could be made into defensive strong points, the Plains Sector was generally under-developed with very few defensive features.

INDIAN PLANS IN THE CHHAMB SECTOR

Unlike the earlier two wars (1947-48 & 1965), Kashmir was not the cause of the 1971 War. It was an external manifestation of an internal despute in Pakistan, whose origins can be traced to the first ever General Elections of that country held in December 1970. By denying the Awami League (which had won the majority) the right to form a government, President Yahya Khan set in motion a series of events, the unintended consequence of which was the Indo-Pakistan War of 1971.

OVERALL STRATEGY

With the launching of Operation Searchlight on 25 March 1971, a brutal military crackdown had been unleashed on the Bengali population of East Pakistan. In order to escape the reign of terror unleashed by the Pakistani army, tens of thousands of people had started to cross into India to seek refuge (at its peak the number of refugees reached a staggering figure of 10 million). The following month on 29 April 1971, Mrs Indira Gandhi called for a meeting wherein were present Mr Jagjivan Ram (Defence Minister), Mr Swaran Singh (Minister of External Affair), Mr Fakhruddin Ali Ahmed (Agriculture Minister) and Mr Y. B. Chavan (Finance Minister). The Army Chief General S.H.F.J. (Sam) Manekshaw was also present as a special invitee. In the course of the discussion, it is leant that Mrs Gandhi wanted the Army Chief to launch an offensive into East Pakistan at the earliest. Major General A. J. S. Sandhu notes in his book Battleground Chhamb:

...He (Manekshsaw) stood his ground. He told her that he needed time to prepare for such a war since there were many deficiencies in armament and equipment in the army; furthermore, the oncoming monsoons precluded military operations in the riverine terrain in East Pakistan and the earliest he could do so was in November. If pushed into undertaking this ill-advised operation immediately, he was even willing to resign... the External Affairs Minister Mr Swaran Singh is said to have counseled restraint and also advocated first exhausting diplomatic measures to resolve the problem. In the event, Prime Minister Indira Gandhi agreed and gave Sam Manekshaw a free hand thereafter.[2]

Although the likelihood of launching of military operations was still an uncertainty, the three defence services started planning for such an eventuality. The politico-military strategy adopted was to launch an offensive into East Pakistan, while maintaining an offensive defensive posture in the Western Theatre. This strategy did not, however, rule out the launching of limited offensives in selected areas in order to improve our defensive posture in the west. This is confirmed by Air Chief Marshal P. C. Lal (Chief of Air Staff) in his book My Years with the IAF, where he wrote that: ...'As defined by the Chiefs of Staff Committee and by each service, it was to gain as much ground as possible in the east, to neutralize the Pakistani forces there to the extent we could, and to establish a base as it were for a possible state of Bangladesh. In the west, the objective was to hold the Pakistani forces.[3]

Based on directions from Army headquarters, the army commands too commenced their planning for a likely military operation. The Western Theatre was the responsibility of two commands; while the bulk of the border stretching from Ladakh in the north to the area of Ganganagar in Rajasthan came under Western Command, the desert region to the south of that up to the Gujarat border (a much smaller area) was under the Southern Command. Initially Western Command, under Lieutenant General K. P. Candeth, consisted of two corps, i.e. 15 Corps (five infantry divisions) which was responsible for the state of Jammu and Kashmir (J &K) as it existed then, (i.e Jammu, Kashmir Valley and Ladakh regions), and 11 Corps (three infantry divisions) which was responsible for the Punjab border as well as the Ganganagar region of Rajasthan. Later in October 1971, 1 Corps (Three infantry divisions and two Armoured Brigades) was placed under Western Command, In addition, 1 Armoured Division and 14 Infantry Division, while being retained as the Army HQ Strategic Reserve, were also moved into the Western Command theatre and located in the Faridkot – Muktsar - Kotkapura area. Lieutenant General Candeth planned to launch 1 Corps into Shakargarh, and 10 Infantry Division and 26 Infantry Division in limited complementary thrusts on either side of the Chenab river into the Pakistan Punjab province. Later, on 1 November 1971 after the visit of Army Chief in this sector, the 26 Infantry Division task was curtailed to only the elimination of the so called 'Chickens Neck' area.

15 Corps under Lieutenant General Sartaj Singh was responsible for the Jammu & Kashmir border (CFL and IB). In addition to the offensives of 10 and 26 Infantry Divisions, the Corps Commander also planned for small-scale, limited attacks in the hilly and mountainous regions of his 25, 19 and 3 Infantry Divisions.

OPERATIONAL PLANS - 10 INFANTRY DIVISION
As brought out earlier the area of responsibility of 10 Infantry Division comprised a Hill Sector to the north, and Plains Sector to the south; and it extended from the CFL in the west to Akhnur in the east. On its ORBAT (Order of Battle) the division had three infantry brigades (28, 52 and 191 Infantry Brigades), an artillery brigade and an armoured regiment (this ORBAT underwent a change later when the division was given an offensive task). However, 52 Infantry Brigade had been designated the 'corps reserve' and was given the responsibility of counter-attack tasks in the Corps Zone; it had therefore to be deployed in depth. 28 Infantry Brigade was responsible for the Hill Sector, while 191 Infantry Brigade was given the task of holding defences in the plains.

The original defence plan (post 1965 war) envisaged holding a defence-line well to the east, along the Tam ka Tilla - Kalit – Troti - Dhon Chak ridgeline, with only a small force of 'Covering Troops' deployed in the Chhamb area. Later, in the run-up to the war, the operational plans of 10 Infantry Division underwent as many as three further changes, the last one on 1 Dec 1971. These frequent changes greatly impacted the preparations of the Division.

INITIAL DEFENCE PLANS - 10 INFANTRY DIVISION
Just six years earlier in the 1965 war Pakistan had launched an audacious offensive in this sector on 1 September 1965 with view to capture Akhnur code-named Operation Grand Slam.

The Pakistani forces literally ran through the Indian defences and by 5 September 1965, had reached within 5 miles of the town.

After the war, 15 Corps had ordered a re-appraisal to be carried out with a view to formulate a stronger defensive layout in this sector. Somehow, the Indian defence planners of that time did not draw the relevant lessons. 'Based on a false notion that the area west of Manawar Tawi River was indefensible), it had been decided to site the 191 Infantry Brigade defences along the Kalit-Troti-Dhon Chak ridge, about 20 kilometres east of the river. Ahead of this, only 'Covering Troops' were deployed in the form of Papa force and Quebec Force; while the former consisted of one infantry battalion and one armoured squadron and was deployed in the Chhamb Salient, the latter consisting of an armoured regiment (less two squadrons) and two infantry companies was located east of the river opposite the Nadala Enclave'.[4] The aim of this 'covering force' was to delay the enemy advance for 48 hours while falling back into the main defences, after which the Indians were to launch an attack on the enemy's stretched line of communications. Such a concept was in the classic mould of 'mobile defence' i.e 'trading space with time'. This strategy though well suited for the long drawn continental wars , clearly flew in the face of a 'short war scenario' in the India- Pakistan context. But such was the mindset of the higher commanders, clearly influenced by their Second World War experience, that this deployment remained in force till November 1971.

The new GOC of 10 Infantry Division, Major General Jaswant Singh, who took over in September 1970, immediately realized the folly of such a deployment. He realized that keeping the main defences so far behind was a recipe for disaster, which the Pakistanis would exploit in any future conflict. On his instructions, an Engineer Appreciation was carried out to assess the construction of permanent defence works of a brigade strength inside the Chhamb Salient, which estimated that this could be done in 'one working season'. The GOC made a presentation the Corps commander Lieutenant General Sartaj Singh in October 1970 recommending the construction of these defence works and moving the whole of 191 Infantry Brigade into the salient to occupy a deliberate defence. This proposal was summarily rejected. The ostensible reason cited was again the 'perceived' indefensibility of the Chhamb Salient.[5]

This defensive layout continued all the way up to 1 November 1971, i.e. till just one month before the outbreak of the war (please see Map 12).

OFFENSIVE PLAN

Even as the above mentioned defensive posture continued to prevail, Major General Jaswant Singh conceptualised an offensive plan. The GOC felt that such an offensive plan (especially if launched in conjunction with 26 Infantry Division to its south) would accrue the following strategic gains: it would pre-empt any Pakistsani plans in this sector and in one stroke remove the threat to Akhnur; threaten the vital areas of Gujrat and Marala Headworks in their Punjab province; and by forcing Pakistan to move troops to deal with this threat, it would facilitate the operations of Indian 1 Corps in Shakargarh Bulge.[6]

The GOC made a presentation of his concept of operations and the additional resources required for this offensive, to Lieutenant General K. P.Candeth, the Army Commander, during a Map Exercise conducted in Shimla in April 1971. Although the Army Commander listened with great interest, he did not give any decision at that point of time. The approval for this offensive finally came during an operational conference held at HQ 15 Corps on 10 Jul 1971. 10 Infantry Division was now allotted additional resources in the form of the newly raised 3 (Independent) Armoured Brigade, 68 Infantry Brigade, 216 Medium Regiment (130 mm guns) and 2 (Independent) Recce Squadron. Furthermore, 52 Infantry Brigade was also relieved of its tasks of being a 'Corps Reserve' and was reverted to 10 Infantry Division. Although its 28 Infantry Brigade remained deployed to defend the Hill Sector, the division still had a formidable strength of an independent armoured brigade, three infantry brigades and six artillery regiments to

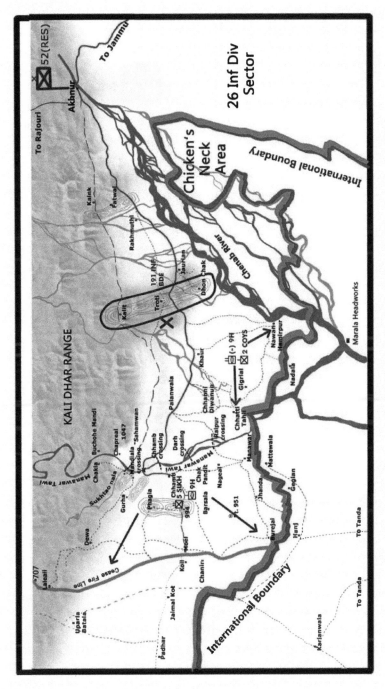

Map 12: 191 Infantry Brigade Initial Defence Posture Upto 1 Nov 1971

launch this offensive. The ORBAT of 10 Infantry Division is given in Appendix G.

This offensive was to be launched with a 48 hours notice: this time had been given to allow 191 Infantry Brigade (which was still holding the defences along the Kalith – Troti - Dhon Chak ridgeline in depth), to move forward into the Chhamb Salient and provide a 'firm base' through which the 'break out' force would launch across the CFL into Pakistan. The plan in outline was:

(a) *Phase1* : One Infantry Brigade supported by an armoured regiment was to establish a brigade-head across the CFL on night D/D plus 1.

(b) *Phase 2* : 3 (Independent) Armoured Brigade along with the second infantry brigade was to break-out towards the Tanda and capture it if possible, failing which isolate it, and then swing towards Marala Headworks.

(c) *Phase 3* : The 'firm base' brigade was to link up with the above force at Marala Headworks.

(d) *Phase 4* : The division was then to re-group and progress operations towards Gujrat on the G.T. Road..

Once the green signal had been given, 10 Infantry Division got busy with preparation and fine-tuning of the offensive task. From mid-July onwards there was a flurry of activity in this regard: reconnaissance by commanders at all levels, 'planning conferences' at the division and brigade level, visits by senior staff officers from 15 Corps HQ to coordinate the staff aspects and so on. The exercises of 52, 68 and 191 Infantry Brigades to test them for their impending task were conducted in the month of October, with the corps commander witnessing the 52 Infantry Brigade exercise. A practice-cum-demonstration of the Crossing Control Organization (to facilitate the passage of the 'break out force') was also organized by 9 Horse at the divisional level. A War Game was conducted by the GOC to fine tune the impending task. Meanwhile, the whole of 10 Infantry Division was operationally deployed on 12 October 1971, according to the then existing plan of only the 'Covering Troops' in the Chhamb Salient and the main defences in depth!

CHANGE IN DEFENCE POSTURE, I.E ADOPTION OF 'FORWARD POISE'.

The third change in the operational plan occurred after the visit of the COAS, General Sam Manekshaw to Akhnur on 1 November 1971. During the briefing by the GOC, the Army Chief questioned the wisdom of having the main defence- line so far back at the Tam Ka Tilla - Kalit-Troti-Dhon Chak line , while leaving the Chhamb Salient relatively weakly defended. The GOC, Major General Jaswant Singh mentioned at the briefing that he had been proposing the deployment of 191 Infantry Brigade into the salient, but this had not been agreed to by the higher headquarters. The Corps Commander, Lieutenant General Sartaj Singh, who was also present at the briefing gave out the reasons for the same, arguing that both he and the Army Commander felt that the Chhamb Salient was 'indefensible' and that the Kalit - Troti - Dhon Chak ridgeline afforded a better defence potential. After much discussion, General Manekshaw went along with the GOC 10 Division's proposal and approved the move forward of 191 Infantry Brigade into the Chhamb Salient, albeit in the shape of what was then termed as a 'Forward Poise'. In other words this brigade was being pre-positioned to provide a 'firm base' to facilitate the division's offensive task, and at the same time give greater defence potential in the front line.

It was this deployment, effected barely one month before the outbreak of the war, that eventually served as the bulwark to the Pakistani attack on the night of 3 December 1971. As a consequence of the adoption of the 'Forward Poise' the following troops (already allocated to the division), were also moved west of the Chenab River and into the divisional sector:

(a) 68 Infantry Brigade.

(b) 72 Armoured Regiment.

(c) 2 (Independent) Reconnaissance Squadron.

(d) 216 Medium Regiment

(Note: 3 (Independent) Armoured Brigade remained east of the Chenab River in order to retain surprise.

The division continued with its preparation for the impending offensive task through the month of November. A 'test exercise' was conducted for 3 (Independent) Armoured Brigade, and Infantry - Tank Cooperation exercise was also held. Movement Tables were finalised and additional artillery ammunition brought forward to the gun areas. The Army and Corps Commanders visited the division and were briefed by the GOC and Brigade Commanders. The IAF officers moved in as Forward Air Controllers (FACs) to form part of the Air Control Team (ACTs). By 30 November 1971, 10 Infantry Division was ready to launch its offensive and eagerly awaited the D Day.

LAST MINUTE CHANGE IN PLANS

Even as 10 Infantry Division waited in its launch pads for the offensive to begin, fate had other plans for it. In a 'twist in the tale' as the old saying goes, on the evening of 1 December 1971, there was a sudden reversal of tasks of this division. The GOC was summoned to Corps Headquarters for an Operational Conference, and ordered to put the offensive 'on hold' and instead adopt a defensive posture by 4 December 1971. This was the FOURTH change in plan of 10 Infantry Division, literally at the eleventh hour, and was to have far reaching consequences as far as the manner in which the battle was later fought.

This change was apparently necessitated due to political considerations at the higher level (i.e. Prime Minister) and not due to military necessity. With troops already in the launch pads, General Sam Manekshaw remonstrated with Mrs Indira Gandhi, but was overruled.[7]

Even as 10 Infantry Division now got busy in reverting to defensive posture, its offensive task had NOT been called off. It was merely put at 48 hours notice. This pre-condition affected the deployment now being adopted, particularly of artillery guns and troops tasked for the initial phase of the offensive (should it be ordered). Furthermore, the Division had to carry out all major activity at night due to the enemy's surveillance capability of forward areas by day. While the Division was still in the process of carrying out its readjustment (the time given to it was till 4 December morning), the Pakistani's launched

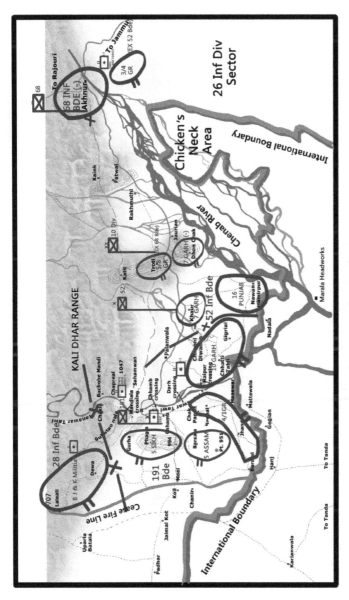

Map 13: Deployment of 10 Inf Div - 3 Dec 1971

Note: Map has been sourced from BATTLEGROUND CHHAMB: The Indo-Pakistan War of 1971 by Major General A.J.S. Sandhu, p.103

their attack on the night of 3 December. Thus, the Division joined the battle in a somewhat initially unbalanced position.

The ORBAT and deployment of 10 Infantry Division as on 3 December 1971 are as shown in Appendix G and Map 13 respectively.

PAKISTANI PLANS FOR THE CHHAMB OFFENSIVE

OVERALL STRATEGY

After a review of the 1965 Indo-Pakistan war, President Ayub Khan (who was also the Supreme Commander) had issued a document : War directive No 4 of 9 August 1967, which enunciated the overall strategic concept for the defence of Pakistan; all three services were to formulate their overall strategy and war plans based on this. As stated in this War Directive, the mission of the armed forces was stated thus:

On commencement of hostilities or as soon as favourable conditions are created, offensive operations will be undertaken to capture and hold as much enemy territory possible, whilst containing and neutralizing the enemy forces elsewhere by all means at our disposal in the West. In the East, contain and neutralize as many enemy troops as possible, inflicting maximum casualtieswithout running risk of annihilation.[8]

This War Directive clearly enunciated that 'even if hostilities commence in East Pakistan, strategic factors dictate that major and decisive battles will be fought from West Pakistan'. In keeping with this concept, Pakistan hoped to launch strong attacks in the Western Theatre and capture enough territory to offset the losses in East Pakistan, and to bring India to the negotiating table. Two types of offensives were planned;

(a) 'Fixing Attacks' by suitably strengthened 'holding' formations; Chhamb Sector was chosen for one such attack.

(b) Major offensives deep into Indian territory, to be carried out by their strategic reserves.

In the absence of a fixed date of attack, Pakistan had formulated a timetable on M-Day basis; M-Day indicated the day the government took a decision to open the Western front.[9] However, as the Hamoodur Rehman Commission notes, this timetable did not 'clearly state the circumstances and factors which the Commander-in-Chief was to take into account in launching the army reserves'. In the event, these strategic reserves were never launched and their potential remained unutilized during the war.

PLANS FOR THE CHHAMB OFFENSIVE

The 1965 Chhamb Offensive, Operation Grand Slam, had been launched at the southern flank of Pakistan 12 Infantry Division's very vast area of responsibility. In order to control this major thrust, the GOC Major General Akhtar Hussain Malik had his headquarters scattered at four locations, i.e the main division headquarter was in Murree, the tactical headquarter at Bhimber, a liaison officer (senior staff officer) located at Kharian as a link with the GHQ while he controlled the first day's battle from the Artillery Brigade Command located at Padhar (near the CFL). This inadequacy in the 'command and control system' was the reason given by Pakistani's Army Chief General Musa, for effecting the change of command on 2 September 1965 to GOC 7 Infantry Division Major General Yahya Khan.[10]

It was based on this lesson that Pakistan had raised a new infantry division to be exclusively responsible for the Chhamb Sector. 23 Infantry Division had been raised in Jhelum in June 1968 and had on its ORBAT-7 AK Brigade, 4 AK Brigade (responsible for the Southern end of the CFL) and 20 Infantry Brigade (responsible for the IB). It also had an armoured regiment (26 Cavalry) and an artillery brigade. This division was responsible of the defence of area opposite Chhamb Sector, which they called the 'Munnawar gap'. It also had a limited offensive task of closing in on to the Manawar Tawi River and capturing maximum territory enroute. Considering the fact that right up to 1 November 1971 the Indians only had a small 'covering force' of one infantry battalion and squadron of armour located inside the salient, this task was clearly 'doable'.

As the war clouds started gathering General Yahya Khan decided to replicate Operation Grand Slam of 1965 once again, but this time with a much larger force. Not only would such an offensive pre-empt any Indian designs through their vulnerable 'Mannawar Gap', but it would enable capturing a large chunk of territory all the way up to Akhnur; the capture of the bridge would also impact the Indian forces deployed in the Rajouri-Punch Sector whose logistic supplies had to be moved over this road bridge.

The Hamoodur Rahman Commission has noted:

This offensive plan had a direct bearing on the overall plans of Pakistan Army, for , this movement was designed to forestall any likely offensive by the Indians towards the Munnawar Gap, and thus 'close the back door' leaving the army to attend to its defensive operations in the south without any danger of being hit at the back.[11]

Accordingly 23 Infantry Division was now boosted up by allotting it additional resources to ensure success of its new operational task; these additional elements included 2 (Independent) Armoured Brigade (a total of three armoured regiments and independent armoured squadron), 66 Infantry Brigade, 111 Infantry Brigade and ten artillery regiments from 17 Artillery Brigade and Corps Artillery. Thus 23 Infantry Division was now a very formidable force. To command this division, General Yahya sent one out of his favourite generals, Major General Iftikhar Khan Janjua. This general had already commanded 6 Armoured Division and was also familiar with the Chhamb sector, as his brigade (6 Infantry Brigade) had also operated here in the 1965 war.

The months of September, October and November were spent with a single minded focus of preparing for their impending offensive (contrast this with the 10 Infantry Division being compelled to having its plans changed four times!). Recconnaissances, war games and exercises were conducted. To quote three examples:

Lieutenant Colonel Khurshid Ali Khan CO of 11 Cavalry noted that ' ... there were endless recces which kept us busy from dawn to dusk with almost no respite. These were followed by war games, planning and coordination between the involved units, and in our case a full-fledged exercise in which we carried out a night march and regimental attack.[12]

Major General Syed Ali Hamid, then the Adjutant of 26 Cavalry recalled 'Soon after its arrival, 11 Cavalry along with 66 Infantry Brigade conducted an exercise in which the force established a bridgehead and advanced twenty miles. During this exercise of forty eight hours, the command echelons of 26 Cavalry were attached with 11 Cavalry as observers. This was a valuable experience...'[13]

Lieutenant Colonel Saeed Ahmad, the GSO1 of the division,

wrote in his book *Battle of Chhamb (1971)*: ...a war game exercise was held from 8 to 15 November... the entire duration of the exercise remaind a busy period for all. Every detail of the terrain was studied. At the end of the exercise a final joint recce was carried out to confirm and clarify one's thoughts. The plan was now completely ready.[14]

By the end of November, Pakistan had assembled a very strong force, comprisng five infantry brigades, an armoured brigade and over 10 artillery regiments or 31 fire units; *it needs to be reiterated that the artillery employed to support this offensive was more than what Pakistan had in the whole of East Pakistan!* The PAF had also assured 'air superiority' over the battle area for the first three days, and had attached a very senior officer, Air Commodore Saeed Ullah Khan at the Divisional Tactical headquarters as 'Advisor' to GOC to coordinate the air effort.

The overall concept of the Pakistani was to attack with two Brigades from the west with a view to establish a bridgehead across the CFL; break-out and contact the Manawar Tawi River line at the earliest; launch an uncommitted brigade across the Manawar Tawi at the Sukh Tao Nala crossing in the north and capture the Kachreal Ridge and the Mandiala Road Bridge; an armoured regiment was then to break-out towards Palanwala. After regrouping, the division was to initially advance towards Jaurian, and then depending on the situation, to Akhnur.[15]

On the morning of 30 November, Major General Iftikhar Khan Janjua was summoned to the Pakistan GHQ and given the 'go ahead' for this offensive. On 1 December 1971 he gave his orders for the initial phase of operations:

(a) 66 Infantry Brigade and 111 Infantry Brigade to attack across the CFL at 2100 hrs (Pakistan time) 3 December and secure lodgments between Khalabat Jhil (in the north) and Ghogi-Barsala (in the south), by first light 4 December. (As Amin says: 'This lodgment would result in the break-up of the main line of Indian forward-defended localities and provide own armour with a firm base for break-out at first light').

(b) At first light on 4 December, 11 Cavalry Group, (i.e 11 Cavalry, one squadron of 26 Cavalry, 4 Punjab, one company of 19 Baluch [Reconnaissance & Support], and 24 Field Company [Engineers] under the overall command of 66 Infantry Brigade, were to break-out from area Munnawali in the northern part of the lodgment, and advance towards Mandiala, cutting road Dewa-Mandiala at Kamali Chappar, and to secure the home bank of Tawi in the Mandiala area by last light of 4 December 1971. 66 Infantry Brigade was to follow behind 11 Cavalry Group and secure the area up to the river line.

(c) In conjunction with 66 Infantry Brigade's advance, 111 Infantry Brigade was to carry out an offensive probe towards Chhamb and Chak Pandit and draw enemy reserves. On 5 December, 111 Infantry Brigade was to advance and capture Chhamb.

(d) Following the capture of Chhamb, 66 Infantry Brigade and 111 Infantry Brigade were to clear the entire salient up to the west bank of Tawi.

(e) *Detailed orders for the operations envisaged across the Manawar Tawi River were to be given later, in relation to the operational situation* (emphasis by the author).

(f) Concurrent to the above, 20 Infantry Brigade in the south was to make demonstration attacks against Burejal, Manawar and Nadala Enclave, to deceive the Indians with regard to the direction of the main attack.

(g) Later, once the main attack of 66 Infantry Brigade and 111 Infantry Brigade in the north had succeeded, this brigade was to advance northwards as far as possible, capturing Jhanda, Mangotian and Manawar.

(h) In the Hill Sector, 7 Azad Kashmir Brigade was to launch local attacks (so as to ensure that 10 Infantry Division had to deal with this sector as well)[16].

The ORBAT of 23 Infantry Division and its Plan of Attack are given at Appendix H and Map 14, respectively

The Chhamb offensive of 23 Infantry Division was codenamed *The Sword of Allah*. In an ironic twist, on the day Major General Iftikhar Janjua gave out his orders for attack, i.e., 1 December 1971, his opposing commander Major General Jaswant Singh was summoned to his corps headquarters and

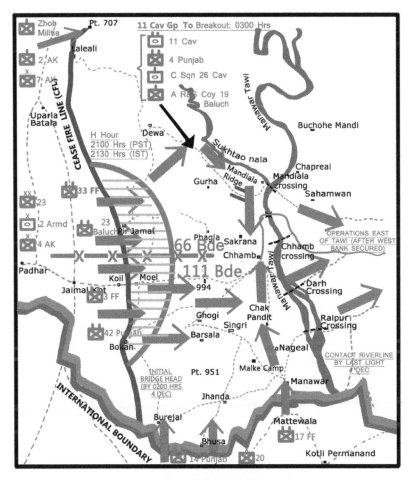

Map 14: Pakistan 23 Inf Div Plan of Attack

Note 1: 66, 111 And 20 Infantry Brigade To progress operations With A view To converge In Area Chhamb- Chak Pandit

Note 2: Map has been sourced from *BATTLEGROUND CHHAMB : The Indo-Pakistan War of 1971 by Major General A.J.S. Sandhu*, p.122

ordered to do the exact opposite, i.e. adopt a defensive posture. On the night of 2/3 December, while the Pakistani troops were moving to their assembly areas for the attack, the Indians were feverishly re-adjusting their defensive position.

Pakistan Air Force's pre-emptive air strikes against selected Indian forward air bases in the evening of 3 December heralded the commencement of the Indo-Pakistan War of

1971. All troops on the western theatre were put on alert. A few hours later, at 2050 hrs (Indian Standard Time) or 2020 hours (Pakistan Time) around 200 Pakistani artillery guns and mortars opened up across the entire front of 10 Infantry Division. The Battle of Chhamb had begun. This toughest, bloodiest and most intensely fought battle of the 1971 war was to play out over the next two weeks.

THE BATTLE

OPERATIONS WEST OF MANAWAR TAWI RIVER
(3-6 DECEMBER 1971)

After 40 Minutes of intense artillery bombardment of Indian defence positions, Pakistan launched its ground offensive (the biggest in the Western Theatre) at 2130 Hours IST (or 2100 hours PST). While 66 and 111 Infantry Brigades attacked from the west cross the CFL, (against 5 Sikh and 5 Assam), 20 Infantry Brigade attacked the forward localities across the IB (against 4/1GR) and elements of 7 AK Brigade attacked Piquet 707 in the Hill Sector (8 J & K Militia). Thus the entire front line of 10 Infantry Division had been activated simultaneously. Although the 'screen postion, at Pir Jamal was withdrawn, the platoon at Moel continued to hold on for another 24 hours! The GOC immediately released the remaining 9 Deccan Horse (RHQ plus B Squadron) to 191 Infantry Brigade, and they crossed over the river and deployed by the early morning of 4 December.

By 0200 hours of 4 December, 66 Infantry Brigade had made in-roads of about 3000 yards and established a bridgehead; however 111 Infantry Brigade to its south was stalled due to 5 Sikh platoon's stoic defence of Moel. 11 Cavalry Group broke out of the bridgehead and headed towards Manawar Tawi River in the area of Mandiala. Their advancing tanks were engaged by RHQ Troop of 9 Deccan horse led by the adjutant Captain Surinder Kaushik .Seven enemy tanks were shot up, and Captain Kaushik and his gunner Jai Singh were awarded Vir Chakras.

By mid-day this battle group had contacted Mandiala

North which was defended by one platoon of 5 Sikh. 4 Punjab supported by tanks and artillery fire, attacked this position. The heavily outnumbered Sikhs stood no chance, and after a brave fight this locality fell to the Pakistanis at 1230 hours. The enemy however, suffered heavy casualties in this attack: 4 Punjab had 20 killed and 30 wounded (including the company commander), while 11 Cavalry suffered 9 killed, 12 wounded and 11 tanks lost.

Anticipating a break through, the Pakistani GOC now gave the following orders, even as the fighting for Mandiala North was still in progress:

(a) 4 A K Brigade to launch an attack across Manawar Tawi River after last light and capture high ground east of Sahamwan village (*i.e. the spur feature near Kachreal*-author).

(b) 28 Cavalry to break-out at first light 5 December, and after capturing Palanwala, *to advance as far eastward as possible* (emphasis by the author). 11 Cavalry was kept in reserve.

(c) 66 Infantry Brigade to follow the advance of 11 Cavalry and close up with River Manawar Tawi.

(d) In conjunction with 4 AK Brigade's main attack, 111 Infantry Brigade and 20 Infantry Brigade were to capture Chhamb and Manawar respectively[17].

Meanwhile, the GOC 10 Infantry Division who had positioned himself at the 191 Infantry Brigade headquarter, realized the ramification of the fall of Mandiala North, which had opened a gateway across the Sukh Tao Nala. Just ahead of this crossing place were deployed the medium gun positions of 216 and 39 Medium Regiments. He summoned 68 Infantry Brigade Commander, Brigadier R. T. Morlin and ordered him to counter-attack Mandiala North immediately with 7 Kumaon, while at the same time moving 9 Jat forward. B squadron of 72 Armoured Regiment was also ordered across the river and placed under 191 Infantry Brigade, who now had the RHQ, two squadrons of 9 Deccan Horse and one squadron of 72 Armoured Regiment. The GOC also ordered a company of 9 Para Commando and a troop of 9 Horse to deploy opposite the Mandiala (which covered the Sukh Tao

Nala gap) and Chhamb crossings.

However, the move of 7 Kumaon got delayed due to the most flimsy reason, i.e., non – availability of Troop Carrying Vehicles (TCVs), which should have been ensured by 68 Infantry Brigade since they had been given the responsibility of counter-attack tasks in the divisional sector. Later, when the R & O Group of 7 Kumaon was moving forward it came under heavy Pakistani artillery fire in which five officers (including the CO) as well as many ORs were injured, resulting in further delay and disorganization of this battalion. In view of all this, 7 Kumaon was now ordered to move forward and deploy east of the Mandiala Crossing / Sukh Tao Nala and plug this gap. Quite surprisingly, the battalion instead made its way to Kachreal hill leaving this vulnerable area undefended. Furthermore, due to communication failure between the battalion and brigade headquarters, this became known only next morning, by when it was already too late. Meanwhile, 4/1 GR had now been tasked to counter-attack Mandiala North. After another unnecessary delay in launching this, the attack finally went in at 8 p.m.. It made good progress against some accurate hostile artillery and small arms fire, and came within a few yards of the top. But with the Company Commander Major Gian Singh injured, one platoon commander dead, and many more casualties, the attack stalled and finally the troops pulled back. Thus the Sukh Tao Nala gap remained thinly defended, and it is in through this gap that 4 AK Brigade launched its attack in the early morning of 5 December.

With the Sukh Tao Nala gap still weakly held, this formidable Pakistani force had a great chance of effecting a break-through and encircling the 191 Infantry Brigades defences form the rear. The brigade commander, Brigadier Ahmad Jamal Khan planned to advance with two battalions in the lead (6 AK on the left and 13 AK on the right); each battalion was to assault 'two companies up' followed by 47 Punjab in its wake. Once the bridgehead had been established, the Manto Force squadron (12 Independent Armoured Squadron operating under CO of 26 Cavalry Lt Col Shamim Yasin Manto) and A Squadron of 26 Cavalry were to move forward for securing this bridgehead and ensuring 28 Cavalry to break-out towards Palanwala, followed by 66 Infantry Brigade and

11 Cavalry. The H hour, after two postponements, was 0400 hours 5 December, 1971.

Unfortunately, 6 AK Battalion got lost and failed to go into the attack at the appointed hour. Thus it was that 13 AK went into the assault, blissfully unaware of this fact (as indeed was 4 AK Brigade). Its first two company 'waves' were led by the CO, Lieutenant Colonel Basharrat Raja, and the following two 'waves' by the 2IC Major Abbassi. They were followed by the leading companies of 47 Punjab. (See Map 15).

In his book Battleground Chhamb, Major General Sandhu has written :

In the darkness, the two 'waves' of 13 AK were unable to maintain direction. While one column veered northwards towards Chapreal, the other continued forward.... The northern column went slam into the two forward batteries of 216 Medium Regiment as well as the 'wagon lines' area of 39 Medium Regiment deployed slightly to their rear. There was confused fighting for the next few hours with the Indian gunners; while the forward batteries were temporarily rendered 'out of action' due to the hand - to - hand combat, the depth battery of 216 Medium Regiment as well as 39 Medium Regiment engaged the enemy by 'direct shooting'. Due to intense firing by both sides, much of the ammunition lying around in the gun area burst, causing damage to five guns of 216 Medium Regiment. When the morning dawned it presented a gruesome sight- the area was littered with bodies of the dead and wounded of both sides. But most importantly, the Pakistani attack had been blunted.

The attack on the gun positions has been covered later in greater detail under 'Artillery Operations'. Major General Sandhu further writes :

This needless engagement with the medium regiments not only caused heavy casualties to 4 AK Brigade, but also distracted them from their main task of capturing the Kachreal Spur. Had the enemy bypassed the guns and headed straight for the spur, they may have got the better of 7 Kumaon who were still in the process of organizing themselves... part of 13 AK which made of to the Kachreal high ground encountered 7 Kumaon who had just reached the spur... After a brief encounter between them, the Kumaonis sent the enemy rolling down the hill. At 0830 hours, the eastern portion of the Chhamb Bridge was reported as having been captured by the Pakistanis: but a quick counter-action by 5/8 GR and a troop of 72 Armoured Regiment from the east, and an ad-hoc platoon of 5 Sikh with RHQ troop of 9 Horse from the west restored it back to the Indians by 1030 hours. This ad-hoc platoon of 5 Sikh consisted of the protection section, orderlies, runners and some signal platoon personnel.[18]

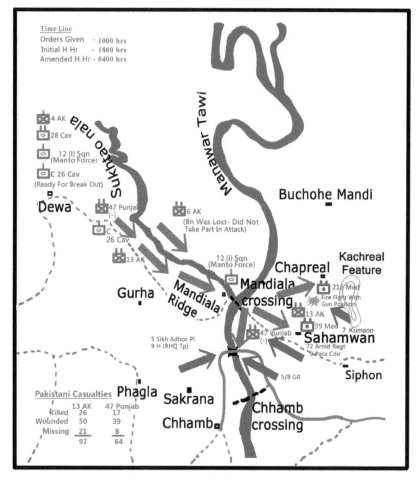

Map 15: 4 AK Brigade Attack along Sukh Tao Nala-0400
Hrs 05 Dec 1971

Note 1: Casualty figures taken from the book "Battle Of Chhamb 1971" by Lt Col Ahmad Saeed

Note 2: Map has been sourced from *BATTLEGROUND CHHAMB : The Indo-Pakistan War of 1971* by Major General A.J.S. Sandhu, p.146

The tanks of Manto Force ad-hoc squadron were not able to cross the Sukh Tao Nala, with many of them shot by the tanks of 9 Horse and the 'direct fire' of 130 Medium Guns. After this bitter encounter with the Indian troops at the Chapreal gun position, Kachreal Spur and the Chhamb Bridge, the 4 AK Brigade attack had completely run out of steam – the expected victory had turned into a defeat. The dejected and demoralised Pakistanis, having suffered heavy casualties, began their withdrawal and re-crossed the Manawar Tavi River. The total casualties suffered, according to GSO1 of 23 Infantry Division, Lieutenant Colonel Ahmad Saeed were:

	Killed	Wounded	POWs/Missing	
(a) 13 AK	26*	50	23**	*Including two officers
(b) 47 Punjab	17	39	08	**Including the CO and 2IC
Total	43	89	31	i.e 163 (a very high casualty figure)

Lieutenant Colonel Saeed has given a detailed account of this botched up operation in his book The Battle of Chhamb (1971). He has written that the Division Operation Room was informed by the Brigade Major of 4 AK brigade that the bridgehead had been successfully established and that the bridge was also in Pakistani hands. (This was false reporting since the fighting at the gun positions and Kachreal was still raging, and the bridge also fell [though only temporarily] much later -author). Saeed further writes that after getting this news the GOC Major General Iftikhar Janjua, along with the commanders of 2 (Independent) Armoured Brigade and 4 AK Brigade, and the GSO1 (Saeed) set out to see the bridge-head. On their way forward to their horror they came across the withdrawing troops and learnt that the attack had failed! The fact that 6 AK did not even go into battle got known much later.[19]

During the first two days of fighting the Pakistanis had not made any worthwhile gains - all the important defended localities continued to hold on. In order to thwart any further Pakistan attack to cross the river, GOC 10 Infantry Division placed 5/8 GR (less company) under command of 191 Infantry Brigade to boost its defence potential; one company continued to be deployed for the defence of Mandiala Bridge. 9 Jat was ordered to cover the Chhamb and Darh Crossings along the river. With the field batteries now in peril of being overrun by the advancing Pakistanis, all artillery deployed forward was ordered to move east of the river to their new gun areas. Later in the morning one more squadron of 72 Armoured Regiment was moved into the salient, thereby giving 191 Infantry Brigade a total of 4 (out of 6) squadrons (i.e. two-thirds of total tank strength of 10 Infantry Division).

Meanwhile, having failed in his attack in the north (with 4 AK Brigade), Major General Iftikhar Janjua decided to pull back his 2 Armoured Brigade to Jaimal Kot, suitably group it with infantry and then assault form the south (area of Bokan – Paur) towards Chak Pandit and reach the river line. The grouping 2 Armoured Brigade was :

(a) 28 Cavalry
(b) One Squadron 11 Cavalry
(c) One Squadron 26 Cavalry
(d) 4 Punjab
(e) 23 Baluch
(f) One Company 19 Baluch (R & S Bn)

This was a fairly strong task force.

On 6 December morning, while 66 and 111 Infantry Brigades continued their attacks on the forward defensive localities from the west, 2 Armoured Brigade Group swung in from the south. Though they not make initial headway, late in the afternoon by a stroke of luck, they ran into the 'dummy', minefield gap and broke through between Point 951 (5 Assam) and Jhanda (4/1GR) and captured Singri. With the situation inside the salient becoming tenuous, the GOC ordered the brigade commander to redeploy 5 Assam and 4/1 GR inwards in order to make his brigade defended sector more compact. 9 Horse and 72 Armoured Regiment were ordered to form a protective ring around the defences. However, due to break-down in communications, before this infantry re-deployment could be effected, and with the enemy having broken through to the river line in the south, 5 Assam and 4/1 GR had withdrawn to the east of the river. The commander informed the GOC of this development stating that both his flanks were now exposed. After consulting the corps commander, GOC 10 Infantry Division ordered 191 Infantry Brigade to withdraw to the east of the river to its original defence line of Kalit-Troti-Dhon Chak. Having made a clean break with the enemy, all troops, vehicles and essential stores had withdrawn across the river by 2330 hours, and the bridge was blown up by the Indian engineers at 2345 hours on 6 December.

191 Infantry Brigade had fought tenaciously against vastly superior enemy forces, and held them for three days. This stoic defence has been analyzed by Pakistani military historian, Major A.H. Amin (see Map 16). Major General A.J.S. Sandhu writes :

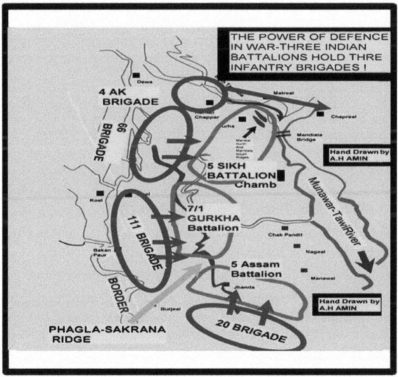

Map 16: Power of Defence - Map by Major A.H. Amin

Map has been sourced from the article Battle Of Chhamb 1971 by Major AH Amin appearing in the internet, http://sphinx-stray-reflections.blogspot.in/2012/06/war-trophies-of-11-cavalry-captured.html accessed on 16th Feb 2015
Amin has mixed the disposition- 5 Assam was in the centre while 4/1 GR (and not) 7/1GR) was in the south. Also, Pakistan employed four and noy three Bdes(20,66,111and 4 AK)

One can now imagine what would have happened if 10 Infantry Division had continued to adopt the original defence plan and only had a 'Covering Force' operating west of the river as the Army Commander (and indeed the Corps Commander) had wanted, the enemy would have perhaps crossed the Manawar Tawi on the first day itself! In the final analysis it was the 'Forward Poise' forcefully argued by the GOC 10 Infantry Division and permitted on 1 November, which had saved the day.[20]

OPERATIONS EAST OF MANAWAR TAWI RIVER
7-10 DECEMBER 1971

Since they did not maintain constant contact with the Indian troops, the Pakistanis remained blissfully unaware that 191 Infantry Brigade had withdrawn to the east of the river, and continued to progress their operations against 'ghost objectives' during the night of 6 December and morning of 7 December! Pakistani military historian Major General Shaukat Riza has written:

111 Infantry Brigade, whose objective was Chhamb had been held up west of Uparli Banian. Brigadier Sardar requested permission to capture Chhamb, the GOCs permission was received at 0400 hours 7 December.

He further describes the plan of attack thus :

(a) 28 Cavalry to attack two squadrons up, making a fire base with the third squadron. 23 Baluch to follow with two companies up.

(b) Out of the attacking squadrons, the right forward squadron to block crossing on Tawi River. The remainder force to advance on Chhamb.

(c) Two divisional artilleries (17 and 23 Divisions) to support the attack.

At 0530 hours 17 and 23 Division artilleries started their preparatory bombardment. At H hour, 28 Cavalry attacked on a broad front south through Khairowal towards Chhamb. 28 Cavalry was closely followed by 23 Baluch.[21]

Thus, a colossal amount of time and resources were unnecessarily wasted in continuing attacks against the vacated Indian positions elsewhere too. Had the Pakistani forces maintained contact with the Indians and followed in the wake of the withdrawing troops, there was a fair chance of effecting a breakthrough at least in one of the four crossing places. Instead, they delayed their plan by one day (just as in the 1965 War!)

The Pakistani plan of attack on night 7/8 December was :

(a) 2 Armoured Brigade (Left Flank): To attack east of Nageal and advance and capture Palanwala.

(b) 111 Infantry Brigade (Right Flank): To attack in the vicinity of Channi Diwanun/ Chhatti Tahli, and capture Lam and Khaur.

On the Indian side, the GOC 10 Infantry Division had already moved 52 and 68 Infantry Brigades forward to the river line. Armoured squadrons were deployed in their vicinity for counter- attack tasks.

As the H hour approached, 2 Armoured Brigade Commander Brigadier Sardar Ahmed, along with Lieutenant Colonel Dagar (CO of 28 Cavalry which was tasked with the break-out from the bridgehead) and Lieutenant Colonel Ehsan (CO of 28 Medium Regiment, the affiliated artillery unit) arrived at the Assembly Area near Nageal and waited for his units to arrive. It was a wait in vain, as both 4 Punjab and 23 Baluch did not turn up; apparently both had lost their way! Hence their attack was called off. On to their right flank, 42 Punjab (of 111 Infantry Brigade) had heard the Artillery Fire Plan being fired, and so assumed that the attack had been launched. Unaware of the cancellation of 2 Armoured Brigade attack, the battalion launched its assault across the Manawar Tawi River. Although they succeeded in capturing some forward posts, the Indians quickly launched counter-attacks and recaptured them. Meanwhile, the news of the aborted attack of 2 Armoured Brigade also reached them; 4 Punjab were thrown back after suffering 46 casualties (10 killed, 21 wounded including an officer, and 15 missing or taken POWs). A captured Artillery Fire Plan and marked map, revealed their plans to capture Palanwala. Thus it was that the second attempt to cross the Manawar Tawi River too failed, and once again due to lost infantry, as in the case of the 4 A K Brigade attack on 5 December 1971.

Clearly disappointed with this setback, Major General Janjua now gave orders to 111 Infantry Brigade to launch yet another attack on the night of 8/9 December. However due

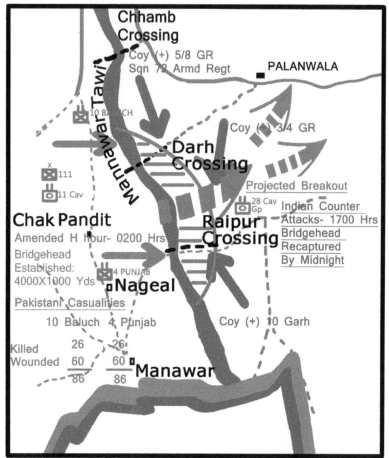

Map 17: 111 Infantry Brigade Attack and Indian Counter Attacks (10 Dec 1971)

Note 1: Casualty figures taken from the book "Battle Of Chhamb 1971" by Lt Col Ahmad Saeed

Note 2: Map has been sourced from *BATTLEGROUND CHHAMB : The Indo-Pakistan War of 1971* by Major General A.J.S Sandhu, p.176

to the change in command of the brigade just one day prior (Brigadier Abdullah Malik having replaced the wounded Brigadier Naseer Ullah Khan Babar) the new commander asked for a delay of 24 hours, which was granted. The attack was now planned for the night of 9/10 December 1971.

The overall plan of 111 Infantry Brigade was to attack with

two battalions in the junction of Darh and Raipur crossings, following which 28 Cavalry was to cross and secure the bridgehead. 11 Cavalry was held back to breakout towards the depth objectives once the bridgehead had been successfully established. In outline, the attack plan was as under (see Map 17) :-

(a) 10 Baluch to attack on the left in the Darh crossing area.

(b) 4 Punjab to attack on the right in the Raipur Crossing area.

(c) 28 Cavalry to follow immediately in the wake of these two battalions to protect the bridgehead

(d) On getting the success signal, 11 Cavalry was to pass through and advance towards Palanwala.

The now desperate GOC of 23 Infantry Division who had been obsessed with getting across the river from the first day, decided to be present in the 111 Infantry Brigade HQ to oversee this third attempt. However, destiny played otherwise. In the evening of 9 December, the helicopter taking him to the brigade headquarter, crashed just before landing. The badly injured and burnt general was immediately evacuated to Combined Military Hospital at Kharian, where he succumbed to his injures. There are varied theories on the cause of this crash, but the most plausible seems to be that while coming in to land (he had made three landings prior including one just a few hours earlier), the pilot swerved to dodge Indian firing in the area and his rotor hit a keekar tree and went down.[22] Brigadier Kamal Matin, recently appointed commander of 23 Artillery Brigade, now took over as the Officiating GOC of the division, and pressed on with the plan of attack. Enemy artillery opened up with a massive artillery bombardment of the forward Indian positions at 0200 hrs. An hour later, the infantry commenced their attack. After bitter fighting the enemy captured some positions. A company of 3/4 GR launched an immediate counter-attack on the lost post in 9 Jat area, but was unsuccessful, losing its valiant company commander in this action. The enemy now progressed the attack towards the depth positions. While this bloody combat was going on, GOC 10 Infantry Division ordered 52 and 68

Infantry Brigades to immediately adopt counter- penetration positions in order to prevent any further advance by the enemy. He also ordered 52 Infantry Brigade to launch a counter-attack with armour, to evict the enemy at Raipur Crossing. However the tanks got stuck in the boggy ground and the infantry too did not make much headway. They were now ordered to 'dig down', and block the enemy.

By mid-morning of 10 December the Pakistanis had managed to secure an area 4000 yards wide and 1,000 yards deep across the river. Its tanks had started moving into this bridgehead. The GOC 10 Infantry Division, Major General Jaswant Singh rang up the BGS at 15 Corps HQ, requesting him to send in additional armour from the neighbouring sector. Accordingly, the Corps HQ ordered the move of Central India Horse and one company of 7 Grenadiers (APCs). With hardly any air support (in spite of demands) the GOC asked the BGS to immediately allocate maximum air effort to the bridgehead site.

Unfortunately, due to the fog of war, there was a lot of false and exaggerated information being sent by the forward troops of 52 and 68 Infantry Brigade painting a very grim picture. Some reports sent to the Division Headquarter even suggested that tanks and infantry had in fact broken through towards the rear. As it later turned out, these reports were patently false, but they did impact the decision making at the higher level. Meanwhile, the Army Chief General Sam Manekshaw, ordered the Corps Commander Lieutenant General Sartaj Singh to go to the divisional sector; he arrived at the time when the bridgehead had been successfully contained but the enemy was poised for a break-out. He was briefed by the GOC and the Brigade Commanders. It was in his briefing at 52 Infantry Brigade HQ, that the brigade commander, Brigadier K. K. Hazari corrected his earlier report of enemy tanks heaving infiltrated towards the rear, by now stating that these was only a few tank-hunting parties!

With the battle having been fought non-stop for seven days, the options now were whether to withdraw to the original, well-prepared defence line in the Kalit-Troti-Dhon Chak area, or to make one more attempt at counter-attacking the enemy.

The uncertainty of information flowing from the front line made the choice even more difficult. Finally, after discussion between the Corps and Divisional Commanders, the Corps Commander advised the latter option.

Accordingly, 52 and 68 Infantry Brigades were ordered to launch counter-attacks on to the bridgehead from multiple directions:

(a) One company (plus a platoon) of 5/8 GR, supported by a squadron of 72 Armoured Regiment was ordered to attack Darh Crossing area from the north.

(b) Simultaneously, one company of 7 Garh Rif was to launch an attack on the Raipur Crossing area from the south.

(c) 3/4 GR was to mount an attack on the Raipur Crossing from the north-west, through a firm base held by 5/8 GR opposite Darh Crossing.[23]

The GOC, Major General Jaswant Singh, located himself at 68 Infantry Brigade Headquarter to monitor these counter attacks. The attacks were launched at 1700 hours, and by 0100 hours all positions had been re-taken. The Pakistanis too chose not to put up a fight and instead pulled back in the face of the Indian attacks from three directions; furthermore, no additional infantry had been pushed into the bridgehead and nor had their ammunition carrying 'F' echelon fetched up. 28 Cavalry too had suffered heavy tank losses and there were reports of Indian re-inforcemens coming into this area - all in all it painted a very grim picture to the Pakistani troops sandwiched in the bridgehead 'box'. Thus it was that the Indian counter attacks did not meet with much resistance. Both the Pakistani battalions (10 Baluch and 4 Punjab) suffered identical casualties of 26 killed and 60 wounded in each, i.e. a total of 172 - a very heavy price for this failed operation. Six enemy tanks were also captured. Enemy maps and documents found in the area gave details of their plans to capture Palanwala, Khaur and Lam.

11-17 DECEMBER 1971

By the morning of 11 December 1971 the Pakistani troops in the bridgehead east of the Manawar Tawi River had been successfully thrown back. Their third attempt too had failed. With the Indian defences having once again stabilized along the river line, GOC 10 Infantry Division started planning for a counter-offensive to recapture the lost positions inside the Chhamb salient. The Army Commander Lieutenant General K. P. Candeth visited the division on 11 December and was briefed by the GOC. On the GOC's request, CIH, 19 Madras as well as a company of 7 Grenadiers (Recce and Support) who had moved into the division sector in the wake of the 111 Infantry Brigade attack, were also made available to him. In addition, HQ of 3 (Independent) Armoured Brigade was also moved in situ. The GOC now issued a new Operational Order No 2, and commenced reconnaissance with his brigade commanders for the counter-offensive.[24]

During this period, while planning for the counter attack was going on, GOC ordered the brigades to concurrently conduct a series of raids on the enemy defences, to retain moral ascendency, as well as cause attraction .Such raids had the desired effect, and also kept the enemy engaged.

Even as the offensive plans were being readied, for some inexplicable reasons the Corps HQ ordered CIH (less one squadron) and 19 Madras to revert to the 26 Infantry Divisional Sector. This was a patently illogical move, since the 26 Infantry Division was relatively dormant, and these troops would have been more gainfully employed in the offensive tasks in 10 Infantry Division Sector. The GOC now had to re-cast his plans; however, the next day even the remaining troops (squadron and company of 7 Grenadiers) were moved out of the sector. This denudation of troops continued with one of the two medium regiments, i.e. 39 Medium Regiment being moved out to the 25 Infantry Division Sector to its north. The GOC now formulated a fresh plan for the counter-stroke across the Manawar Tawi River. However, just before the counter-attack was to be launched the Unilateral Ceasefire was declared which put paid to the GOC's plan. This cease fire came into effect at 2000 hours as 17 December 1971. On this last day of battle, 10 Infantry Division let loose a very heavy barrage of artillery fire on to the enemy positions. The Battle of Chhamb, so fiercely fought by both side had finally come to an end.

It needs to be reiterated that 10 Infantry Division had commenced the battle from an initially unbalanced position, as it was still in the process of re-adjusting its defences (due to last minute change in plans), when Pakistan attacked on the night of 3 December 1971. In spite of this handicap, the Division fought magnificently to thwart Pakistani designs to capture Akhnur, by holding them on the Manawar Tawi River.

Commending the gallant and determined fight put up by 10 Infantry Division, the Army Commander Lieutenant General K.P. Candeth wrote in a D.O. letter to the GOC:

> The main weight of Pakistani's pre-emptive attack on land came against your Division, and although you had to give ground, you inflicted such attrition on him that his advance ground to a halt without achieving a major success.[25]

A word about the Unilateral Ceasefire. On 16 December 1971, the Pakistani forces in East Pakistan had surrendered to Lieutenant General Jagjit Singh Aurora, GOC-in-C of the Indian and Bangladeshi Forces in the Eastern Theatre. Having achieved her political objective having been achieved, Mrs Indira Gandhi did not feel the necessity to continue the war in the west. She therefore announced her intention to declare a Unilateral Ceasefire in the Western Theatre. The wisdom and logic of this decision continues to be debated to this day. After all, although the Pakistanis had been inflicted a resounding defeat in East Pakistan, the military situation in the west was a mixed bag – both sides had made gains and losses. Even though India had captured a much greater area, the Pakistanis too had made some inroads into Indian territory, one of which was in the Chhamb Salient. With our resources in the East (army and air force) now available, India had a clear strategic edge to progress operations for a few days more in the west in order to recapture the lost territories. One does not know what, if any, advice was given by the three service chiefs to the Prime Minister in this regard, but Mrs Indira Gandhi baulked at taking this tough decision. Perhaps it was due to

International pressure. However, what is inexplicable is that even in the Shimla Agreement, the return of lost territories was not made a pre-condition, even though India held the trump card of holding over 92,000 Pakistani POWs. After all a precedent did exist, i.e. following the 1965 war, as part of the Tashkent agreement, India had to agree to return the strategically important Haji Pir Bulge to Pakistan. Thus Mrs Indira Gandhi could (and should) have insisted on the return of the Chhamb Salient, which she apparently did not.

ARTILLERY OPERATIONS

Pakistan Artillery Orbat And Deployment – Chhamb Sector

In keeping with the importance accorded to this offensive by the their GHQ, Pakistan amassed a huge artillery force to support 23 Infantry Division. As mentioned earlier, the artillery employed by Pakistan in the Chhamb Sector was more than they had to defend themselves in East Pakistan (now Bangladesh). Their artillery resources included 23 Artillery Brigade, 17 Artillery Brigade and other ad-hoc units created by equipping them with guns from their School of Artillery as well as Ordnance Depots (See Table 5.1). In an interview given to Major A. H. Amin of the Pakistan Defence Journal in 2001, Brigadier Naseer Ullah Khan Babar, the commander of 23 Artillery Brigade mentioned how he innovated in creating these additional assets:

> In addition some other innovations were also taken in hand. The locating battery had not been issued their equipment (radars and sound ranging) and to be used purposefully they were issued old vintage 105 mm howitzers and made history by fighting as a gun battery! Elements of Mujahidin had been provided, and to use them purposefully they were organized into a mortar battery and issued 120 mm mortars. To befool the Indians, two heavy guns from the School of Artillery, suitably deployed and directed to fire on Jaurian – indicating the presence of corps artillery.[26]

TABLE 5.1 PAKISTAN ARTILLERY ORBAT IN CHHAMB SECTOR

---

1. 11 Field Regiment Group
   (a) 11 Field Regiment (25 pounders)
   (b) 100 Medium Battery ex 28 Medium Regiment (155 mm howitzers)
   (c) 2x7.2 inch heavy guns
   (d) 285 Division Locating Battery (6x105 mm howitzers)*
2. 39 Field Regiment (25 Pounders)
3. 50 Field Regiment (122 mm Chinese howitzers)
4. 63 Field Regiment (122 mm Chinese howitzers)
5. 51 Composite Mountain Regiment
   (a) 8x105 mm Italian howitzers
   (b) 4x3.7 inch howitzers
6. 71 Mountain Regiment Group
   (a) 18 x 105 mm Italian howitzers
   (b) 81 AK Battery (8x25pounders)
7. 28 Medium Regiment less Battery (one battery attached with 11 Field Regiment Group) (155 mm howitzers)
8. 64 Medium Regiment (155 mm howitzer)
9. One Mujahid Battery (120 mm mortars)**
10. 16 x17 pounder guns were distributed all along the front and named by Mujahids.

Note. Sourced from Major General Shaukat Riza, 'Izzat-O-Iqbal' School of Artillery, Nowshera, pp. 386-87.
*Although in his book it is shown as 3.7 inch howitzers, in actual fact the battery was equipped with 105mm howitzers as mentioned by the Commander Artillery, Brigadier Naseer Ullah Khan Babar .
**This has also been confirmed by Brigadier N.U.K Babar, though erroneously missed out by Major General Shaukat Riza.

The above mentioned artillery of over 10 artillery regiments was indeed a very formidable force; it effectively translated to 31 fire units or 186 guns! This devastating fire power was concentrated over a very narrow front.

DEPLOYMENT

Keeping in mind the attack plan of 23 Infantry Division, Pakistan artillery was deployed to the west of the CFL and just south of IB. This somewhat 'L' shaped pattern of deployment allowed them to fire inwards, (i.e. west to east and south to north) thereby ensuring concentration of fire on the selected Indians defensive positions. Furthermore, in order to ensure maximum range of fire, Brigadier Naseer Ullah Khan Babar, deployed his artillery well forward, in fact even ahead of their minefield. In the aforementioned interview to Major Amin, Brigadier Babar says:...`I planned an extremely unconventional deployment of artillery unorthodoxly close to the front line, with field guns at 2,000 yards from the FDLs and medium guns at 4,000 yards, and ahead of our own minefield. This paid great dividends in terms of fire support.[27]

The reconnaissance of the gun areas had been carried out discreetly in the weeks before the war, as also the survey of the targets for the projected Artillery Fire Plan. The Pakistani artillery regiments moved into their deployment areas on the night of 2/3 December 1971. By the morning of 3 December approximately 186 Pakistani artillery guns/howitzers/ mortars were in position. The day was spent in preparing the ammunition and coordinating various aspects of the Artillery Fire Plan which was to be fired that night.

10 INFANTRY DIVISION ARTILLERY ORBAT
Initially, 10 Artillery Brigade consisted of the normal complement of artillery units i.e. three field, one medium and one light regiment. However after the division was tasked to launch an offensive into Pakistan, it was allocated another medium regiment which was equipped with 130 mm guns. In addition, it also had one Air Defence Battery of L-70 guns and one Air Defence Troop of L-60 guns (See Table 5.2).

TABLE 5.2:10 ARTILLERY BRIGADE ORBAT

1. 12 Field Regiment ⎫
2. 18 Field Regiment ⎬ (25 Pounder Guns)
3. 81 Field Regiment ⎭
4. 39 Medium Regiment (5.5 inch guns)
5. 216 Medium Regiment (130 mm guns)
6. 86 light Regiment (120mm Mortars)
7. 65 AD Battery ex 45 AD Regiment (L-70 guns)
8. `E' Troop ex 151 AD Regiment (L-60 guns)
9. 127 Divisional Locating Battery

---

10 Infantry Division artillery consisted of 18 Fire Units i.e. 108 guns - as compared to Pakistan's total quantity of 186 artillery pieces; thus Pakistan enjoyed a vastly superior ratio of 1.7:1. Notwithstanding this, the Indian artillery played a decisive role in blunting the Pakistani offensive in this sector.

DEPLOYMENT

The artillery of 10 Infantry Division (18 batteries or fire units) was deployed in five groups, i.e. three batteries (one field and two light) in the Hill Sector in support of 28 Infantry Brigade, five field batteries in the Chhamb – Sakrana area west of the Manawar Tawi, two batteries east of river at Nikkiar, six medium batteries east of the river in the Kachreal/Chaprecal area and two batteries (one each of field and light) in the Akhnur Sub Sector to cater for a possible threat from the Chicken's Neck area.

The deployment as on 3 December is given below and also depicted in Map 18:-

(a) 12 Field Regiment
    (i) Regiment less two batteries -Sakrana
    (ii) One battery   -Hill Sector
    (iii)One battery   -Akhnur Sub Sector
(b) 18 Field Regiment
    (i)Regiment less one battery   -Nikkiar
    (ii) One battery   -Sakrana
(c) 81 Field Regiment   -Sakrana
(d) 39 Medium Regiment   -Kachreal
(e) 216 Medium Regiment   -Chapreal

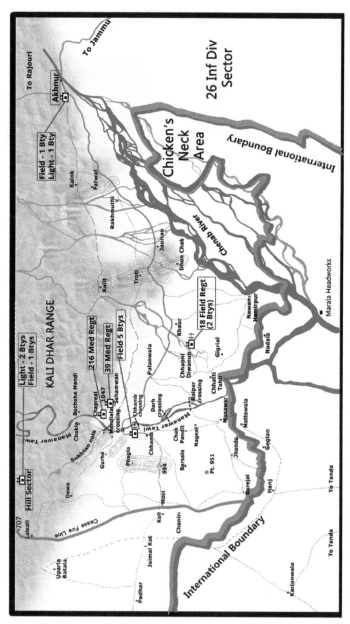

Map 18: 10 Infantry Division Artillery Brigade: Initial Deployment as on 3rd December 1971

(f) 86 Light Regiment
    (i)Regiment less one battery   -Hill Sector
    (ii)One battery   -Akhnur Sub Sector
(g) 65 AD Battery
    (i)Echo Troop   -Medium Gun Area near Kachreal/Chapreal
    (ii)Foxtrot Troop   -72 Armoured Regiment Harbour
(h) Echo Troop 151 AD Regiment   -Sakrana Gun Area
(j) 10 Artillery Brigade FDC   -Sakrana

The following points need emphasis:

(a) With three batteries in the Hill Sector and two in the Akhnur Sub Sector, only thirteen (seven field and six medium) were available to support the Plains Sector for the first three days; the two batteries at Akhnur were reverted only on 6 December after the 26 Infantry Division attack into Chicken's Neck went in the night prior. These two batteries had been deployed there at the orders of the Corps Headquarter to deal with the so-called threat, which appears to have been grossly exaggerated by 26 Infantry Division.

(b) 216 Medium Regiment had moved into their new gun position at Chapreal only the night before and were still in the process of preparations on 3 December.

(c) The FDC was ready to move to its new location east of the river, but the GOC revoked this during his chance visit on the evening of 3 December.

Regarding the aborted move of the FDC, Brigadier (then Major) AN Suryanarayanan, who was the Brigade Major of 10 Artillery Brigade has written in The Tribune dated 21 December, 2010:

It was 6.40 pm on Friday, December 3, 1971. Some of us were sitting outside our dugouts being filled in forward area and distributing jawans' pay, under low-wick-lanterns. Suddenly, the speeding General Officer's jeep screeched to a stop before my Fire Direction Centre (FDC); he bombarded me from within: "Surya, what are you people doing outside the dugouts? Why are your vehicles hooked up? Why are the dugouts being filled? Where is your Commander?"

I explained that the Commander had gone to witness a newly arrived regiment moving from Hide to Temporary Gun Position by night; we were closing up and moving my FDC to another position, approved by his HQ! He shouted at me: "Don't you know the PAF has attacked our Forward airfields? Ground attack is expected tonight. You better re-occupy this very position! I shall send your Commander here" and off he went.

The Commander came after an hour and saw us re-digging. He said sheepishly: "I should have listened to you and left the dugouts unfilled but camouflaged" (my suggestion that morning)! He had flown off the handle and called us "softies"! My reasoning, which I couldn't tell him, was: every Friday, there used to be Mirages on photo-recce over the Divisional sector, which did not happen that day, conveying some foreboding; secondly, Yahya had said in an interview the previous week that "Next Friday, I will be off fighting a war!"[28]

As mentioned earlier, although on the evening of 1 December, the Corps HQ had ordered 10 Infantry Division to adopt a defensive posture, the offensive task had NOT been called off; it had merely been put `on hold', with the caveat of 48 hours notice to launch! This term of reference not only resulted in a kind of 'duality of aim', but also affected the deployment and layout of formations and units, in particular that of the artillery; a careful balance had to be maintained between the defensive and offensive tasks, since the division was for all purposes still on 48-hour notice to launch its offensive.

THE BATTLE BEGINS

At 2050 hours IST more than 10 Pakistani artillery regiments, (i.e. 186 guns) opened fire with all their fury upon the Indian defensive positions. The firing of this Pakistani Fire Plan heralded the beginning of the Battle of Chhamb. The aim of this massive pre-H hour artillery bombardment was to pulverize and soften the Indian defences to facilitate the attacks by their infantry. Why this peculiar time of ten minutes to 9 o'clock' (2050 hours IST 2020 hours PST)? There is an interesting anecdote narrated by Major General Shaukat Riza in his book Izzat-o-Iqbal.:

Watches were synchronized at 2000 hours (PST-author) 3 December. At 2015 hours Major General Eftikhar and Brigadier Babar stood outside the artillery command post to watch the first salvo of preparatory bombardment break through the night. This was to be at 2030 hours. At about 2020 hours

(2050 hours IST – author) about 3000 yards on the left there was a flash followed, a few seconds later by the sharp crack of a high velocity gun. There was a second shot. It was too much to hold back the rest. The gun position officers released the tension in their lungs with full throated 'Fire'. Eftikhar and Babar checked their watches. The preparatory bombardment had gone off ten minutes ahead of schedule. Babar scowled and was about to jump into the command post when the general restrained him and said 'It is all right. Let the boys have fun.' The premature bombardment had been triggered by a zealous Mujahid...[29]

The Battle of Chhamb had begun ten minutes early. Within minutes the Indian artillery retaliated in full measure. Soon the sky over the battlefield was filled with flying projectiles from both sides. causing death and destruction on the troops on ground. The smell of cordite filled the nostrils.

PAKISTANI ARTILLERY OPERATIONS

Pakistan commenced its grand offensive Sword of Allah (the codename of this attack) with a very heavy pre-H hour bombardment of the Indian defences. Major General Jaswant Singh GOC of 10 Infantry Division, later recalled to veteran radio journalist Melville de Mellow that '... the attack started with a very heavy artillery bombardment at about 8.50 P.M at night, and in a matter of 70 minutes this artillery bombardment had gone through the entire depth of our forward positions.[30]

At that moment Captain (later Brigadier) Tariq Ali Khan, 2IC (Squadron, 11 Cavalry FF, was on the move with his tank column towards the CFL as his regiment was tasked to break-out from the bridgehead and advance towards Mandiala Crossing. He writes:

As the sun was setting it presented a breath-taking scene. The mountains loomed ahead as the rolling countiryside turned into foothills with flat plains receding behind us. We had been briefed about the number of guns which would open up before H hour to support our assault across the LOC. At the appointed hour our artillery opened up and I could see flashes of guns being fired all across the horizon from our side. Just at that moment, I looked up into the mountains and our forward post of Pir Batala started its machine gun fire on the Indian post across it. I saw the traces flying in the dim twilight. The war had begun.[31]

EMPLOYMENT OF ARTILLERY BY PAKISTAN

Pakistan used its overwhelming superiority in the artillery recourses in the Chhamb Sector to good effect. It employed the concept of 'massed artillery fire' very effectively. Its opening Fire Plan on 3 December (codenamed Broken Jaw according to captured Fire Task Table), was a taste of what to expect right through the battle. In stages, it covered the entire forward defence system of the Division, including forward companies, depth companies, gun positions and later the depth areas. The opening Pre-H hour bombardment was intense and sustained. Its effect is best narrated by the Indians who faced this devastating artillery fire.

In an interview with the author, Major General (then Major) P.K. Puri, who was commanding B Company, 5 Assam, at the forward defended position of Barsala, recalled:

I was ahead of my company locality supervising the laying of protective minefields, assisted by Second Lieutenant M. K. Ghatraj, when the Pakistanis opened up with their pre-H hour artillery fire. The fire was very heavy and intense, and my first thought was to quickly reach the safety of my bunker. I remember that I ran so fast that I could have beaten Milkha Singh (the Indian Olympic sprinter – author) that day. Unfortunately, Second Lieutenant Ghatraj was wounded when a splinter went through his neck - he was perhaps 10 Infantry Division's first officer casualty of the war![32]

Brigadier (then Captain) A. P. Deo, who was the Adjutant of 18 Field Regiment during this battle, recounted:

On 3 December 1971, while listening to the 7 P.M news on All India Radio we came to know of PAF'spre-emptive air strikes an some of western air bases. The war was now on. We were listening to a later news bulletin and suddenly around 2050 hours hell broke loose. The earth started shaking as if an earthquake was happening - we had never heard such explosive sounds. It was probably the heavy or medium guns of Pakistan artillery. The ear-deafening sounds of shells exploding around us was fearsome. It was like a big bang first, followed by spreading of a tremendous sound-wave, followed by a blast-wave. We all dived into our bunkers.[33]

In other accounts to the author, Major General (then Major) J. R. K. Bhattacharjee, Battery Commander (BC) 39 Medium recounted: ...'On night of 3 December, after dinner I retired to my rest area to take off my boots and have a wash. I was mid way when suddenly the environment was full of loud booming sound and the western horizon was lit with bright pink and yellow light; and we could hear loud whistling noises of projectiles rushing through the wind'[34]. Major General (then Captain) S.V. Thapliyal of 86 Light Regiment, who was an Observation Post officer with B Company 5 Sikh at Point 994, recalled : ...'There was lack of intelligence about the enemy. No one knew that Pakistan had amassed a large force under 23 Infantry Division, including a large quantum of artillery from neighbouring sectors/formations; as a result that when the artillery commenced its Pre-H hour bombardment on the night of 3 December, the quantum and ferocity of artillery fire completely unnerved us (italics by the author)[35].

In all its initial attacks on the defended localities in the 191 Infantry Brigade area in the Chhamb Salient, Pakistan made optimum use of its artillery. Artillery FOOs (Forward Observation Officers) and BCs were grouped with all attacking infantry battalions, as well as armoured regiments. It was able to do so because there was no dearth of artillery resources! Prior to the battalion attacks, the Indian defensive localities were subjected to a concentrated dose of artillery fire and when the attack actually went on, the FOOs were able to control and progress the artillery fire to keep pace with the advancing infantry. In his book 'Izzat-O-Iqbal' Major General Shaukat Riza has narrated numerous examples of how FOOs and BCs provided such support; one such example of Captain Qamar-uz-Zaman (71 Medium Regiment) who went on as FOO in two successive (but failed) attacks in given below;

3 / 4 December. (This was a two-company attack on Piquet 707, called Mandhar by the Pakistanis, launched just after midnight: one company of Zhob Militia was on the left, and one company of 2 A K battalion on the right). Riza writes:

In the north a company from 2 A. K. Battalion and a company of Zhob Militia were ordered to capture Mandhar post 2000 yards north-east of Laleali. Captain Qamar-ur-Zaman (71Medium Regiment) accompanied as forward observer. At 0200 hours 4 December the company of Zhub Militia approached within 200 yards of enemy bunkers. Suddenly the angry buzz of machine gun fire bullets filled the air. The company oommander of Zhob Militia crawled to within a few yards of one bunker and lobbed a grenade.

As soon as he got up, a second machine gun shattered his chest. The Indians set up for a quick counter- attack. Qamar stopped the enemy with battery concentrations. By this time, the Zhob were themselves subjected to air burst. By first light they were back in their original position. The company of 2 AK Battalion reached the top and held off Indian attacks (until forced to fall back- author). The two companies lost 27 killed and 33 wounded in this short and sharp action.[36]

6/7 December (One company of 2 AK Battalion made a determined bid to capture the Laleali post; once again the FOO was Captain Qamar-uz-Zaman. This attack too was repulsed by the Indians with heavy casualties to the Pakistanis). Maj Gen Shaukat Riza further writes.:

At 0300 hours 7 December the second company of 2 AK battalion was ordered to capture Laleali Hill. This company was commanded by Major Mohammad Faruq. Captain Qamar-uz-Zaman accompanied as forward observer. The company was guided to the forming up place with artillery concentrations indicating the objective. In the forming up place they were greeted by hostile shells (italics by the author). Faruq and Qamar led the assault. About 100 Yards short of the objective Faruq was killed. The company lost 24 killed and 29 wounded. Faruq was awarded Sitara-i-Jurat and Qamar got *Tamga-i-Jurat.*[37]

A more detailed version of these attacks and how they were successfully beaten back by 8 J & K Militia, supported by 86 Light Regiment, appears in the book Battleground Chhamb : The Indo Pakistan War of 1971 by Major General AJS Sandhu.

Pakistan made many determined attempts to cross the Manawar Tawi River in order to progress operation eastwards, towards Palanwala and Akhnur; they succeeded on three occasions, only to be beaten back, i.e. on night of 4/5 December, 7/8 December and 9/10 December. All these have been covered earlier in this chapter. The common thread in each of them was the optimum use of artillery in support of the infantry. In each case thirty to forty five minutes prior to the assault there was a heavy barrage of all available artillery brought down on the selected objectives; the aim was to soften up the defences sufficiently in order to facilitate the attacks of the infantry which followed in the wake of the barrage. All Indian accounts mention heavy enemy artillery fire prior to the Pakistani attacks.

The Pakistani FOOs and OP officers were always on the lookout for 'opportunity' targets. Two examples stand out. One was the artillery shelling of the 7 Kumaon 'R and O' Group during its move forward for a counter attack. While it was on the move, it came under very heavy artillery fire in which its CO, four other officers and some personnel were injured resulting in temporary loss of command and control. The second example is of 6 December, and narrated to the author by Brigadier (then Captain) Ashok Kunzru , of 72 Armoured Regiment:

Brigadier Morlin (Commander 68 Infantry Brigade), my CO Lieutenant Colonel I.J. Chopra and Major Amarjit were discussing counter-attack plans on a map near the tank of Captain Safaya. I was standing a few yards away. As soon as the enemy artillery shelling started, Brigadier Morlin and Lieutenant Colonel Chopra jumped into a nearby trench, Major Amarjit ran towards the squadron 2IC's tank while I dived behind my jeep. Captain Safaya who was standing inside his cupola was hit by a splinter and slumped inside his tank. Major Amarjit got some shrapnel as he was climbing the tank and he fell on to the ground. As the shelling stopped, I along with my operator ran and picked him up. He was critically injured and died in my arms before he could be evacuated to the Advance Dressing station. Captain Safaya too had succumbed to his injuries. They were replaced by Major A.S. Sandhu and Captain Surinder Khanna.[38]

Although Pakistan used their artillery resources with great effect, military historian Major General Shaukat Riza, is critical of their dispersal of resourses. In his book Izzat-o-Iqbal he writes:

The deployment of artillery fire power available to 23 Infantry Division was in contravention of the principle of concentration. The division was supported by eight regiments (actually it was 10 regiments plus one battery as he himself has tabulated in the same book - author). This fire power was distributed to support simultaneous attacks by four brigades. The distribution of artillery support militated against the suppression of hostile weapons to a level of acceptable opposition. West of the Tawi the Indians had border security forces backed by covering troops from regular forces. Their purpose was to delay and define Pakistani attack; by distributing our artillery power over 30,000 yards the Indians were enabled to attain their aim.[39]

10 Artillery Brigade Operations
Indian Artillery Retaliates

Although vastly outnumbered `gun-to-gun' by the Pakistanis, the Indian gunners rose to the occasion and performed extremely well during this battle. When Pakistan launched its preparatory artillery bombardment at 2050 hours IST on 3 December, the Indian retaliation was swift. Within minutes, the Indian artillery had opened fire. Major (later Brigadier) A.N. Suryanarayanan of 10 Artillery Brigade was busy re-establishing the FDC, when the Pakistani artillery commenced its pre-H hour fire. In an article in The Tribune he recalled:

We had not even finished re-digging when intense enemy shelling started over my FDC and the gun positions at 8.48 pm (actually it was 850 p.m. – author)! I ordered breaking of wireless silence; and immediately, frantic calls for fire from 108 Field-guns under my control as Brigade Major , came from 26 Observation Post officers all over the front!

I occupied the half-re-done FDC; and our return fire commenced. Within the first hour my living bunker and jeep got direct hits and were written off; I lost my personal effects and had no jeep for the remainder of the war! Non-stop action went on for the next five days nights, when we couldn't get a wink of sleep! The GOC directed the operations mostly from my FDC till December 6, due to excellent communications.[40]

The then Adjutant of 18 Field regiment, Brigadier AP Deo, recalled to the author:

The raging Pakistani artillery fire was still on when the radio set blurted '1 for 1 and all stations Sierra (The Regimental Signals Net Call sign was based on the first initial of the COs name : S N Verma). War is on, fire as per orders' Just as this message was over came a call '45 for 45 Uniform 2040, fire'. This was Captain Y.R. Tyagi our OP at Pir Jamal forward post. Within the next 10 seconds 18 Field Regiment guns started booming for the first time against a real enemy. (All DFs. [Defensive fire] were to be fired upon by all available guns at Three Rounds Gun Fire. This could be repeated thrice).

At the same time we heard Captain Ravinder Kaura (of 39 Medium Regiment) who was located at the Moel BOP, asking for fire on target in 2047. We immediately shifted from 2040 to 2047.[41]

Captain (later Colonel) Prakash Pande was the Adjutant of 39 Medium Regiment at Kachreal. In his account to the author he wrote:

The war started on 3 December 1971. The enemy commenced heavy artillery shelling on all our forward defences at about 2050 hours. The entire border was lit with orange and crimson colour, visible from our gun position, accompanied by the booming sound of bursting shells. This propelled 'Team 39' into immediate action. Everyone was at their designated posts in the gun position, ready for action . Immediately our OP officers at Moel (5 Sikh), Bhusa (4/1GR) and Laleali (8 J and K Militia) called for fire on DFs in front of them. Other OP officers too started calling for artillery fire on DFs in front of their defended positions. Immediately, fire orders were passed to the guns and within a minute the regiment fired the first salvo at the designated targets with a full throated Jaikara: Bole So Nihal Sat Sri Akal. The firing continued throughout the night and thereafter.[42]

108 Indian guns of assorted calibres (25 Pounders, 130 mm medium guns, 5.5 inch medium guns and 120 mm mortars) were soon, spewing their deadly artillery projectiles upon the Pakistanis. (Coupled with the 186 Pakistani guns, this was indeed a very concentrated dose of artillery fire over the battlefield area)

Over the next two weeks, the guns of 10 Artillery Brigade remained busy in support of the infantry and armour. There was never a dull moment nor any respite. The gunners indeed lived up to the old adage – 'The guns must never remain idle'. Whether it was breaking up enemy attacks by bringing down Defensive Fire (DF), attacking hostile battery locations, supporting own counter-attacks to regain lost positions or simply resorting to Harassing Fire (HF), the gunners were everywhere, true to their motto *Sarvatra :Izzat-O-Iqbal* Everywhere with Honour and Glory. Since Pakistan had launched their initial attacks all across the divisional front, there were simultaneous demands placed upon the gun positions, to bring down artillery fire. The Brigade Major, Adjutants of the regiments as well as Gun Position Officers were often put under tremendous pressure, but never once did they falter.

It is not possible to go into detail about the Indian artillery operations. However, the few actions narrated below, give a sense of how the artillery supported the 10 Infantry Division operations. Incidentally, since the Field Cashier had not been able to get cash on either 1 or 2 December, all the artillery units and the brigade HQ were engaged in the Pay Parade on that fateful day of 3 December; and when the attack actually started later in the evening some units still had not finished distributing pay to their personnel. Brigadier (then 2nd Lieutenant) J. Dhasmana a GPO of 39 Medium Regiment recalled:

3 December was the 'pay day' and the cash arrived by late afternoon. Later we learnt from the All India Radio that Pakistani Air Force had attacked several Indian Air Bases including Pathankot Air Base. Around 7 p.m., after men had their dinner, I along with couple of JCOs and NCOs sat down in a small tent erected for pay distribution. Since all stations had to be manned, men came one by one from various detachments to collect their pay and sign the documents. By 8.50 pm we were half way through the payment when we suddenly started hearing continuous booming sounds from a distance. I was quite puzzled and did not know how to react because it was the first time in my life I had heard the rolling thunder of an artillery barrage being fired in my direction. The JCOs and the NCOs in the tent were veterans and had fought in the 1965 war in the same area. The Senior JCO, Subedar Mohinder Singh said *"Saab ladai lag pai"*. I then realized that the war had started!! When I came out of the tent the entire horizon as far as could be seen had turned a strange mixture of red, orange and bright yellow. I quickly collected all the cash, pushed it in the deep pockets of my great coat, told the TA Havildar Gurbax Singh to keep the cash payment papers safely and ran to the Command Post. By now the louder sound of Pakistani shells bursting over our forward positions could also be heard. Having dealt with our forward positions, it was a question of time before enemy Counter Bombardment (CB) started targeting us. I later learnt from some Pakistani accounts that their actual 'H' hour was later than 8.50 pm but some zealous Razakar due to excitement or confusion prematurely pulled the firing lever and everyone else had followed. The cash was to remain in my coat pockets for the next fourteen days.[43]

Grouping of OPs and BCs

All the infantry and armoured units had been provided OPs and BCs from their affiliated artillery regiments. They had in fact even trained alongside their infantry brigades as well as with 3 (Independent) Armoured Brigade, for the offensive task which had now been put 'on hold' on 1 December. After being asked to adopt a defensive posture, 191 Infantry Brigade had been provided additional OPs / BCs over and above their normal affiliation. Brigadier A. N. Suryanarayanan, wrote in an article published in the 'Fauji India' magazine that

(a) 24 OPs were provided to the Plains Sector of which 12

(including 9 Field and 3 Medium) OPs were for 191 Infantry Brigade.

(b) Although many infantry post commanders were JCOs, ALL our OPs were OFFICERS (We lost 3 within the first 36 hours).[44]

These OP officers and BCs did a splendid job in bringing down concentrated artillery fire in the form of DF Tasks, to disorganize and break-up the Pakistani attacks. Some examples are given below.

ATTACK ON MOEL

This was a forward post on the CFL, which covered the road Koel-Moel-Pt 994-Chhamb. It was held by a platoon of 5 Sikh, with Captain Ravinder Kaura of 39 Medium Regiment, as the OP officer. Moel was attacked in the first rush itself on 3 December and all through the day of 4 December. The resolute Sikhs held out stubbornly supported by the continuous fire support provided by the OP officer. Lieutenant Colonel Ahmad Saeed, then GSO-1 Operations) of 23 Infantry Division, noted that 'A well entrenched enemy company (actually a platoon – author) held their advance ... When the day broke, 111 Infantry Brigade still stood much short of their objective with leading two battalions separated by Moel post'.[45] This post finally fell in the evening of 4 December.

Captain Ravinder Kaura displayed cool courage and exemplary leadership, and continued to bring down very effective artillery fire on the attacking enemy. In his book *Indian Gunners at War*, Major General Jagjit Singh writes:

Captain R. Kaura of 39 Medium Regiment, the OP officer at Moel, distinguished himself by his courage, leadership and accurate shooting, which helped break up successive Pakistani assaults. On the morning of 3 December, this officer was to be relieved, as a matter of routine. Kaura requested permission to stay on, since he was well acquainted with the ground and as such could deal with the enemy better in the event of an attack. In the final Pakistani assault, Kaura kept inspiring and encouraging the men at Moel to hold on to their position. He repeatedly exposed himself to danger, undeterred by heavy shelling, while bringing down accurate artillery fire, till he was killed by an enemy shell. This brave officer was awarded the Vir Chakra (Posthumous) for his gallantry, determination and leadership of a very high order, fighting an unequal artillery battle against the overwhelming gun superiority of Pakistan.[46]

There are other reports which suggest that there was an additional artillery officer present, by virtue of which greater concentration of artillery fire was achieved at Moel. Major General A. J. S. Sandhu has written : ...'In an interesting development there were two artillery OP officers at this post and hence were able to bring down very heavy artillery fire on enemy forces. Captain A. S. Malik of 39 Medium Regiment had been sent on 3 December to relieve Captain Ravinder Kaura but the latter decided to stay on and asked Malik to return to the regiment the following morning. However, the war started on the night of 3 December with Malik still at Moel... Captain Malik was listed as missing...'[47]

ATTACK ON BUREJAL

Another heroic and brave act in the face of an overwhelming enemy attack was that of Captain D. S. Jamwal of 81 Field Regiment, who was the OP Officer at Burejal. This post, located in the south at the tip of the CFL, was held by one platoon of 5 Assam, commanded by Captain G. R. Singh. They were attacked by 14 Punjab on 4 December; this attack was preceded by very heavy artillery bombardment in order to soften the defences. While the heavily outnumbered Assamese fought very bravely, Captain D. S. Jamwal continued bringing down artillery fire on the advancing enemy till the post was overrun. He died when he was shot by a Pakistani in his bunker while still directing fire. Brigadier Vijay Chopra (81 Field Regiment) met a Pakistani officer of 14 Punjab, at a flag meeting after the ceasefire, who narrated to him the account of their attack:

My company was tasked to attack Burejal on 4 December. On the onset of the attack we were affectively engaged by accurate artillery fire. We kept the momentum of attack and were in the process of running over the Burejal BOP defences when I encountered an officer who was in the process of passing orders for artillery defensive fire on as close as his own position (DF RED RED RED). He was poised to shoot at me with his sten gun, when one of my Havildars noticed him asked me to duck and immediately fired a burst from his own sten gun, resulting in the Indian officer's death. Captain

Jamwal was a fearless and daring officer, who laid down his life fighting to the last. I salute him for his commitment to his task and daredevil spirit. Later, we laid him to rest near the post itself.[48]

To authenticate this episode, the Pakistani officer mentioned to Brigadier Chopra, the name of the book from the regimental library lying in his bunker, besides other nick-knacks belonging to him.

Shooting of a Pakistani Helicopter

This incident was recounted to the author by Colonel (then Captain) R. I. Singh (39 Medium Regiment), who was OP officer at Red Hill Post in the Hill Sector (28 Infantry Brigade), as part of 8 J and K Militia:

Around 7 or 8 December (I do not remember the exact date), I observed a helicopter flying from the enemy's side and going towards Laleali/Picket 707 from our rear. I was certain it was a reconnaissance flight with some senior officer on board. I quickly moved to the MMG Post and asked the NCO to bring out the MMG from the bunker and fire on the helicopter on its return. He was not sure if he could hit the helicopter. Not wanting to miss an opportunity, if it arose, I once again familiarized myself with the firing of the MMG from the NCO. Sure enough, after a few minutes, I saw the helicopter returning and after taking sufficient 'lead', I fired a few bursts from the MMG. I think the helicopter was hit as it was seen going into quick descent, and force-landing at nearby Pir Jamal post.[49]

Harassing Fire By Anchor OPs

The Anchor OPs located on the heights of Red Hill, Buchohe Mandi and Kachreal had a very good observation of the Chhamb Salient, and any movement of enemy after 6 December, was an obvious target. Colonel (then Captain) R. I. Singh who was located at Red Hill told the author : 'During day time I brought down effective fire on tanks, vehicles and troops as and when they were seen in the plains. This not only caused casualties on them, but also imposed caution on their day-time movement'[50]. Another Anchor OP, Major General (then Captain) Virpal Singh of 81 Field Regiment recounted to the author:

After 6 December I was located at Buchohe Mandi as OP with 7 Kumaon. From its commanding heights. I had excellent observation of the Chhamb salient which had by then been captured by the Pakistanis. I was thus able to bring down very effective fire on the Pakistani troop movement as well as defensive positions. I used 'airburst' ammunition with good effect. The results were visible - I could see their vehicles scramble in different directions to escape this artillery fire. After the Cease Fire at a Flag Meeting, I was satisfied to hear from the Pakistani contingent leader that the harassing fire brought down by the OP at Buchohe Mandi played havoc with them.

Seeing the nuisance being caused by me, the Pakistanis tried many times to neutralize my OP position by frequent 'precision shoots', but luckily due to the layout of the terrain, their rounds fell either 'over' or 'short' into the dead ground. In any case I would change my position by a few yards every day and move away from the prominent concrete bunker, which they thought was the OP locations.[51]

That the Indian artillery shelling was very affective is borne out by the Pakistani accounts as well. Major (then Lieutenant) Mahin Malik and Brigadier (then Captain) Tariq Ali Khan, who were Troop Leader and Squadron 2IC respectively in 11 Cavalry, have written about the effectiveness of the Indian artillery in their war reminiscences. Major (then Lieutenant) Malik writes that after the day's battle on 6 December, 11 Cavalry had leaguered just behind Kamali Chappar village (leaguer was an area where the tanks 'harboured' for the night - author). He notes that: 'Here was a potpourri of tanks, infantry, artillery, engineers, langars and all. The leaguer was formed behind 4 AK Brigade Headquarter that was perhaps 600 - 800 yards towards the Mandiala ridges'. He then writes:

Suddenly all hell was let loose. The Indian observation posts (OPs) had figured out this mass of tanks, vehicles and men in an area about 1,000 square yards. I cannot figure out who the hell chose this location as our leaguer. The artillery barrages that commenced were fierce and unrelenting. I could see many dead and wounded all around. This went on for about 45 minutes when there was a lull. Somebody from 4 AK brigade shouted that the brigade headquarter had been run over and the enemy tanks had launched a counter-attack. We knew that the Indian T-55s had night vision. In a leaguer tanks are sitting ducks at night, also with intense flares going on above us. So an order to evacuate the leaguer was given. Now this break-out almost became a hasty retreat till Major Awan got hold of the situation and ordered us (B Squadron) to turn around and go back to our prior day positions that were beyond Gurha and short of the Mandiala defile. That's what we did. There had been no counter-attack.[52]

In his account Brigadier Tariq Ali Khan recounts how a severe Indian artillery bombardment caused great damage to the regimental 'O' Group in the morning of 7 December:

We were asked to assemble in village Gurha in the morning for some briefing and orders. I remember that morning clearly. It was a sunny day. We parked the jeeps, both mine of C Squadron 2IC and Major Awan's, behind a cactus hedge close to the track. A tank was also located close by. I remember Risaldar Mian Muhammad had also stayed back in the morning after the echelons had left. He wanted to be with the squadron, and particularly with Major Awan now being the Squadron Commander, to boost the morale of the squadron of which he was the Senior JCO. He was doing it out of his own commitment to the squadron, otherwise his position should have been in the rear areas looking after the administration of langar, getting food prepared and dispatching the remains of shaheeds to their homes, etc. He was, however, a soldier to the core. He therefore was with the troops and standing beside Major Awan's Rover chatting with the driver and operator.

An intense artillery barrage suddenly hit the site of this gathering. I remember walking a few steps till I saw a trench in which stood two infantry men. I jumped inside and stayed in it while shells rained all around us. This was the heaviest shelling that I experienced throughout the war. It seemed that the Indians had opened up all guns in range for an intense shoot for at least 15 minutes. After the shelling ceased we witnessed the death and destruction it had wrecked. Both the jeeps had direct hits and were completely destroyed. B Squadron commander's driver and operator were killed. Risaldar Mian Muhammad was also killed, his body charred. My jeep driver, a reservist named Sarfraz, who was a good soldier, was pulled out by Major Khadim with his lower torso on fire. We tried to put out the fire as quickly as we could. I thought he may survive but very calmly he began to recite the kalima and closed his eyes. That spectacle of calm acceptance of death by a truly devout soldier will remain forever etched in my mind. Major Khadim was there as usual keeping his nerve and thinking clearly. He saw that the tank standing next to the jeep had also begun to catch fire. He ordered someone to immediately remove the camouflage net and extinguish the fire. This prompt action saved the tank.

It was a very dark hour for us. The FOO of B squadron Captain Bashar, my course mate and a Bengali, who had throughout shown a lot of courage, was also wounded in the shelling. He was attended to by Lieutenant Mahin, bandaged with 'shell dressing', given morphine and evacuated. He was given an award for his bravery.[53]

Major Mahin Malik too was present at this 'O' Group and has written an equally lucid account of the devastation caused by the accurate Indian artillery fire, brought down by an Anchor OP situated on one of the commanding heights. He ends his account by making a telling statement: The 'Order Group' was disbanded - rather demolished - by the Indian Artillery. There were many casualties.[54]

UNCONVENTIONAL PROCEDURES

As usually happens in war, artillery fire discipline and procedures are thrown to the wind and unorthodox methods of fire are adopted. Colonel (then Captain) R. I. Singh told the author; 'At times guns had to resort to unconventional methods to fire on to targets. Guns even engaged targets when they were going outside the maximum range. We also resorted to engagement of multiple targets by the same sub-unit by engaging a target by one or two guns, while the remainder guns of the battery engaged other target(s). An example of a 5.5 inch gun firing beyond the maximum range was narrated to the author by Brigadier (then 2/Lt.) J. Dhasmana:

One evening Captain (later Colonel) R. I. Singh called me on the telephone line, gave his own location and the necessary target data for engagement of a Pakistani attack which was building up. The target was close to the maximum range of the gun, hence it warranted 'Charge Super'. The first ranging round was fired and an 'Add' correction was received. On passing the correction to the gun, the gun Number 1 reported 'Elevation Expended', implying that the gun could not be elevated any further, hence the correction could not be applied. Now there was a real dilemma in my mind. Technically as well as by training there was nothing I could do. However, during discussions in the Mess and with men I had heard that similar situations had occurred during the 1965 war, but the fire support was provided by adding an additional Charge One bag with the Charge Super bag in the gun chamber!! The requirement for fire was becoming urgent by the minute. Since there is no accepted terminology to pass such unconventional orders, the No 1 was explained the situation and told to order 'Stand Clear', and fire the gun from a safe distance using a lanyard. A 'Drop' correction was received and fire was successfully adjusted on the enemy. Thereafter, only the ranging gun was used for greater punishment on the target.[55]

DIRECT SHOOTING

There were many occasions when the guns were employed in the 'direct firing' role, firing at the enemy targets over 'open sights' with great effect. Three examples are given below:-

(A) BUNKER BURSTING AND DAMAGE TO THE MATTEWALA TOWER.

Before the war GOC 10 infantry Division had directed his Artillery Brigade Commander to be prepared to employ the medium guns in the direct-firing role against enemy bunkers and strong points closed to the IB/CFL. Accordingly Brigadier K. Srinivasan had tasked 39 Medium Regiment to recce possible targets close to the CFL/IB, which could be engaged by their medium guns in direct firing role. The CO of the regiment, Lieutenant Colonel B. C. Gaurishankar had nominated one gun per battery for this task; these guns had been 'zeroed' at the required range by live firing at the Dewa Field Firing Ranges. In his book *God of War: History of the Regiment of Artillery*, Major General Anjan Mukherjee writes that 'At about 0300hrs on 6th December (it was actually 4 December – author), the Divisional Commander Major General Jaswant Singh ordered one 5.5 inch medium gun to move forward across the Manawar Tawi river to destroy enemy bunkers at Mattewala.' On 4 December, the CO personally took one gun (A-1 gun of 122 Medium Battery) to the previously reconnoitered area opposite the Mattewala Tower. The gun was deployed within the forward defended locality next to Manawar Post, which was then under attack. The gun destroyed / damaged six enemy bunkers and hit the pylon of the Mattewala Observation Tower causing it to tilt to one side, and rendered it unusable. Havildar Piara Singh was Mentioned-in-Dispatches for this action.[56]

(B) ENGAGEMENT OF ENEMY TANKS BY 216 MEDIUM REGIMENT.

During the attack by 4 AK Brigade across the Sukh Tao Nala on 5 December morning, the Pakistanis had attempted to push through tanks of 12 (Independent) Armoured Squadron for the protection of the bridgehead. These were spotted and engaged by the guns of 216 Medium Regiment as well as the tanks of 9 Deccan Horse. In his book, Battle of Chhamb (1971), Brigadier

Ahmad Saeed has written:

When they reached near the foot track from Matreal to Khani, a battery
of 130 mm deployed north of Chapreal just on the opposite bank of Tawi
opened up a barrage of direct fire. The medium guns were deadly against
the tanks. Three out of six tanks were hit and immediately caught fire.
Fourth received a hit tilting it on acute angle but without doing any serious
damage... The companies of 47 Punjab crossing the river in broad daylight
were caught in a cross-fire of the enemy tank squadron which was now in
position behind an embankment and these guns. Many fell dead in this
unexpected but accurate fire.[57]

This little known action was perhaps the only example of
Indian artillery guns successfully engaging enemy armour
by ʻdirect fireʼ during the 1971 War, i.e. 130 mm guns of
216 Medium Regiment. Quite surprisingly this anti-tank
engagement has not got the publicity it deserves.

(C) ENEMY INFANTRY ATTACK ON THE MEDIUM GUN
POSITIONS.
4 AK Brigade attack launched across the Sukh Tao Nala in the
early morning of 5 December has already been covered earlier
in this chapter; here only the attack on the medium gun areas
is discussed. This was the only battle incident during the 1971
Indo-Pakistan war, when artillery gun positions were subjected
to an infantry battalion attack. 216 Medium Regiment bore the
brunt of this unexpected but deadly onslaught. The surprised
gunners put up a brave fight against a much stronger force.
Some of the attacking infantry made its way to the Wagon
Lines of 39 Medium Regiment and were successfully engaged
by their gunners. During this brief but intense engagement
between 4 AK Brigade and the Indian Medium Gun Positions,
while the two forward batteries of 216 Medium Regiment
were involved in hand-to-hand combat, its depth battery
brought down effective gun fire by direct shooting. 39 Medium
Regiment also came to the aid of this regiment; while two of its
batteries continued to provide fire support to the forward OPs,
one battery opened fire on this enemy attack over open sights.
The attack on 216 Medium Regiment has been a subject of
debate and discussion ever since the war; unfortunately much

of it is uninformed and based on mis-perception, half-truths and even disinformation. This author has put it in perspective in his book Battleground Chhamb, an extract of which are given below:

The attack on the gun position needs some elaboration as it has been a subject of much discussion and differing perceptions, and regrettably some distortion. The records of 10 Artillery Brigade and 216 Medium Regiment show that at about 0430 hours, forward patrols had reported suspicious movement of personnel in khaki clothes. Since the Indian BSF troops (who also wore khaki uniform) had been ordered to fall back to depth positions, this information was referred to Commander 191 Infantry Brigade for confirmation, by the Brigade Major of 10 Artillery Brigade. However, before any clarification could come from 191 Infantry Brigade, the enemy attacked the two forward batteries of 216 Medium Regiment (i.e. P and R Batteries). Major G. S. Chopra (the battery commander of P Battery who happened to be present in the gun area) and Subedar Vasant Mulay (of R Battery) were severely wounded in the first rush itself. While the forward batteries fought on tenaciosly, the depth battery (Q Battery) under the GPO Subedar Phadtare, as well as 39 Medium Regiment resorted to 'direct fire' on the enemy, possibly causing casualties to some of their own troops as well. With this sudden and heavy onslaught of the enemy and with none of the infantry to defend them it was natural that there was confusion, panic and possibly some flight. But the number of dead and wounded gunners found alongside their guns as the day broke, is ample testimony to the courageous fight put up by 216 Medium Regiment, which sadly has not been acknowledged. The Pakistani casualties were very high. Many wounded Pakistanis were later taken as POWs from this area. In fact, in the evening of the same day, even as 4 AK Brigade had retreated across the river, the Q Battery command post was fired upon by the Pakistanis. The Adjutant Captain M. L. Mahajan led a patrol in the direction of the trench from where the fire was coming and captured two Pakistani stragglers, one of whom was very severely wounded and dying.[58]

About the attack on the Wagon Lines of 39 Medium Regiment, Colonel (then Captain) Prakash Pande, the adjutant of the regiment recounted to the author:

In a disorganized state, some men of 13 AK Battalion now went towards Kachreal heights, while some went southwards, where they ran into our Wagon Line and started attacking our drivers and B echelon personnel. Our alert men fought them. A hand-to-hand fight ensued. Bayonets not being issued to artillery units, we were at a disadvantage. We lost seven men. Enemy too suffered many casualties. Driver Paramjit Singh snatched the bayonet from one of the enemy's rifles and killed two Pakistanis. The enemy left behind his dead, an assortment of ammunition and 17 filled magazines.

Later in the evening, the fleeing enemy soldiers tried to escape carrying their injured 2IC Major Rashid Abbassi on their shoulders, passing close to our RHQ area. When challenged by our Quick Reaction Team (QRT), they dumped the officer on the ground and vanished, taking advantage of the darkness. This happened near my command post. Hearing the commotion, I ran to the spot and prevented the men from hitting him. He was taken to the command post , where he was interrogated by the CO. Later he was handed over to the Division staff.[59]

Incidentally, the same evening the injured CO of 13 AK Battalion, Lieutenant Colonel Basharrat Raja, was also captured along with two others, by Captain (later) Colonel Deepak Kaul of 'E' Troop, 151 AD Regiment; air defence units were part of the Regiment of Artillery at that time. Hence, the gunners can rightfully claim the capture of these two Pakistani officers. Lieutenant Colonel Basharrat Raja, was the senior most Pakistani officer to be captured as a POW in the Western Theatre.

Meanwhile, continuing with the action at the gun position, Brigadier (then 2/Lt) J. Dhasmana narrated to the author, how he fired his guns by direct fire on the Pakistani:

Some gunners of my battery noticed men in Khaki uniform climbing up the Kachreal hill. My BC, Major Dhindsa who was in the gun position, asked me to check with the adjutant (Captain Pandey) if he had any information of any BSF movement in that area (since BSF too wore Khaki uniforms). On looking through my binocular I observed that those facing in our direction had two pockets on their jerseys, clearly indicating that they were Pakistanis (since BSF did not have pockets on the jerseys.) I accordingly informed my BC and adjutant.

I then ordered Havildar Dalip Singh (of Gun Number 5) to turned around his gun in that direction and I engaged the enemy troops with HE shell fitted with 'percussion super quick' Fuze 117, using the direct firing sight. Later, I also fired HE 213 Airburst with a minimum fuze setting of 0.5 in order to cover the 'folds' between the spurs of the Kachreal ridge. Later, I ordered Gun Number 3 (of Havildar Nirmal Singh) to also engage the enemy by direct fire. We could see the enemy troops running helter skelter and taking cover.[60]

The dead bodies of the Pakistanis near the gun position bear testimony of the resolute fight put up by the gunners. A fair amount of the total 161 casualties of 4 AK Brigade (killed, wounded, missing/POWs) were due to this infantry-gunner combat. 216 Medium Regiment too suffered a heavy toll of 102 casualties, of which 63 were martyrs. But the Pakistanis had been denied their bridge head, and were forced to withdraw back across the river.

In his book Pakistan's Crisis in Leadership, Major General Fazal Muqeem Khan has alluded to the role of these medium gunners in successfully thwarting this attack; he writes:

... 13 AK by the sheer determination and drive of its commanding officer succeeded in crossing and immediately hit the strongly defended Indian Artillery area. The Indian reaction was extremely swift with their artillery (italics by the author), and in the morning their air become very active. There was confused fighting for about 24 hours in which both sides suffered heavy casualties. The next night the bridge head was withdrawn.[61]

There has also been much debate on how many of the 130mm guns of 216 Medium Regiment were destroyed citing exaggerated figures. Brigadier (then Major) A. N. Suryanarayanan who as the Brigade Major of 10 Artillery Brigade compiled the 'After Action Report' of the war, clearly states that although five of them suffered varying degree of damage, only one was completely destroyed. In an article in Fauji India magazine of February 2018 he writes:

There is a mistaken belief that the enemy blew up some guns of this Medium Regiment; it is TOTALLY FALSE. NO GUN OF ANY ARTILLERY UNIT WAS BLOWN UP BY ENEMY IN 1971 IN CHHAMB SECTOR. Five guns of the Medium Regiment were badly damaged (solid tyres were burnt out until wheel-discs touched the steel plates below) due to air strikes, sympathetic detonation of own ammunition during enemy shelling by DIRECT observation from Mandiala (which was lost) and Kachreal heights (never occupied). During the intense phase of operations and under repeated air attacks from 5 to 7 December, Artillery Brigade Commander Brigadier K. Srinivasan, with his Intelligence Officer, Captain C. K. Passi (later Colonel and now retired), assisted by the 2IC of the Medium Regiment, Major (later Lieutenant Colonel) R. C. Passi were advised on technical aspects 'in situ' by Major M. N. Kelkar of Field Workshop, who also supervised retrieval of the five damaged guns from Chapreal and damaged Kraz towers from Kachreal. Of these, four guns were repaired at the Base Workshop and only one was declared 'Beyond Economic Repair' and is now held at Artillery Museum at Artillery Centre, Nashik Road. One each of 25 Pounder and L-60 guns was damaged badly due to airstrikes/enemy shelling. NO gun of the other Medium Regiment was damaged.[62]

Downing of a Pakistani F-86 Sabre Jet by E Troop 151 Air Defence Regiment on 8 December 1971.

The Pakistani Air Force (P.A.F.) had been very active in the Chhamb Sector, flying daily missions in support of their ground offensive. On 8 December 1971, during one such mission consisting of two Sabres, one aircraft was shot down by a detachment of E Troop 151 A.D. Regiment. This engagement was observed by the Corps Commander and Divisional Commander who were on their way to the frontline. Col. (then Capt.) Deepak Kaul who was commanding E Troop narrated this incident to the author:

We were deployed in our new gun position east of the Manawar Tawi River. By now we had also received a replacement for the fourth gun which had been disabled earlier. On 8 December, while I was sitting on the Number 3 layer's seat of one of the gun detachments (whose Number 1 was Hav Uttam Jawalge), I saw two Pakistani Sabres in hot pursuit of three of our SU-7s who were returning from a mission over enemy territory. I immediately ordered the detachment to load, at the same time guiding the Number 2 to lay on the leading Sabre for 'elevation' while I laid for 'line'. As soon as I had him in sight, I ordered 'Fire'. We fired four rounds, all of which hit the fuselage of the leading Sabre which went down in front of our eyes, killing the pilot. Coincidentally, this engagement had been observed by the Corps Commander, Lieutenant General Sartaj Singh and GOC, Major General Jaswant Singh, who were on their way forward from the Divisional Headquarters. As soon as Sartaj (who was an artillery officer) entered the gun area, he said: 'This is how I want Colonel Commandant to be received when he comes to a gun area!' He then asked: 'Who is the detachment Commander of the gun which shot down the aircraft?' When he was told that it was Havaldar Uttam Jawalge, the Corps Commander awarded him the Vir Chakra on the spot! I still have the four cartridges of the rounds which shot down the aircraft, which I was allowed to retain by my Commanding Officer as a war trophy.[63]

Artillery Leadership

Pakistan's 23 Infantry Division had three artillery brigadiers viz. Brigadier Naseer Ullah Khan Babar (23 Artillery Brigade (upto 5 December), Brigadier Kamal Matin (23 Artillery Brigade from 7 December) and Brigadier Jamal Saeed Mian (17 Artillery Brigade). The initial planning and deployment was done by Brigadier N. U. K. Babar. He was able to muster additional batteries by getting guns from School of Artillery, equipping the Divisional Locating Battery with 105 mm guns and converting them into a fire support role, and also getting Mujahids to man as many as 18 guns/mortars (equal to a regimental strength). As mentioned earlier he deployed his guns boldly and in an unorthodox manner. On 5 December he was shifted to command 111 Infantry Brigade, and relieved by Brigadier Kamal Matin who took over on 7 December. Brigadier Jamal Saeed Mian had little role to play other than coordinating the deployment and employment of his artillery resources according to the overall artillery plans of 23 Artillery Brigade.

Brigadier (then Captain) Tariq Ali Khan of 11 Cavalry has written that, 'The Division Artillery Commander Brigadier Naseer Ullah Khan Babar was the artillery brigadier who matched Major General Janjua in his courage, and till he was wounded while commanding an Infantry Brigade, was always by his side. Later, after retiring from the army as a Major General he became a prominent public figure and occupied ministerial posts in the PPP government'.[64]

Brigadier K. Srinivasan, the Commander of the Indian 10 Artillery Brigade was an outstanding gunner with a good professional reputation. He was always available to the GOC to give sound advice on artillery matters. He had meticulously planned the artillery support for the 10 Infantry Division offensive task, till it was abruptly put 'on hold' on the evening of 1 December. Thereafter he became involved in coordinating the Defence Fire (DF) Tasks across the divisional front. He ensured adequate availability and re-supply of artillery ammunition to the units, as is borne out of the fact that no regiment ran out of ammunition.

Colonel (then Captain) Mahesh Chadha who as the ADC to the GOC, saw the Commander Artillery at close quarters, had this to say:

Brigadier K. Srinivasan took over the 10 Artillery Brigade around March 1971. I think he had come from his assignment of Military Attaché in Vietnam. Right from the beginning he left a deep impression on me of being a professional Gunner. As the war clouds gathered, the C Artillery was intensively involved in the planning of both offensive and defensive operations. I do not know why he was nicknamed as Henry - may be that he behaved like King Henry the Vth! He was always there to render useful advice to the GOC as and when called for.

As early as November 1971, two FDCs were established, which presented a totally war-like picture - the one where C Artillery was present with his Brigade Major, acted as the 'Main' around which the whole Divisional Artillery swung into action. With a cigarette between his lips Brigadier Srinivasan was always on his toes. I do not think that he ever sat down or had even a wink of sleep during the intense battle for 13 days. DFs, DF SOS, CB, guns in 'direct firing' role and Air OP were something for me to be seen to be believed. The Commander was a cool courage personified, pursuing his mission with zeal and relentless spirit of a gunner who believed in keeping all the guns in roaring more for destruction and not only for neutralization. But for the artillery support, we may not have successfully sustained the initial onslaught of the enemy on our FDLs for more than 72 hours. The Commander Artillery was indeed the man of the hour-confident, determined and above all a gunner par excellence. Even when one of the regiments was attacked by infantry, he was there to hold the hand of the CO saying this can happen in war, so 'stand up and fight'. My salute to him and the team he led so courageously despite the FDCs being targeted many times, endangering him and his staff.[65]

CONCLUSION

Artillery played a vital role in the Battle of Chhamb, with both sides using their artillery very effectively in support of their operational plans. *In fact during the first three days of combat this battle saw what was perhaps the maximum concentration of artillery units in a divisional battle during the 1971 war, i.e. a total of approximately 300 guns firing in a small area of the Chhamb Salient.* Considering the overall availability of artillery resources almost half a century ago, this was a considerable amount of fire power on a 'per square kilometre' basis.

As far as Pakistan is concerned, they had amassed more artillery in support of 23 Infantry Division, than they had to defend in the entire East Pakistan Theatre! Every infantry / armour attack was preceded by a heavy dose of artillery bombardment.

Considering the availability of artillery resources available to them (23 Artillery Brigade, 17 Artillery Brigade as well as other ad-hoc units), they were able to group FOOs and BCs with all the infantry and armour units, thereby assuring artillery support to the attacking forces at all times. Their artillery observers were always on the look-out of random targets as well. Their shelling of the 'Reconnaissance and Orders' Group of 7 Kumaon at a vital point, injuring the CO, four officers and many others, as well as the artillery fire brought on Commander 68 Infantry Brigade, CO 72 Armoured Regiment and C Squadron, resulting in the death of the squadron commander and 2IC, are examples of this.

On the Indian side, although vastly outnumbered 'gun-to-gun', they made very optimum and efficient use of their artillery. The first-hand accounts (appearing earlier in this chapter) of Pakistani officers who witnessed the havoc caused by the Indian artillery, bear testimony to this fact. This battle was also a good example of the use of artillery in the 'direct shooting' role - the guns were successfully used to engage enemy tanks, to do bunker-bursting, for the destruction of an Observation Tower, as well as engaging enemy infantry by 'open sights'? The attack by 13 AK Battalion on the 216 Medium Regiment gun areas, is the only example of an artillery unit getting embroiled in a hand-to-hand combat with the infantry in the 1971 war. This also resulted in the blunting of the offensive of 4 AK Brigade and capturing of CO and 2 IC of13 AK Battalion.

Whenever artillery fire was called for, the gunners rose to the occasion, often using unorthodox procedures and methods, to meet the demands of artillery support. Even during a lull in battle, the Indian OP officers continued with harassing fire on the enemy. Brigadier Tariq Ali Khan writes: '...during the day we were constantly harassed by Indian artillery. I remember CO 33 FF, Lieutenant Colonel Feroz Alam as a very calm and professional CO. He told his unit to deploy and dig in wherever they halted so as to protect themselves from Indian shelling. He passed orders that if anyone in 33 FF gets hit by shelling being in the open, he will be charged by the CO for indiscipline!'[66] Two Indian artillery OP officers were martyred while bringing down artillery fire, while one remains missing to this day. It is also on record that most of the casualties (on both sides) were caused by artillery fire.

It is pertinent to note that although the battle started with the heavy artillery bombardment of Indian positions on 3 December, it ended with heavy shelling of Pakistani positions by the Indian artillery on the night of 17 December. With the Unilateral Ceasefire due to come into effect at 8 p.m. that night, 10 Infantry Division fired a heavy artillery barrage on the Pakistanis with devastating effect. In an interview given to Melville de Mellow of All India Radio, Major General Jaswant Singh, GOC of the division, recalled that 'on the last day of the war one of his (enemy's - author) stations cut into our own wireless net and acknowledged that he was an enemy station, but said for God's sake stop your guns.'[67]

Of the 21 gallantry awards (three Maha Vir Chakras and 18 Vir Chakras) awarded to 10 Infantry Division, the gunners got three Vir Chakras :

Captain Ravinder Kaura- 39 Medium Regime
(Posthumous)
Captain S.S. Gill   - 18 Field Regiment
Havildar Uttam Jawalge - 151 AD Regiment (part of
                               Artillery in 1971)

In conclusion, it will be fair to state that the gunners of 10 Infantry Division lived up to their motto *Sarvatra: Izzat-O-Iqbal,* and played a vital role in blunting the biggest Pakistan land offensive of the 1971 war. Instead of capturing their intended objective of Akhnur, the enemy was halted on the western bank of the Manawar Tawi River, and all attempts to cross the river were thwarted. Unfortunately, just when 10 Infantry Division was poised to launch a counter-stroke to recapture the lost territory, the Unilateral Ceasefire intervened and put paid to its plans.

APPENDIX G
Orbat of 10 Infantry Division

GOC : *Major General Jaswant Singh, VSM*

Armour

9 Deccan Horse (9 Horse) (T-54) (Integral Regiment)

72 Armoured Regt. (T-55). This regiment was raised just before the war and initially allotted to 3 (Independent) Armoured Brigade; however, in November 1971 it was placed under command 10 Infantry Division for offensive tasks.

2 (Independent) Recce Squadron

C Company 12 Guards

Group 9 Para Commando

Infantry

28 Infantry Brigade *(Brigadier R. H. Bajina, Vr C)*

52 Infantry Brigade *(Brigadier K. K. Hazari)*

68 Infantry Brigade *(Brigadier R.T. Morlin)*

191 Infantry Brigade *(Brigadier R. K. Jasbir Singh)*

Artillery

10 Artillery Brigade *(Brigadier K. Srinivasan)* (See Table 5.2 for detailed ORBAT)

Engineers

61 Engineer Regiment

106 Engineer Regiment

Signals

10 Infantry Division Signal Regiment

68 Infantry Brigade Signal company

Paramilitary Force:

51 BSF (less two companies) and 57 BSF

APPENDIX - H

Orbat of Pakistan 23 Infantry Division Group

GOC : *Major General Ifitikar Khan Janjua (up to 9 December, died in battle > Brigadier Kamal Matin (officiating) > Maj Gen Ghulam Umar from 11 December)*

19 Baluch (Reconnaissance & Support Battalion)

Company SSG

Armour

2 Armoured Brigade ex 6 Armoured Divison (Brigadier Sardar Ahmed), consisting of 11 Cavalry (T-59), 28 Cavalry (T-59), and 12 (Independent) Armoured Squadron (M36B2).

26 Cavalry (Sherman tanks) was the Divisional integral regiment.

Infantry

4 Azad Kashmir Brigade *(Brigadier Ahmed Jamal Khan)*

7 Azad Kashmir Brigade *(Brigadier Fazlur Rahim)*

20 Infantry Brigade *(Brigadier Sayed Zair Hussain)*

66 Infantry Brigade / 17 Infantry Division *(Brigadier Qamar-us-Salam Khan)*

111 Infantry Brigade *(Lieutenant Colonel John Tressler (officiating) > Brigadier Naseer Ullah Khan Babar wounded in battle > Brigadier Abdullah Malik)*

Artillery (Brigadier Naseer Ullah Khan Babar > Brigadier Kamal Matin)

Besides integral artillery, this included 17 Artillery Brigade and units from 1 Corps Artillery) (See also Table 5.1).

Note. Orbat primarily sourced from Major General Shaukat Riza, The Pakistan Army 1966, pp. 177-80; although in the book the Orbat is given in the form of 'grouping'; this Orbat has been corroborated from other books as well (i.e. Battle of Chhamb 1971 by Lieutenant Colonel Ahmad Saeed and An Atlas of the 1971 Indian - Pakistan War by John H. Gill).

APPENDIX I

Casualties to Personnel and Equipment

PERSONNEL

Indian	Officers	JCOs	OR
Killed	23	20	397
Wounded	36	35	652
Missing/POW	05	03	182
	64	58	1,231
			(i.e. Total 1,353)

Pakistan*	Officers	JCOs	OR
Killed	20	15	337
Wounded	61	35	1,638
	81	50	1,975
			(plus 110 missing/POWs. Total 2,216)

*Sourced from the book *Battle of Chhamb (1971),* by Lieutenant Colonel Ahmed Saeed, p.87.

EQUIPMENT

Indian	T-54	T-55	2.5 Pdr	5.5 In	130 mm	120 mm	AD Guns
Destroyed	09	08	01	01	01	01	02
Damaged	01	-	05	01	05	04	-
	10	08	06	02	06	05	02

Pakistan (Estimated)	T-59	Sherman	Unidentified Tanks	Arty Guns
Destroyed	28	08	-	Unknown
Damage	-	-	12	
	28	08	12	

Notes: 1. Major General Fazal Muqeem Khan (Pakistan's Crisis in Leadership, p.280) has given the figures of Pakistani casualties in this war as follows:

(a) Western Theatre :

Killed	-	1,405
Wounded	-	3,078
Missing/POWs	-	475
Total	-	4,958

(b) Eastern Theatre :

Killed	-	1,293
Wounded	-	2,539
Missing	-	393
Total	-	4,225

2. It can be seen that the casualties suffered by Pakistani's 23 Infantry Division Group in the Battle of Chhamb (2,216 personnel), were approximately 53 percent and 45 percent respectively, of those suffered by their army in the Eastern and Western Theatre - a very heavy toll.

APPENDIX - J
DO Letter of Lt. Gen. K.P. Candeth

Lieut General KP CANDETH, PVSM

DO No 10000/2/Scott
HEADQUARTERS,
WESTERN COMMAND
SIMLA-3.

17 Jun 72

      I was responsible for the raising of 10 Infantry Division whilst Deputy Chief of Army Staff and moving it to your present Sector of operations and soon afterwards, in 1966, the formation came under me when I took over as GOC XV Corps. I have thus watched it grow from a collection of hetrogeneous units to a fighting formation.

      The main weight of the PAKISTAN's pre-emptive attack on land came against your Division and although you had to give ground, you inflicted such attrition on him that his advance ground to a halt without achieving a major success.

      I would like to thank your formation and unit Commanders for all the work that they have done in peace and war whilst under Western Command, and would be grateful if this is conveyed to them. I am very proud of the steadfastness and determination displayed by your formations and units and now that you are passing out of my Command, I would like to wish you and your formation success in any future operations.

               With my best wishes,

               Yours Sincerely

Maj Gen HS KLER, MVC AVSM
General Officer Commanding
10 Infantry Division

NOO
   Copy to :-
      Maj Gen JASWANT SINGH
      Chief of Staff
      HQ I Corps

NOTES

1. *Hamoodur Rehman Commission of Inquiry with Respect to the 1971 War, Vanguard* Books, Lahore, p.213.
2. Maj. Gen. A.J.S. Sandhu, *Battleground Chhamb : The Indo - Pakistan War of 1971*, Manohar, New Delhi, 2017, p.78.
3. Air Chief Marshal P.C. Lal, *My Years with the IAF*, Lancer International, New Delhi, 1986, p.79.
4. Maj. Gen. A.J.S. Sandhu, *Battleground Chhamb*, p.84.
5. Ibid., p.85, Maj Gen Jaswant Singh has written in detail on this issue in a letter dated 21 January 1972 to Lt Gen J.S. Dhillon (former GOC 11 Corps during the 1965 war and later GOC-in-C, Central Command from 1967 to 1970).
6. Ibid., p.87-8.
7. Ibid., p.100, quoting a talk given by Field Marshal S.H.F.J. Manekshaw to the students of the Higher Command Course Serial 19, at Army War College, Mhow in January 1991.
8. 'War Directive No. 4 of 9 August 1967', as extracted from the Hamoodur Rehman Commission Report.
9. Ibid., p.173, gives out the movement schedule of Pakistani Forces from M Day to M+9.
10. Gen Mohammad Musa, *My Version : India- Pakistan War 1965*, ABC Publishing House, New Delhi, writes : 'Abdul Malik's nerve centre - tactical headquarters - constrained him to rely much more on ...Corps artillery headquarters... (it is) not designed for such purpose... (hence) was unable to exercise effective personal control... at the very crucial stage of fighting...', p.41.
11. *Hamoodur Rehman Commission*, p.213.
12. Lt Col M.Y. Effendi, *Punjab Cavalry*, Oxford University Press, Karachi, 2007, p.248.
13. Maj Gen Syed Ali Hamid, *Forged in the Furnace of Battle : The War History of 26 Cavalry Chhamb Operations*, Sang-e-Meel Publishers, Lahore, 2014, p.12.
14. Lt. Col Ahmad Saeed, *The Battle of Chhamb (1971)*, has given a detailed account of the preparation and planning of 23 Infantry Division, pp.1-5.
15. Maj Gen AJS Sandhu, *Battleground Chhamb*, pp. 118-19, gives out the overall concept of the 23 Infantry Division plan in detail.
16. Extracted from Lt. Col. Ahmad Saeed, *Battle of Chhamb (1971)*, p.15, Maj. A. H. Amin, *Battle of Chhamb*, Defence

Journal, September 1999, pp.18-19, and Maj. Gen. Shaukat Riza, *The Pakistan Army 1965-71*, p. 181.

17. Lt. Col. Ahmad Saeed, *Battle of Chhamb (1971)*, p. 27.
18. Maj. Gen. A. J. S. Sandhu, *Battleground Chhamb*, pp. 144-47, covers this attack in detail.
19. Lt. Col Ahmad Saeed, *Battle of Chhamb (1971)*, pp. 38-42, in which he gives a detailed account of this failed attack.
20. Maj. Gen. A.J.S. Sandhu, *Battleground Chhamb*, pp. 162-3.
21. Maj. Gen. Shaukat Riza, *The Pakistan Army 1966-71*, p. 185.
22. Maj. Gen. A. J. S. Sandhu, *Battleground Chhamb*, pp. 173-4; also Lt. Col Ahmad Saeed, *Battle of Chhamb (1971)*, pp. 74-6.
23. Ibid., *Battleground Chhamb*, pp. 177.
24. Ibid., pp. 182-88, gives a detailed account of the activities between 11 to 17 December.
25. Demi Official Letter dated 17 June 1972, wriiten by Lt. Gen. K.P. Candeth to GOC 10 Infantry Division.
26. Maj. A. H. Amin, *Remembering Our Warriors : Babar The Great*, Defence Journal, April 2001, p.17.
27. Ibid., p.17.
28. Brig. A. N. Suryanarayanan, *The Tribune* Chandigarh dated 21 December 2010.
29. Maj. Gen. Shaukat Riza, *The Pakistan Army 1966-71*, p.181 and *Izzat-O-Iqbal, History of Pakistan Artillery*, pp. 388-9.
30. Maj. Gen. A. J. S. Sandhu, *Battleground Chhamb*, p. 130.
31. Brig. Tariq Ali Khan, (Pakistani 11 Cavalry), account in *Battleground Chhamb*, p.221.
32. Maj. Gen. P. K. Puri (then B Company Commander with 5 Assam) in an interview with the author on 3 March 2015.
33. Brig. A. P. Deo (then Adjutant of 18 Field Regiment) in an email to the author.
34. Maj. Gen. J.R.K. Bhattacharjee (then BC with 39 Medium Regiment) in an email to the author.
35. Maj. Gen. S. V. Thapliyal (then OP Officer with 5 Sikh) in an email to the author.
36. Maj. Gen. Shaukat Riza, *Izzat-O--Iqbal*, pp. 389-90.
37. Ibid., p.390.
38. Brig. Ashok Kunzru (then Intelligence Officer in 72 Armoured Regiment) in an interview with the author on 23 March 2015.
39. Maj Gen Shaukat Riza, *Izzat-O-Iqbal*, p. 405.
40. Brig. A. N. Suryanarayanan, *The Tribune* dated 21 December 2010.
41. Brig. A. P. Deo in an email to the author.

42. Colonel Prakash Pande (then Adjutant of the 39 Medium Regiment), in an email to the author.
43. Brig Jitendra Dhasmana (then GPO in 39 Medium Regiment), in an email to the author.
44. Brig. A. N. Suryanarayanan, *The True Position of Artillery Support in Chhamb - 1971*, Fauji India, February 2018.
45. Lt. Col Ahmad Saeed, *The Battle of Chhamb (1971)*, p. 20.
46. Maj. Gen. Jagjit Singh, *Indian Gunners at War: The Western Front 1971*, pp. 81-2.
47. Maj. Gen. A. J. S. Sandhu, *Battleground Chhamb*, p. 142.
48. Brig. Vijay Chopra (then OP Officer with 81 Field Regiment), in an email to the author.
49. Col. R. I. Singh (of 39 Medium Regiment, who was OP Officer with 8 J & K Militia), in an email to the author.
50. Ibid.
51. Maj. Gen Virpal Singh (of 81 Field Regiment, who was OP Officer with 7 Kumaon), in an email to the author.
52. Maj. Mahin Malik's (Pakistani 11 Cavalry) account in *Battleground Chhamb*, p.206.
53. Brig. Tariq Ali Khan's account in *Battleground Chhamb*, p.229-30.
54. Maj. Mahin Malik in *Battleground Chhamb*, p. 208.
55. Brig. J. Dhasmana in an email to the author.
56. Maj. Gen. Anjan Mukherjee, *God of War: History of the Regiment of Artillery (1966-2009)*, Akshay Media Pvt Ltd, New Delhi, 2010, p. 193.
57. Lt. Col. Ahmad Saeed, *Battle of Chhamb (1971)*, p. 45.
58. Maj. Gen. A. J. S. Sandhu, *Battleground Chhamb*, pp. 145-7.
59. Col. Prakash Pande in an email to the author.
60. Brig. J. Dhasmana in an email to the author.
61. Maj. Gen. Fazal Muqeem Khan, *Pakistan's Crisis in Leadership*, Alpha and Alpha Pakistan, New Delhi, 1984, p. 198.
62. Brig. A. N. Suryanarayan, *Fauji India*, April 2018.
63. Col. Deepak Kaul in conversation with the author on 7 April 2017; also see Battleground Chhamb: The Indo-Pakistan War 1971, by the author, p. 260.
64. Brig. Tariq Ali Khan's account in *Battleground Chhamb*, p. 232.
65. Col. Mahesh Chadha's (who was ADC to GOC 10 Infantry Division) in an email to the author.
66. Brig. Tariq Ali Khan's account in *Battleground Chhamb*, p. 230.
67. Maj. Gen. Jaswant Singh, in an interview with Melville de Mellow, broadcast on All India Radio in January 1971.

CHAPTER-6

Battles of Tololing And Tiger Hill

(Operation Vijay)

(May – June 1999)

The Kargil Conflict

The war in Kargil will go down in history of India as a saga of unmatched bravery,grit and determination displayed on the battlefield by the Indian Army; a symbol of great pride and inspiration.

GENERAL V.P. MALIK

(former COAS) in his book KARGIL : Surprise to Victory.

INTRODUCTION

India and Pakistan fought a short but intense conflict between May and July 1999 on the icy heights of the Kargil District of the Indian State of Jammu and Kashmir. This was a war thrust upon India, and remained localized to that region. Ever since the partition of the sub-continent in 1947. Pakistan has sought to annex Jammu and Kashmir by violent means, but failed every time. Even today, Pakistan continues to wage a proxy war in that state by sending terrorists and in indulging in other cross border activities.

During the winter of 1998/99 the Pakistani army posing as Jehadis, occupied many mountain peaks along the Line of Control (LOC) on the Indian side, between Mashkoh (121[I] Infantry Brigade) and Sub Sector West (102 Infantry Brigade) in the 3 Infantry Division Sector. These intrusions were along a rather long stretch, and came to light only in May 1999. Undoubtedly, this was a case of intelligence failure at national, strategic and tactical levels. Although Pakistanis claimed that these intruders were Kashmiri Jehadis, it was soon clear that they were the regular troops of the Pakistan Army, dressed to look like militants.

With diplomatic efforts to get the intruders to vacate the

posts illegally occupied across the LOC having failed, India decided on a military response to evict them. There was however, a government caveat which greatly constrained the army and IAF in their operations : the LOC will not be crossed under any circumstances.

After the failure of the initial attacks, it was decided to first build up adequate forces into the Kargil Sector, and then launch well planned, deliberate operations, backed by sufficient artillery fire support. Thus 8 Mountain Division was moved from the Kashmir Valley into the Dras area. Importantly, many artillery units were also moved to Kargil from outside formations; these included the 155 mm Bofors howitzers and the GRAD 122 mm Multi Barrel Rocket Launchers (MBRLs). The Bofors were to become the symbols of success of the numerous attacks launched after 12 June 1999, (i.e. the Battle of Tololing). The build up of Artillery is given in Table 6.1[1]

This war received wide media coverage, with on-the-spot of journalists often giving live reports of ongoing operations. The battles being fought were literally brought to the drawing rooms of the public. Writing about the battle of Tiger Hill, General V.P. Malik notes in his book *KARGIL : From Surprise to Victory*, `For the first time in India's military history, a TV channel covered the battle live: a sign of progress and transparency, not to mention the on-screen depiction of our confidence[2]. Such intense coverage also stirred a strong sense of patriotism in the Indian citizenry and united the country.

A word about the terrain of the area where these battles were fought. The Kargil Sector extends approximately 170 kilometers. The LOC ran along high mountain peaks and ridges with heights reaching up to 17,000 feet; Tiger Hill was at a height of 16,600 feet. These high ridges were rocky and bare, with no vegetation at all. The area remained snow – clad for a major part of the year (October to June). There were many rivulets and *nullahs* (big and small) which flowed north to south, between the spurs of these ridges. The temperatures were sub-zero.

TABLE 6.1 : THE BUILD-UP OF ARTILLERY IN THE KARGIL SECTOR

Between 8 May, two days after One Alpha (NH 1 A – author) was opened to traffic, and 12 July, more and more artillery units were moved into the sector, to be added to the artillery regiments already supporting 121 (I) Brigade, which comprised: 141 Field Regiment, 286 Medium Regiment, 1861 Light Regiment and one battery of 307 Medium Regiment. They totalled over 108 105 mm Indian field guns (IFG), and 132 130 mm and 155 mm medium guns amongst others – over 280 additional guns, mortars and rocket launchers, with a number of guns and missile batteries for air defence:
4 Field Regiment
15 Field Regiment
315 Field Regiment
197 Field Regiment
41 Field Regiment
255 Field Regiment
108 Medium Regiment
307 Medium Regiment
158 Medium Regiment
305 Medium Regiment
253 Medium Regiment
114 Medium Regiment
155 Medium Regiment
One battery 139 Medium Regiment
1889 Light Regiment
One battery GRAD BM-21
212 Rocket Regiment
Two batteries 160 mm mortars
244 Heavy Mortar Regiment

Note. Extracted from *A Ridge Too far*, by Amarinder Singh, Motibagh Palace, Patiala, 2001, p.73.

The lifeline to Ladakh, National Highway 1 A ran along the southern tip of the Kargil Heights. The road was under the observation of the enemy perched atop the illegally occupied posts and could be interdicted by artillery fire. The area occupied by the intruders could be divided into five sub-sectors;

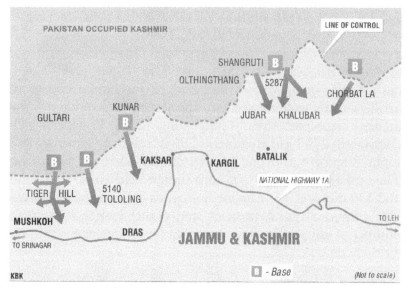

Map 19: Pakistan Army's Intrusion Plan-Kargil Sector

Note : Map has been sourced from *KARGIL 1999 : Blood, Guts and Firepower* by
Colonel Gurmeet Kanwal, p.12

Dras, Kaksar, Kargil, Batalik and Sub Sector West (See Map 19).

It was in this inhospitable terrain and extremely high mountain peaks that India fought a very successful offensive campaign over two months in the summer of 1999. The codename given to this operation was Operation Vijay. The Regiment of Artillery played a stellar role in this victory. By 20 July all territory had been recaptured by the Indians, but the cost had been heavy: 527 dead, and 1363 wounded.

Since the number of battles which were fought in the Kargil War are too numerous to recount, this chapter narrates two famous ones, ie. the Battles of Tololing and Tiger Hill.

PART 1 – BATTLE OF TOLOLING

TOPOGRAPHY

Tololing Ridge was a striking geographical feature which overlooked the Indian NH 1 A. The Pakistanis now sitting on the ridge had clear observation of the vehicular movement on this critical Srinagar – Leh highway, and could bring down effective artillery fire to disrupt this movement. Other dominating high features in its close proximity viz. Point 5140 and Point 4590, further added to the defence potential of Tololing. In this book *Kargil : Turning The Tide*, Lieutenant General Mohinder Puri notes:

Tololing feature was representative of the deepest penetration made by Pakistan in Drass. One actually has to stand at Drass and look towards this feature to believe the extent of its domination. From his deployment on the feature, the enemy could dominate the highway both by observation and fire, and interdict any movement or build-up besides cutting off troops along the Bhimbat Valley by direct firing weapons. By holding features of Hump, Point 5140, Point 4700 and Area Three Pimples, the enemy had ensured a secure route of maintenance for his troops at Tololing.[3]

Tololing is a ridgeline which runs in a north-south direction, starting from Point 5140 and culminating at Tololing Top, after which it separates into spurs running south-east and south-west (See Map 20). The entire feature could be split into distinct objectives of Point 4590 and Tololing Top (which dominated the area around it), two Humps (North Hump and South Hump) with a saddle in between, Rocky Knob, Point 5140, a little distance to west of which was Black Tooth. While 1 Naga was in contact with Rocky Knob in the north-west, 18 Grenadiers had formed a firm base around the rest of the ridgeline from the west, south and east. Due to the geographical configuration, the attack had to be launched uphill along the south-west and south-east spurs.

THE ATTACK PLAN

GOC 8 Mountain Division, Major General (later Lieutenant General) Mohinder Puri, directed Brigadier Amar Aul, commander of 56 Mountain Brigade, to launch a two-battalion attack with a view to capture Tololing and Point 5140 simultaneously by 2 Raj Rif and 18 Garh Rif respectively. He had decided to include Point 5140 as part of the attack on Tololing, since it was a dominating height to the north of the Tololing ridge and could interfere with the capture of Rocky Knob and the area of the Humps. The attack, earlier planned

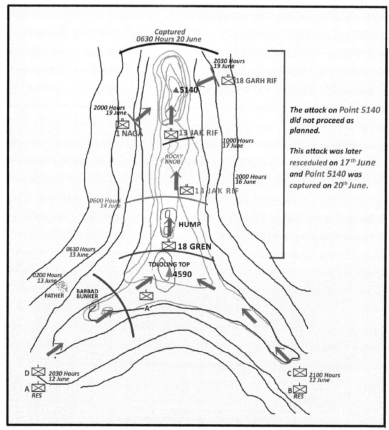

Map 20: Battle of Tololing

Note : Map has been sourced from *KARGIL : Turning The Tide*, by
Lt Gen Mohinder Puri, p.64

for the night 10/11 June was postponed twice by 24 hours each time, in order to give 18 Garh Rif more time to assemble their troops in the launch area. A request for further postponement was turned down by the GOC. In his book, Lieutenant General Puri recalls.:

I called the respective COs over alongwith Commander 56 Mountain Brigade (...on 4 June ...), discussed with them plans for the capture of Tololing and Point 5140. By noon the discussion was over and I asked Lieutenant Colonel Ravindranath, CO 2 Raj Rif to capture Tololing, and Colonel SK Chakraborty, SC, SM, CO 18 Garh Rif to capture Point 5140 from the north. However, the attack had to be postponed since 18 Garh

Rif which had to be launched from the north-east of Point 5140 through Bhimbet Nala, took some time to move, settle and carry out reconnaissance. It was a difficult move for the battalion as they could only move during hours of darkness due to enemy's domination over the Bhimbat Valley which lay on the induction route. I therefore decided to launch the attack on night 11/12 June. However, while the battalion was ready for their task, I was informed by CO 18 Garh Rif on 11 June morning that since the day was a Friday, the unit was requesting for postponement of the attack on grounds that the day would be lucky for the enemy. We men who are from a rural background are very superstitious and at such times I thought it was wise to concede to their request. There was a bit of murmuring that the 12th which happened to be a Saturday and the 13th which is at is considered unlucky, would also be inauspicious days to commence our operations, but this time I was determined to launch the attack and gave the go-ahead for commencement of our offensive on the night of 12/13th June. We, the army and the nation, badly needed a success and I had been particularly very deliberate in our planning process to ensure a cent percent chance in our first operation, although the thought of having delayed the attack did bother my mind several times.[4]

It was appreciated that the Tololing Ridge was occupied by a platoon plus, ie. around 40 personnel, equipped with light and medium machine guns, infantry mortars with assured artillery support. Perched on the dominating heights, this was indeed a well defended enemy position. Brigadier Aul was tasked to capture Tololing with 2 Raj Rif by 0600 hours and Point 5140 with 18 Garh Rif by 0700 hours of 13 June. The aim was to mount a multi-directional attack, i.e. while 2 Raj Rif was attacking from the south-west and south-east direction, 18 Garh Rif was launching its attack on Point 5140 from the north-east. (18 Garh Rif operations are not discussed here).

Colonel Ravindranath's plan was to launch a two-company attack as under:-

(a) D Company (Major Mohit Saxena) with A Company (Major P Acharya) in reserve was to attack along the South-West Spur in the direction of Point 4590 (under the overall control of the 2IC Major SS Bajaj).

(b) C Company (Major Vivek Gupta) with B Company (Lieutenant SS Rautela) in reserve, was to launch its attack along the South-East Spur towards Tololing Top (under the overall control of the CO).

(c) The Commando Platoon (Captain N. Kengurose) was tasked to establish a `block' between Hump and Tololing, the aim being to interdict enemy movement and deny re-inforcements coming into the area.

(d) It was planned to stagger the timings of launch of the two companies; whereas the attack by D Company along South-West Spur was to commence at H hour, C Company was to be launched 30 minutes later. The CO hoped that the enemy, by re-adjusting his defences to deal with the former, would facilitate the operations of C Company.

H hour was 2030 hours on 12 June. The infantry assault was to be preceded by artillery bombardment of not only the intended objectives, but their gun areas as well. A couple of hours before the commencement of the artillery fire plan, 18 Grenadiers which was in contact with the enemy and providing a firm base for the attack by 2 Grenadiers, was to withdraw its forward line by 150 metres. This was done in order to provide a clear corridor for the Bofors to fire on their targets and minimize attrition to our infantry.

THE INFANTRY ATTACK COMMENCES

The Indian Artillery commenced its pre-H hour bombardment at 1936 hours, and after it had pounded the enemy defences sufficiently, the attack commenced with C and D Companies making their way upwards along the South-East and South-West spurs. It was indeed a tough operation in the rocky outcrops of the Tololing feature.

The advance by D Company along South-West Spur made steady progress under Major Major Mohit Saxena. The reserve A Company followed in its wake. By a little after midnight, the forward two platoons of D Company were able to capture their initial objectives of Pathar and Rock. The reserve platoon was now launched and Barbad Bunker too was in Indian hands by 0200 hours of 13 June.

The attack by C Company along the South-East Spur was slower as compared to the advance on its west; this was primarily due to the very heavy and accurate small arms and artillery fire it drew from the enemy at Tololing Top. They continued to advance and soon captured the area of Flat. Sensing an opportunity, Major Vivek Gupta decided to change direction and personally lead his reserve platoon to attack Tololing Top. In his unpublished article Colonel Shafi Sheikh notes: `Major Vivek Gupta himself led the reserve platoon of his company to launch an attack on Tololing Top from a different direction as the capture of Flat had provided a new opening. The officer was grievously wounded at this stage but continued to lead his men and made the supreme sacrifice but not before the enemy had been evicted from Tololing Top.'[5] At this stage, the young artillery FOO Captain M.K. Singh, took temporary change of the company and rallied the men to beat off as many as three determined counter-attacks launched by the Pakistanis to recapture this feature. Due to the dogged resistance put up by the men of C Company 2 Raj Rif, Tololing continued to remain in Indian hands.

Although most of the Tololing ridge had been captured by 0600 hours, Point 4590 proved a harder nut to attack. The enemy holding this post continued to offer stiff resistance to the attackers. Colonel Ravindranath assessed the situation, and now launched his reserve company, supported by massive artillery fire. Soon Point 4590 too capitulated, and the CO sent a radio message to his Brigade Commander and GOC that Tololing was now in Indian hands. This was a major Indian victory which set the tone for further successful operations.

ARTILLERY OPERATIONS

DIRECT FIRING EXPERIMENT
One week before the attack on Tololing, Brigadier Lakhwinder Singh, commander of 8 Mountain Artillery Brigade, decided to try out the concept of 'direct fire' by artillery guns from lower heights on to targets at higher altitudes. On 6 June 1999, he moved two Bofors (155mm Hows) and two 105 mm Field Guns to the area of Bhimbat; these were from 108 Medium Regiment and 197 Field Regiments respectively. The best detachments were selected for this task. The objective for

carrying out this experimental 'direct fire' was the Tololing feature. Communications were set up with the CO of 18 Grenadiers Colonel Kushal Thakur, as well as the Forward Observation Officer located with him near Tololing, who was to control this fire. Colonel Kushal Thakur was also told to pull back his troops temporarily along the flanks so as to ensure there was no collateral damage to them during this experimental fire.

Brigadier Lakhwinder Singh was present at Bhimbat to personally observe this firing along with the commanding officers of 108 Medium Regiment and 197 Field Regiment, Colonels Prabhat Ranjan and Alok Deb respectively. They were joined by Commander 56 Mountain Brigade, Brigadier Amar Aul, who had been tasked to capture Tololing. Initially the targets were registered by one Bofors gun, which was immediately followed by the 'direct fire' of both the medium guns on to the objectives. Their shells landed squarely on to the Tololing feature. The enemy immediately retaliated by directing its artillery on to this gun position. Undeterred and enthused by the effect of the Bofors guns, they now directed the 105mm Field Guns on to the objective. These guns too, were on target. Brigadier Lakhwinder Singh recalls: By the time we had fired a few rounds, our troops around the target could hear the enemy in complete disarray. The radio intercepts proved how devastating was the impact on the enemy: *Hamare par kehar aa gira hai. Hamein Bachao.* (All hell has broken loose on us, save us.)[6] Lieutenant General Y. M. Bammi also notes in his book *KARGIL: The Impregnable Conquered* '...direct fire of Bofors became a very decisive battle winning factor in all attacks'.

ARTILLERY GROUPING WITH 2 RAJ RIF
The following officers were grouped with 2 Raj Rif to provide artillery support during the attack on Tololing:

    (a) Battery Commander   -Major A.S.Kasana,
                                    41 Field Regiment
    (b) FOO with D Company -Captain A. Saxena,
                                    1889 Light Regiment

(c) FOO with C Company   -Captain Mridul
                                 Kumar Singh, 197
                                 Field Regiment

In addition to the above officers who were to go into assault with the attacking troops, two sets of Anchor Observation Posts (OPs) were also established in the East (under Colonel Alok Deb) and West (under Colonel Mediratta) to coordinate the artillery fire along both the approaches. This was to ensure registration of targets initially, and subsequently for correction of artillery fire. Adequate signal communications had been provided to both these 'Anchor OP hubs' so that they could remain in contact with attacking troops, guns and headquarters.

ARTILLERY FIRE PLAN

Considering the importance of this attack, it was decided to build up maximum artillery to support 2 Raj Rif. Lieutenant General Mohinder Puri writes : By 12 June, a number of artillery units had been placed under my command. I had two medium regiments less a battery, three field regiments, one light and heavy mortar regiment each and a troop of rocket regiment. There was enough artillery support available for the operations.'[7] This totalled a staggering 20 fire units to support a battalion attack.

It was a challenge to find suitable gun areas for so many artillery units in the mountainous terrain. Whereas the mortars could be moved inwards, the field and medium guns and MBRLs had to be deployed along the National Highway. Adequate artillery ammunition was dumped to support this attack.

The Fire Plan formulated for the attack was code named *Nischay Vijay* (Certain Victory) and involved the coordination of the fire of 108 guns and three Multi Barrel Rocket Launchers (MBRLs), including six guns in the `direct fire' role. In the words of Brigadier Lakhwinder Singh:

The technique was to surround the target by selecting the gun areas around it, engage the objective with a combination of low and high angle fire, and superimpose direct firing guns to maximize the impact. Such deployment ensured that maximum shells were captured by the crest of the target and the objectives engaged effectively from multiple directions, giving no respite to the enemy. Direct firing of Bofors and MBRLs on selected pin points added exponentially to the effect of Fire Assault.[8]

The outline Fire Plan Nischay Vijay is given in Table 6.2.[9]

TABLE 6.2 : DIAGRAMMATIC FIRE PLAN FOR CAPTURE OF TOLOLING BY 2 RAJPUTANA RIFLES

DUKAS		MARPOLA		FARANSHAH		BENAZIR		MOHARRAM	
MED 6	MED 6	MED 8	MED 6	MED 5	MED 6	MED 7	MED 6	MED 8	MED 6
MINUS 54 FD- MINUS 49	MARO TO MARO PLUS 10	MINUS 48 MINUS 43 MED 4 MINUS 4 TO MINUS 1	MARO PLUS 54 TO MARO PLUS 59	MINUS 42 FD MINUS 37	MARO PLUS 8 TO MARO PLUS 11	MINUS 34 TO MINUS 31	MARO PLUS 12 TO MARO PLUS 15	MINUS 30 TO MINUS 35	MARO PLUS 12 TO MARO PLUS 15

RESOURCES

FD-12
MED-9
HY-2
LT-2
MBRL-1

RIDGE   PIMPLE

FD-5 MED-4	ON CALL	FD-1	ON CALL

TOP

FD-8 MED-2	MINUS-20 TO MINUS 13	MARO PLUS 28 TO MARO PLUS 35	MINUS 8 TO MINUS 3	ON CALL FD-2 MED -2 HY-2

MMG BUNKER

FD-5	MINUS-20 TO MINUS 15	MARO PLUS 25 TO MARO PLUS 30	FD-6 MED - 6
ROCKETS	MINUS 10 TO MINUS 5	FD-1 MED-1	ON CALL

THREE STONES & SPINE

FD-6	MINUS 4 TO MINUS 1	MARO PLUS 30 TO MARO PLUS 35	FD-5 MED-4	ON CALL LT-2

BLACK TOOTH PT 5140

FD-6 MED-2 LT-2 FD-2	ON CALL

Explanatory Notes

1. Dukas, Marpo La, Faranshah, Benazir and Moharram were the suspected gun positions of Pakistan Army. Besides the enemy gun positions, the other known, identified and suspected enemy positions to be engaged were named as Pimple, Ridge, Medium Machine Gun Position, Top, Three Stones and Black Tooth.

2. Resources available to support the attack are indicated in battery (of six guns each). Field and Medium indicate the type of gun, while mortars are indicated as Heavy and Light. Multi Barrel Rocket Launcher Troop is indicated, separately.

3. While enemy gun positions and few other targets were to be engaged as per a 'timed' fire plan starting at H (Hotel Hour, when the assaulting troops cross a line or are released from a place), 'minus' indicates minutes before

H hour. Similarly, 'H Plus' indicates duration of engagement after H, all in minutes. 'On Call' denotes targets that could be engaged as and when they become active, on the orders of the Forward Observation Officers or the Anchor Observation Posts.

4. *MARO* (Hit) was the codeword to start the fire plan.
Note. Sourced from *Kargil 1999: The Impregnable Conquered*, by Lt. Gen. Y. M. Bammi, Gorkha Publishers, NOIDA, 2000, p.215.

THE ATTACK COMMENCES

H hour for 2 Raj Rif was 2030 hrs. The Fire Plan commenced 54 minutes prior (1936 hours) by pounding the enemy's suspected gun areas at Dukas, Marpola, Faranshah, Benazir and Muharram with all available artillery, after which it shifted on to the infantry objectives according to plan. Commenting on the effectiveness of the artillery fire, Lieutenant General Y.M. Bammi writes '...its intensity turned the whole feature of Tololing into a flaming red burning hill... The devastating artillery fire did cause casualties and demoralize the enemy...'[10] The GOC, Major General Puri who was on the spot to observe this fire, wrote `The effect of Bofors and MBRLs on the target was tremendous.'[11]

At H hour, D Company under Major Mohit Saxena alongwith the FOO Captain A Saxena, commenced its assault along the South-West Spur. As the company made steady progress towards its objectives, the Anchor OP at Dras Transit Camp under Colonel Mediratta ensured accurate artillery fire by ordering corrections where necessary. Close behind the reserve company, was the CO's party of Colonel Ravindranath and his Battery Commander, Major A.S. Kasana, who controlled the fire of the supporting guns and lived up to the Gunner credo of *Sarvatra : Izzat-O-Iqbal*. His unit history records, 'During these operations the officer displayed exceptional courage and very effectively directed accurate artillery fire causing heavy enemy casualities. The officer entered the minefield and succeeded in retrieving infantry casualities; his brave deed and professionalism was commented by his infantry comrades'. None other than the COAS, General V.P. Malik also extolled the officer's courage, writing in his book :

In the different battles for Tololing, Major Amrinder Singh Kasana of 41

Field Regiment showed himself to be an indefatigable and an exemplary gunner officer. He was a battery commander with 18 Grenadiers, but he volunteered to continue with 2 Raj Rif during its assaults. He participated in four consecutive attacks on Tololing, Hump, Rocky Knob and Point 5140'.[12]

Major Kasana was awarded the Vir Chakra for his valour.

Meanwhile, as planned, C Company was launched along the South-Eastern Spur with a stagger of 30 minutes. The FOO with this company, Captain M.K. Singh ensured accurate artillery fire on the enemy along this approach. The progress was slow but determined. While closing on to the Tololing Top, the company commander Major Vivek Gupta was fatally wounded. At this stage the FOO, Captain M.K. Singh took charge and fended off the enemy counter attacks to re-capture the position. Once again, to quote the COAS, General VP Malik, 'At this critical hour, Captain Mridul Kumar Singh, a young artillery FOO took over the company, rallied the men and deployed them on the objective to successfully ward off the counter attacks'.[13] As mentioned earlier, Tololing was captured by 0600 hours. Major Vivek Gupta and Captain MK Singh were awarded the Maha Vir Chakra and Sena Medal respectively.

Tololing was India's first victory, and the turning point of the Kargil War. Buoyed by this success, the Indian forces went on to achieve a string of victories hereafter. The Artillery played a decisive role in the Indian victory at Tololing.

PART – II THE BATTLE OF TIGER HILL

Topography

Tiger Hill was a conical feature, which rose majestically into the skyline at a height of 5060 meters (approximately 16,600 feet). It drew its importance from its height, dominance and visibility from the National Highway 1A. Due to the intense media coverage it had already become a household name in India. In the words of General V.P. Malik, 'As the sharp triangular top of Tiger Hill was clearly visible from the highway, and appeared almost impossible to capture, the media had projected it as a national challenge'.[14]

Although Tololing Top was a relatively narrow feature, the Tiger Hill complex was a larger objective, extending 2200 metres west to east, and 1000 metres north to south. On either side of Tiger Hill flowed the Sando and Tingel nullahs. The entire complex consisted of many smaller features. The Conical Top had two prominent `cuts' along its sides called Tooth (to the east) and V cut (to the west). As the top sloped downwards towards the west, there was India Gate, Helmet and further down was Rocky Knob. Two prominent spurs sloped downwards from Tiger Hill Top in the southern and south-eastern direction, and provided possible avenues for an attack on this feature. Along the South-East Spur was a smaller feature called Tongue. A panoramic view of Tiger Hill is shown in Map 21.

By virtue of its configuration, Tiger Hill was a very difficult feature to assault. The enemy had deployed one company of the 12 Northern Light Infantry (NLI) battalion to defend this feature, along with adequate infantry support weapons such as Medium Machine Guns (MMGs) and mortars, as well as an Artillery Observation Post. The deployment was designed to cover all the approaches to the Tiger Hill Top. General V.P. Malik further writes: 'After the recapture of Tololing and the adjacent features, evicting the enemy from this well-fortified position became a priority'.[15]

THE ATTACK PLAN

The attack on Tiger Hill took place three weeks after the capture of Tololing. In the third week of June, Major General Mohinder Puri started planning for the attacks on the Twin Objectives of Tiger Hill and Point 4875, by 192 and 79 Mountain Brigades, commanded by Brigadier M.P.S. Bajwa and R.K. Kakkar respectively. In his appreciation, Point 4875 had greater tactical importance, though Tiger Hill had become more well known due to intense media coverage. Major General Puri initially earmarked two battalions each for the two objectives; however, he later changed the grouping by allotting three battalions, i.e. 2 Naga, 13 Jak Rif and 17 Jat for Point

4875, and one battalion (18 Grenadiers) plus the company of 8 Sikh in reserve for Tiger Hill, as he wanted to concentrate his effort on what he termed as 'the point of decision.' Although he wanted to attack these objectives simultaneously, it was not possible to marshal adequate artillery to support both assaults; hence he staggered the operations by launching the attack on Tiger Hill 24 hours in advance. The GOC also hoped thereby to divert the enemy's attention from Point 4875. The attack was planned for the night of 3 / 4 July 1999.

An earlier attack by 8 Sikh on Tiger Hill in May had failed, but the battalion was able to reach close to Tiger Hill upto a place called *Parion Ka Talab*. It then 'firmed in' around Tiger Hill and continued to engage the enemy with intermittent harassing fire.

After doing a detailed reconnaissance of the area, Colonel Kushal Thakur, the CO of 18 Grenadiers, decided on a multi-

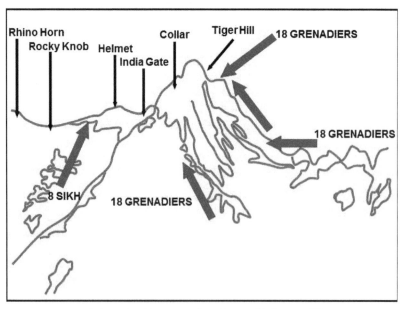

Map 21: Panoramic View of Tiger Hill

Note : Map has been sourced from *KARGIL : Turning The Tide*, by Lt Gen Mohinder Puri, p.91

directional attack by three companies, with one company in reserve. 8 Sikh was to provide the firm base and one company in reserve.

The outline plan of attack was as under (see Map 22):

(a). The Ghatak (Commando) Platoon (Lieutenant Balwan Singh) and C Company (Major P.J. Mijar) to attack from the North-East.

(b). A Company (Major R.S. Rathore) to attack from the South.

(c). D Company (Captain Sachin Nimbalkar) to attack from the East.

(d). B Company (Major Y.S. Tomar) to act as reserve.

(e). In addition 8 Sikh was tasked to earmark one company as reserve to 18 Grenadiers.

H Hour for the attack was 2100 hours on 3 July 1999. Preparatory bombardment was to commence 90 minutes earlier.

THE ATTACK COMMENCES

The assault on the Tiger Hill Complex by 18 Grenadiers was preceded by a heavy artillery bombardment of the objectives, initially by `direct firing' (eight Bofors and three MBRLs), followed later by the rest of the artillery (120 guns), as part of the Fire Plan. This pounding was designed to degrade the fighting potential of the enemy.

18 Grenadiers commenced their three pronged assault at 2100 hours. It was a very tough and arduous climb, especially along the North – Eastern Approach where the troops had to negotiate nullahs and boulders.

A Company under Major Rathore made steady advanced and was able to capture Tongue by 0130 hours. However, they were unable to make further progress due to heavy fire from enemy positions at Tiger Hill Top and positions at Helmet and India Gate.

The Ghataks under Lieutenant Balwan too managed to reach within 30 metres of the Top by 0400 hours, when they were detected by the enemy who opened fire on them. He quickly launched a small team to fix ropes and attack the

Top. In this action, young Grenadier Yogender Singh Yadav, though wounded, charged the enemy unmindful of his injuries and killed four Pakistani Soldiers. He was awarded India's highest gallantry award - the Param Vir Chakra. Meanwhile C Company under Major Mijar, following in the wake of the Ghataks, established themselves behind them.

While the above action was going on, D Company under Captain Nimbalkar also reached in the close vicinity of Balwan's Ghatak Platoon. After intense artillery bombardment, Nimbalkar and Balwan launched a coordinated attack and reached the Top by about 0600 hrs. This news was broadcast by the media channels in their morning bulletins. The writing was now as the wall for the Pakistanis – withdraw or face the Indian assaults. Ironically this news reached Pakistani Prime Minister Nawaz Sharif just hours before he was to meet US

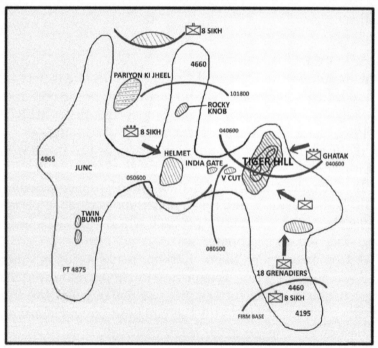

Map 22: Battle of Tiger Hill

Note : Adapted from the map appearing in the book *KARGIL : Turning The Tide*, by Lieutenant General Mohinder Puri (opposite page 93)

President Bill Clinton in Washington.

Although Tiger Hill Top was in Indian hands, enemy continued to hold his positions around it. They launched a series of counter attacks on 5 July to recapture the Top, but were beaten back. At this stage Brigadier M.P.S. Bajwa directed 8 Sikh send its reserve company to occupy Helmet and India Gate. This movement was designed to block the routes of reinforcement and resupply by the enemy which was holding the reverse slopes of Top. This 8 Sikh Company was formed around the nucleus of their Commando platoon, boosted by jawans from the other companies, and comprised of two officers, four JCOs and 46 soldiers. They moved swiftly and occupied Helmet, but their movement to India Gate was met with heavy enemy fire. Undeterred they continued towards the objective and managed to capture India Gate. They continued to hold on inspite of suffering casualties due to enemy fire and counter -attacks. One of these counter-attacks was led by Captain Karnal Sher Khan who was killed later in this action. His body was returned to the Pakistanis. He went on to receive the Nishan-e-Haidar, the highest Pakistani gallantry award. *The Battle of Tiger Hill was a rare instance of two soldiers – one Indian and one Pakistani - having been conferred the highest gallantry awards of their countries in the same battle.*

By 7 June, the complete Tiger Hill Complex was in Indian hands.

ARTILLERY OPERATIONS

ARTILLERY GROUPING WITH 18 GRENADIERS

The following officers were allocated to 18 Grenadiers to provide artillery support to 18 Grenadiers:

(a).Battery Commander -Major Arun Sharma (41 Field Regiment)

(b).FOOs - Major AS Bevli (41 Field Regiment) -Captain Anil Sharma (197 Field Regiment)

In addition to the above, Anchor OPs were established under Commanding Officer of 41 Field Regiment Colonel G.S.

Mann, along with Major A.S. Kasana and Captain Amitabh Roy.

ARTILLERY FIRE PLAN

Just as he had done for the Tololing battle, Brigadier Lakhwinder Singh once again amassed a formidable artillery force to support the attack on Tiger Hill – a total of 21 fire units. These guns were a healthy mix of 155 mm Bofors howitzers, 105 mm field guns, 120 mm mortars, 160 mm heavy mortars as well as one troop of MBRLs. Sufficient ammunition had been made available to all the artillery units. Signal communications had also been tied up in detail.

The Fire Plan to support this attack code – named *Final Blow*, was prepared by Colonel GS Mann, Commanding Officer of 41 Field Regiment. In addition, eight Bofors guns (six from 108 Medium Regiment and two from 158 Medium Regiment) along with three MBRLs were deployed in the 'direct firing' role. The 'direct firing' was to be coordinated by Colonel Prabhat Ranjan (108 Medium Regiment) assisted by Major Amul Raj.

Fire Plan *Final Blow* was designed to commence 51 minutes prior to the infantry assault (2009 hours) in order to ensure sufficient pounding of enemy positions. After bombarding the selected infantry objectives, the guns were to move on to the enemy guns positions just before H Hour. The stage was now set for the Battle of Tiger Hill.

THE ATTACK COMMENCES

The 'direct firing' by the Bofors and MBRLs commenced at 1930 hours. This was witnessed by many media persons gathered near the gun positions. Some of these visuals were also beamed live on TV. This direct firing was very accurate and battered the enemy's defensive positions on Tiger Hill. Brigadier Lakhwinder Singh who was present in the gun area recalls:

I was in the Gun Area standing next to a Bofors Gun, when the firing started. We were firing a mix of High Explosive Extended Range (HEER) and High Explosive (HE) shells. The extended range ammunition burns at the tail to reduce the drag and in doing so leaves a bright trail. The visible trail and direct hits on the target, enthused own troops and possibly the whole nation watching the live telecast. The Direct Firing can sometimes give a violent backlash. I faced one while overseeing the Bofors engaging Tiger Hill. The backlash was so severe that my turban flew off my head. Hats off to the brave gunners who continued to fire unflinchingly despite so much din and smoke.[16]

Fire Plan *Final Blow* commenced at 2009 hours. 120 guns of assorted calibres opened fire simultaneously. It was a sight to see. General VP Malik writes in his book; `The Commanding Officer of 41 Field Regiment drew up an elaborate artillery fire plan. Individual guns were ranged so as to cover each objective. Bofors guns were used in direct firing role once again, with inspiring accuracy. On the day of the assault, nearly 120 field and medium guns, 122 mm MBRLs and mortars rained death and destruction on Tiger Hill'.[17]

Major General Mohinder Puri who witnessed this massive artillery fire, recounted in his book, 'The sight of the artillery rounds falling on the objective made an awesome scene which remains etched in my memory till date'.[18]

As the three companies and the Ghataks made their way towards their objectives, artillery guns continued to bring accurate fire on the enemy positions and suspected gun areas. The FOOs with the companies, as well as the Anchor Ops, ensured the accuracy. The incessant pounding by the artillery ensured sufficient degradation of the enemy's fighting potential, thereby facilitating the task of our assaulting infantry. The BCs/FOOs/OPs displayed exceptional courage and devotion to duty during the assault, by directing accurate artillery fire on to the objectives while themselves exposed to enemy fire.

Once again to quote Brigadier Lakhwinder Singh:

The guns engaged each objective with a fusillade of 100 guns firing a mix of ammunition, supplemented by eight direct firing guns and three MBRLs. The fire assaults hit each objective like a mini nuclear explosion, literally pulverizing the enemy. It must have joyed the infantry to see the enemy getting blasted. The Pakistani radio intercepts revealed that they were scared to death. They could be heard saying, "Kehar se sholay baras rahe hain" (a shower of fire from hell !).[19]

Interestingly, artillery fire was also employed to help in the navigation of the assaulting infantry in the darkness. Artillery was later used extensively to beat back the numerous counter-attacks launched by the enemy to try and recapture their lost positions. At one stage in the morning of 6 July, when the enemy launched a determined counter-attack on to India Gate, the 8 Sikh platoon deployed there called for artillery to fire 'Defensive Fire Save Our Souls' (DF [SOS]), ie. artillery fire in the immediate vicinity of own positions.[20]

After the capture of Tiger Hill, Major General Mohinder Puri extolled the role of gunners saying, 'you have done it again. The infantry marched sling-arm to reach the top'.[21]

CONCLUSION

In the words of the Chief of Army Staff, General VP Malik, 'The war in Kargil will go down in the history of India as a saga of unmatched bravery, grit and determination displayed on the battlefield by the Indian Army; a symbol of great pride and inspiration'.[22] The Regiment of Artillery lived up to its motto '*Sarvatra : Izzat-O-Iqbal*' (Everywhere : with Honour and Glory), and played a decisive role in the Kargil Operations. The gunners were a battle-winning factor in the battles of Tololing and Tiger Hill. The synergy between the infantrymen and their artillery comrades was in full display during the attacks on the seemingly insurmountable peaks.

The artillery fire plans were prepared by the Commanding Officers with ingenuity to suit the infantry attack plans; they were a mix of `timed' and `on call' firing tables. More than 100 guns were amassed to support each battalion attack, and sufficient ammunition was allocated. Deployment of guns in the mountains is always a challenging task, but the artillery commanders managed to tuck in the guns in the folds of the mountains along the Srinagar – Leh Highway.

The Battery Commanders and FOOs were in the forefront with their infantry commanders, and ensured timely and accurate artillery support at all stages of the battles. Extolling their performance, General Malik writes in his book:

Several FOOs and Battery Commanders while moving with assault troops, who exposed to small arms fire and, in the process, got injured or killed. On some occasions when a company commander became a casualty, the FOO took over command of the rifle company and led it to capture the assigned objective.[23]

It may be recalled that during the Battle of Tololing, when the C Company Commander Major Vivek Gupta was killed, it was the FOO Captain M.K. Singh who took charge and led the men to the top.

During the entire Kargil Operations the artillery fired close to 3,00,000 shells of assorted types. The details of the quantity and type of ammunition fired is shown below:[24]

TABLE 6.3 : TOTAL AMMUNITION FIRED

105 MM Field Gun	
High Explosive	1,85,000
Smoke	4000
Illuminating	1000
Total	1,90,000
120 mm Mortar	
High Explosive	15,500
Smoke	600
Total	16,100
130 mm Medium Gun	
High Explosive	3400
155 mm Bofors	
77B	42,500
High explosive extended range	23,500
Cargo	2700
Smoke	1000
Illuminating	100
Total	69,800
160 mm Mortar	9000
Rockets Multi-Barrel Rocket Launcher	5300
Total	2,93,600

Note. Sourced from Kargil 1999 : The Impregnable Conquered, by Lt. Gen. Y.M. Bammi, pp. 382-3.

Each and every gunner (officers, JCOs and men) worked indefatigably, night and day, to ensure the success of this operation. And to provide inspiring leadership was the dynamic commander of 8 Mountain Artillery Brigade, Brigadier Lakhwinder Singh. He marshalled his artillery resources optimally to ensure concentrated artillery fire to support every attack; as can be seen from the above narrations, the battles of Tololing and Tiger Hill were supported by 100 to 120 guns. He deserves full credit for evolving and fine tuning the concept of `direct fire' by the Bofors and MBRLs at high altitudes, where such firing had never been undertaken till then. Infantry attacks were also supported by six to eight guns and three MBRLs in the 'direct firing' role. Brigadier Lakhwinder was always present at the gun areas or Anchor OP positions at the time when the artillery Fire Plans were executed. Due to his gutsy and inspiring leadership, he earned the sobriquet of the *'Enraged Bull of Dras'*. ('Bull' is the codename of a artillery commander).

In an unpublished note shared with the author, Brigadier Lakhwinder Singh summed up the role played by the artillery in the Kargil conflict:

> The analyses of Kargil war conclusively brings out that the Artillery Fire Power continues to retain it's primacy in the ground operations. Artillery deployed imaginatively and innovately is an all weather assured firepower available for ground operations... In Kargil, the Fire Power enabled the infantry to attack and capture the enemy positions in day light withoug any casualities. It also saw the attacking troops reaching the objectives slung arms without firing a single shot from pers weapons. Infantry had then to carry out mopping up and ground holding of the captured area.[25]

It is pertinent to quote the views of a U.S. Army officer who has done extensive research on the Kargil War. In a thesis titled *High Altitude Warfare: The Kargil Conflict and the Future*, submitted at the Naval Post Graduate School, Montery, California, USA in 2003, Captain Marcus P. Acosta extolled the performance of artillery.

Artillery emerged as the primary source of fire power on the high altitude battlefield. Massive artillery barrages provided the cover of suppressive fire under which Indian infantry advanced. Indian batteries engaged in both direct and indirect fire, and produced devastating effects. Without artillery fire, Indian infantry stood no chance of taking the heights, as they were vulnerable to Pakistani forces firing freely down upon them while they made the slow and difficult trek up the slope. Recognizing this need after early setbacks, the Indian Army deployed fifteen artillery regiments containing over three hundred artillery pieces to the theater. Indian artillery fired more than 250,000 rounds over the course of the campaign...

He further writes:

The controversial Bofors FH-77B emerged as the Indian Army's most reliable and lethal artillery piece on the high altitude battlefield of Kargil. Its long-range, heavy caliber shell readily destroyed poorly constructed fighting positions. Indian batteries reported that the 24-km maximum range at sea level extended beyond 40-km in the thin air of Kargil. The concentrated fire of multiple batteries overcame the loss in accuracy that accompanied the increase in range. One of the howitzer's most important features became its ability to execute high-angle fire. The tube could be elevated to angles over 70°, making it capable of shooting over the high mountain crests of Kargil.[26]

The contribution of the Regiment of Artillery in the success can be gauged with the number of gallantry awards, Honour Titles and COAS Unit Citations awarded to it These are as under:

(a). Vir Chakras	-	4
(b). Yudh Seva Medal	-	3
(c). Sena Medal	-	34
(d). Mention-in-Dispatches	-	22
(e). Honour Title of `KARGIL'	-	9 Units (41 Field Regiment, 141 Field Regiment, 197 Field Regiment, 315 Field Regiment, 108 Medium Regiment, 158 Medium Regiment, 286 Medium Regiment, 1889 Light Regiment and 2122 Rocket Battery.
COAS's Unit Citation	-	3 Units (141 Field

Regiment,   197   Field
Regiment and 108
Medium Regiment.

In the end it is appropriate to quote the Corps and Division Commanders on the performance of the artillery in the Kargil conflict. Lieutenant General Krishal Pal, GOC 15 Corps, commented:

Artillery created such fire supremacy and environment on the battlefield that the enemy was physically and psychologically degraded to such an extent that subsequent ground operations were pre-destined to success. Daring, bold dynamic handling and unconventional way of employment of artillery resulted in positive execution and was a good force multiplier.[27]

Major General Mohinder Puri, GOC 8 Mountain Division writes in his book:

That the artillery became the major facilitator in most successes during the operations was acknowledged by all commanders. And the large percentage of own and enemy casualties sustained owing to artillery fire was emblematic of that .... He further writes... *Notwithstanding the enormous constraints, the gunners acquitted themselves with unremitting merit throughout the operation in a range of tasks, from destruction of enemy defences in the intrusion areas; disrupting enemy reinforcements; harassing fire in the depth areas including logistic bases; preparatory bombardment to supporting fire for the assaulting troops; engagements of targets on reverse slopes which was not possible from ground or by the Air Observation Post (Air OP).*[28]

General Puri has willy nilly covered every facet of artillery operations in his comments.

The code-name given to the Indian military response to the Pakistani intrusions in the Kargil Sector was *Operation Vijay* (meaning Operation Victory). And it was indeed the Indian Army that got Vijay or Victory!

As a tail-piece I am appending a short first - hand account of artillery operations as seen by an intrepid journalist of the Indian Express, Mr Vikram Jit Singh, who was in the frontline at Kargil during *Operation Vijay*.

ARTICLE

Artillery Battles in the Kargil War as witnessed by a War Correspondent, then stationed with The Indian Express, at Srinagar, October 1997 to October 1999.

-BY VIKRAM JIT SINGH

Bofors HEER shells arched across the night sky like red shooting stars.

Twilight had turned the austere Batalik mountains to hues of orange. The night sky, a milky bed of stars from a vantage point at 15,876 feet. Fired in trios, the High Explosive Extended Range (HEER) shells of the Bofors came up like red shooting stars from gun pits on the Indus river and behind the mountains, arched in the sky and then travelled silently across, searing at the infinite whiteness. The shells dipped towards Kukarthang ridge, disappeared and fell across the LOC. Huge red and silver flashes of fire lit up the sky with the attendant, crashing roars of 43 kg of TNT as Pakistan Army positions were targeted. The blood redness of the HEERs was due to the burner on the shells that reduces air drag and fetches extended range for the howitzer. What I had witnessed was a section of the 23,500 HEER shells fired during the Kargil War.

The HEER firing evoked a poetic description in the night's celestial amphitheatre. But what would the Pakistani soldiers be thinking as the red orbs advanced menacingly upon them? Would the beauty of the nocturnal cosmos appear a murderous canvas for the enemy targets? Certainly, many poetic verses would be reserved for the epitaphs on their graves back home, if this was the last night they would ever see. But verses none for those unlucky to die within Indian territory and buried in unmarked graves fashioned by Indian soldiers or for those whose splintered bodies were flung deep into the Batalik abyss by fleeing comrades of the Northern Light Infantry.

It was July 7, 1999, and I was in the pup tent of Colonel V.S. Bhalothia, CO, 12 JAK Light Infantry, and sharing the tight space with Major M. Indrabalan, BM 70 Infantry Brigade. We were located in the Point 4812 complex on the southern extremity of the Khalubar ridge. This was the second occasion

I had been granted permission by HQ 15 Corps, to accompany troops into battlefields at high-altitude towering thousands of feet above the valleys of Drass, Mashkoh and the Indus, the only mediaperson bestowed this unique privilege of the Kargil War.

Fortunately, I did not end up adding to the long list of casualties inflicted by Artillery. An estimated 80 per cent of casualties on both sides were claimed ownership by the omnipresent splinter. My climb to Point 4812 that afternoon and relocating to the CO's tent at dusk was fraught with fire. We had to negotiate the western cliff face of Khalubar to reach the tent and suffered exposure to Pakistani observation posts on the Kukarthang ridge to the south west. The path along the cliff was suited for an Ibex but I had to negotiate a tightrope act. One mis-step, one intense convulsion or exaggerated shudder would have sent me plunging thousands of feet below into the Gragario nallah.

The chaperone attached to me was Signals Subedar Karan Singh, also the CO's radio operator. As the Pakistani OPs directed ground-burst shells of 81 mm mortars onto us, we would take shelter amid rocks, move forward for a few minutes and then again duck into whatever cleft we could find in the cliff face. Singh rendered some consoling artillery-evasion advice to me: "Protect your head, Sir. If that goes, nothing of you will remain. If legs go, we can always amputate them."

The Pakistani artillery fire at us was augmented by withering bursts from thier Infantry's UMGs and RPGs. I requested Colonel Bhalothia in a jocular vein: were I to write my Will amid the respite of rocks,would he be kind enough to deliver it back home? But we reached his tent safely after taking two hours to negotiate 150 m of cliff face. Singh blandly consoled me: "Sir, Pakistan OPs did not have good coordination with mortar detachment, that is why we got through".

The ensuing night was replete with a piece of artillery irony. We enjoyed a dinner that included egg curry, which had been carried up the Khalubar inclines by soldiers in empty, black-coloured and two-parts-fused 82 mm mortar casings!

That night of July 7 and 8, Colonel Bhalothia was the

coordinating officer for the 5 PARA's assault on Point 4100 flanking the enemy' nerve centre at Munthodalo. He was also coordinating the fire of HEER shells across LOC to curb Pakistani 'harkat' (harassing fire). His radio set crackled incessantly like cicadas chirping on a monsoon night. The Yaldor nallah was whistling with 105 mm shells of the Indian Army's field guns as they softened the 'Area Spring' and Point 4100. The Pakistani artillery response was more measured because it was riddled with uncertainty. I estimated a few hundred Pakistani shells and RPGs whistled by our location and burst to our left and right on Khalubar that night. "Pakistanis are firing virtually blind as their key OPs have been over-run. They are firing into areas where they speculate our assaulting troops will come from," explained Col. Bhalothia.

An artillery officer came onto the CO's frequency: "Golf to Sultan. We are going to obliterate Point 4100". Eight hundred rounds of 160 and 120 mm heavy mortars, Bofors, 105 mm field guns and multi-barrel rocket launchers were released in 600 seconds to impact a 300 m x 300 m area. The high-intensity fire assault trapped the NLI intrusions as an observation grid of Indian forward observation officers (FOOs) and observation posts (OPs) was directing Artillery from all sides. At 3 am on July 8, the wounded mountains lapsed into a sullen silence. At 5.30 am came a triumphant message from an officer of 5 PARA: "Alpha for Sultan. Point 4100 taken. Casualties suffered minimum. Three cheers."

AMID TINY FLOWERS, PERILS OF AIR BURST ARTILLERY
Air burst artillery claimed a significant share of casualties incurred by Indian assaulting troops. On July 1, six days before the Khalubar odyssey, I had gone up the Bhimbet nallah (Drass LOC sector, flows north-south on the eastern flank of Tololing) to 16,000 feet with the 18 Garhwal Rifles. I was to join up with with Colonel SK Chakravarti, CO, 18 Garhwal Rifles, who was launching assaults on 'Junction' and 'Black Rock' on the LOC. As I trudged up the nallah with a patrol of 18 Garhwal Rifles led by Major Sharma and deputed for my odyssey to the LOC, the soldiers pointed out the wreckage of

the Mi17 helicopter brought down by a Stinger missile on May 27. But Pakistani OPs positioned on ridgelines overlooking the nallah spotted our movement. They directed air burst artillery upon us from mortars and mountain guns. The Garhwali solders directed me to conceal my red and green checked shirt under an olive green jacket with the plea: "Sir, the Pakistanis must think there is a VVIP going up the nallah with soldiers, so they are delivering an extra dose of shelling."

Splinters showered upon on us from the cool mountain air like gigantic, inverse Diwali 'anaars'. The soldiers directed me to lie face down amid rocky outcrops. "Sir, everything is in Dharti Mata's (mother earth) hands now as we are completely exposed. It is kismet if air bursts don't hit us. We can do nothing but pray to Mata," was the sage counsel rendered to my numbed ears by a stoic Garhwali soldier. I replied to him that I was with them in whatever might happen.

Tiny bluebells, irises and daisies, the only flora at those austere heights, stared me in the face as I lay flat in the gravel and stone. I plucked those flowers with minimal movements as we waited out each bout of shelling. I sent them home to my terror-stricken fiancee, Hemani, later in a letter to Chandigarh from Drass. "Which fiancee has flowers sent to her from the battlefield," I had written. I guess I won her for life with those flowers laced with the cordite of battle and the novelty of love budding at those heights. We negotiated shelling till we reached the fork in the Bhimbet nallah where the Pakistani OPs were rendered blind by the topography.

Artillery Crunches Lit up Drass like A Celestial Diwali

If the advance of HEER shells across the Batalik night sky were an ethereal spectacle, the Artillery crunches on Tololing in June were cosmic in scale. Like a Grand Diwali, the intense fire assaults would light up our evenings at Drass and serve as an augury for the eventual triumph of good over evil. Infantry Commanders would chew their nails in anxiety; only a few weeks remained before winter would set in and shield the entrenched enemy. The artillery assault on Tiger Hill on July

3 packing 5,000 shells and rockets was witnessed by me from the comfort of 56 Mountain Brigade HQs with a running commentary on the firepower deployed by artillery officers who had worked the fireplan.

As put so eloquently by an artillery commentator: "The deafening thunder of hundreds of simultaneous explosions rent the air, rumbled over the mountains and then echoed back and forth till the next volley arrived and the cycle was repeated." The effects were palpable: Infantry soldiers would cheer the artillery crunch but turn quiet and stoic when IAF flew sorties as they knew the latter would inflict limited damage on enemy bunkers. The artillery's results were effective: shells blew off bunkers and degraded enemy's fighting morale. This had registered deeply in the soldier's mind: from gate sentries at Brigade HQs to assaulting Infantry.

I was staying at 56 Mountain Brigade HQs, Drass, and was privileged by the insights afforded into high-altitude artillery warfare by none other than the very articulate Colonel Alok Deb, CO, of the highly-decorated 197 Field Regiment. He had drawn up the massive Tololing firing plans in conjunction with Colonel GK Mediratta, CO 1889 Light Mortar Regiment. Colonel Deb's was the only Artillery regiment in support of 56 Brigade when it moved to Drass in the panic and rush of early May. I was enabled enough to pen in detail the first media dispatches from the battlefield on the Artillery's pivotal role in the Tololing breakthrough.

The initial assaults in May and June, 1999, by 18 Grenadiers had deployed heavy fire from Infantry support weapons like rocket launchers and mortars but troops suffered heavy casualties. It then dawned upon the higher command that without massed artillery and a deliberate execution of firepower, Infantry assaults would result in serial suicides and tragic citations for bravado sans victory.

Detailing the fire assault on Point 4590 in the Drass sector, I had written then for *The Indian Express*: "For a month, 125 intruders entrenched in bunkers spanning Tololing ridge-Saddle-Hump-Point 4590-point-Point 5190 and overlooking the national highway weathered Infantry assaults and piecemeal Artillery fire. With the IAF strikes in the Drass sector not bringing in the desired results, it was left to Infantry and Artillery to give the first major breakthrough."

The opening paragraph of my June 1999 dispatch was: "It was an offensive unparalleled in Indian artillery warfare: a 120-gun Bofors-led broadside that not only pulverised bunkers and left the intruders dead in their sleeping bags but saw boulders fly 200 m, lowered the height of a mountain --- Point 4590 --- and turned the snows of the peaks into an acrid, petrol colour unfit for consumption."

Artillery had truly lived up to its motto: *Sarvatra: Izzat-O-Iqbal* (Everywhere --- With Honour and Glory).

TAIL PIECE

On some Drass evenings, when 56 Brigade Commander Amar Aul had some moments to spare from his nerve-wracking manouevres, we would take a stroll along the highway for a short distance or in the HQs complex and share our anxieties and moments of success. One late afternoon, Brigadier Aul bundled me into his Maruti Gypsy and told me: "Vikram, I am taking you for a Bofors shoot". We drove along the national highway west of Drass to a point where the ridgeline ran to Point 5140 and was under the area of operations of 1 NAGA.

Brigadier Aul was flushed with confidence. He had on June 17 initiated a daring, out-of-the-box assault by 13 JAK Rifles by deploying Bofors in a direct fire mode during daylight. The troops had assaulted and captured Humps 9 & 10 and Rocky Knob (a part of the point 5140 complex held by the enemy) by late evening after being fired in by the Bofors at 3.30 pm. "The momentum built up after the fall of Tololing on June 13 was in danger of faltering as the troops had been bogged down for two days. So, I initiated the daytime assault making innovative use of Bofors and it went off well," Brigadier Aul had told me.

What transpired that late Drass afternoon kindled memories of childhood days --- of a duck shoot at dusk over spillage ponds flanking the Satluj at Ropar. One Bofors gun that had driven along with us now wheeled itself in a position along National Highway 1D and lowered its barrel to a direct firing mode. The gun crew was ordered by the Medium Regiment's CO to target a fibre-glass hut of the Pakistani intruders serving as living quarters. It was like shooting a wild duck with a .22 LR rifle fitted with a telescope! Tactically located in a cleft of the cliff face, the hut did not constitute a sitting duck for the Bofors! The hut was one of the few the Pakistanis had transported to the frontlines of the incursions as otherwise the standard recourse of the NLI for shelter was to tentage and 'rock sangars'.

The Bofors corrected fire in an arc and the shells one by one crept menacingly towards the hut as we watched with powerful field glasses. We did not have much time as we knew the Pakistanis possessed ANTPQ 36 gun-locating radars. And, then 'POOF', a Bofors shell registered a direct hit and the hut crumbled like a cheesecake smashed on a birthday boy's face. The hut's remains tumbled down from those forbidding heights and lie buried in the eternally-lonely abyss. The duck down, we along with the Bofors crew resorted to a 'shoot and scoot' from the spot and to a well-earned 'peg-sheg-chicken leg' in the battle mess of 56 Brigades HQs.

NOTES

1. Amarinder Singh, *A Ridge too Far: War in the Kargil Heights 1999*, Motibagh Palace, Patiala, p.73.
2. Gen. V.P. Malik, KARGIL : *From Surprise To Victory*, Harper Collins, NOIDA, India, 2010, p.172..
3. Lt. Gen. Mohinder Puri, KARGIL : *Turning The Tide*, Lancer, New Delhi, 2016, p.61.
4. Ibid., pp.57-8.
5. Col Shafi Sheikh, in an unpublished article on Operation Vijay.
6. Maj. Gen. Lakhwinder Singh, *KARGIL 1999*, appearing in the book 'Themes of glory: Indian Artillery in War' by Brig. Darshan Khullar, Vij Books, New Delhi, 2017, p.128.
7. Lt. Gen. Mohinder Puri, *KARGIL : Turning The Tide,* p.61.
8. Maj. Gen. Lakhwinder Singh, *KARGIL 1999*. p.129.
9. Lt Gen Y.M. Bammi, *KARGIL 1999: The Impregnable Conquered*, p.215.

10. Ibid., p.216.
11. Lt. Gen. Mohinder Puri, *KARGIL: Turning The Tide*, p.64.
12. Gen. V. P. Malik, *KARGIL: From Surprise to Victory*, p.162.
13. Ibid., p.161.
14. Ibid., p.169.
15. Ibid., p.169.
16. Maj. Gen. Lakhwinder Singh, *KARGIL 1999*, p.140.
17. Gen. V.P. Malik, *KARGIL : From Surprise to Victory*, p.170.
18. Lt. Gen. Mohinder Puri, *KARGIL: Turning The Tide*, p.92.
19. Maj. Gen. Lakhwinder Singh, *KARGIL 1999*, p.141.
20. Lt Gen Y.M. Bammi, *KARGIL 1999: The Impregnable Conquered*, p.258.
21. Maj. Gen. Lakhwinder Singh, *KARGIL 1999*, quotes Maj Gen Mohinder Puri, p.142.
22. Gen. V.P. Malik, KARGIL: *From Surprise to Victory*, p.13.
23. Ibid., p.222.
24. Lt Gen Y.M. Bammi, *KARGIL 1999 : The Impregnable Conquered*, p.382-3.
25. Maj Gen Lakhwinder Singh, in an unpublished note shared with the author.
26. Capt Marcus P. Acosta, U. S. Army, in a Thesis titled *High Altitude Warfare: The Kargil Conflict and the future*, submitted to the Naval Post Graduate School, Montery, USA, 2003, pp. 55-6.
27. Maj. Gen. Lakhwinder Singh, *KARGIL 1999*, p.148.
28. Lt. Gen. Mohinder Puri, *KARGIL: Turning The Tide*, p.116.

BIBLIOGRAPHY

BOOKS AND ARTICLES

CHAPTER 1: INTRODUCTION

Graham, Brigadier General, C.A.L, *The History of the Indian Mountain Artillery*, Gale and Palden, Aldershot, 1957.

Mckenney, Janice E, *The Organisational History of the Field Artillery: 1775-2003*, Centre of Military History, United States Army, Washington D.C., 2007.

Palit, Major General, D.K., *History of the Regiment of Artillery; Indian Army*, Palit and Dutt, Dehradun, India, 1971.

CHAPTER 2 : BATTLE OF GETTYSBURG

Cole, Philip M, *Civil War Artillery At Gettysburg*, Colecraft Industries, Orrtanna, PA, USA, 2002.

Gottfried, Bradley M, *The Artillery Of Gettysburg*, Cumberland House, Nashville, Tennessee, USA, 2008.

Haskell, Frank A, *The Battle Of Gettysburg*, Eyre & Spottis, Norwich, Great Britain, 1959.

Wood, W Birbeck and Edmonds, Brigadier General Sir James, *The Civil War In The United States*, Methuen & Co Ltd, London, 1937.

Young, Jesse Bowman, *The Battle of Gettysburg: A Comprehensive Narrative*, Hamper and Brothers Publishers, New York, 1913.

CHAPTER 3 : BATTLE OF VIMY RIDGE

Berton, Pierre, *Vimy*, Pen & Sword Military Ltd, Barnsley, UK, 2003.

Cave, Nigel, *Battleground Europe- Arras: Vimy Ridge*, Pen & Sword Military Ltd,Barnsley, UK, 2013.

Douglas, Tom, *Valour at Vimy Ridge*, Altitude Publishing, Canada, Ltd, Canmore, Canada, 2007.

Edited by Geoftry Hayes, Andrew Iarocci, Mike Bechthold, *Vimy Ridge: A Canadian Re-assessment*, Wilfred Laurier University Press, Ontario, Canada, 2010.

Sheldon, Jack, *The German Army on Vimy Ridge 1914-*

1917, Pen & Sword Military Ltd., Barnsley, UK, 2008.

Hopkins, J. Castell, *Canada at War 1914-1918*, George H. Doran Company, Canada, 1919.

Turner, Alexander, *Vimy Ridge 1917 : Byng's Canadian Triumph at Arras*, Osprey Publishing, Oxford, UK, 2010.

CHAPTER 4: BATTLE OF BIR HACHEIM (POINT 171)

Effendi, Colonel M.Y., *Punjab Cavalry : Evolution, Role, Organization and Tactical Doctrine 11Cavalry (Frontier Force) 1849 – 1971*, Oxford University Press, Karachi, 2007.

Mukherjee, Colonel Anjan, *Har Maidan Fareh : History of 2 Field Regiment (SP) Point 171 and Letse*, Vishal Publishers, Jammu, 1997.

---News item in *Daily Telegraph*, London, 27 May 1982.

Sandhu, Major General Gurcharan Singh,

---*I Serve : The Eighteenth Cavalry* Lancers, New Delhi, 1991.

---*The Indian Armour : History of the Indian Armoured Corps 1941-1971*,Vision Books, New Delhi,1987

Singh, Lieutenant General P.K., *2 Indian Field Regiment And The Battle of Bir Hacheim – Point-171*, Salute Magazine, April – May 2019, New Delhi.

Shergill, Lieutenant General M.S., *To Honour A Past, U.S.I. Journal*, April – June, 2005, New Delhi.

Statement of Sir Winston Churchill, Prime Minister of Great Britain, in the House of Commons; HC 02 June 1942 Vol 380 cc 528-34.

War Diary of 2 Indian Field Regiment.

CHAPTER 5: BATTLE OF CHHAMB: THE INDO-PAKISTAN WAR OF 1971.

Amin, Major Agha Humayun,

----'The Battle of Chhamb 1971', *Defence Journal*, September 1999.

---- 'Remembering Our Warrior : Babar the Great', *Defence Journal*, April 2001.

Candeth, Lieutenant General K.P. (Retd) *The Western Front : The Indo-Pakistan War 1971*, Allied Publishers; New Delhi, 1984.

Effendi, Colonel M.Y. *Punjab Cavalry: Evolution, Role, Organization and Tactical Doctrine, 11 Cavalry (Frontier Force) 1849-1971*, Oxford University Press, Karachi, 2007.

Hamid, Major General Syed Ali, *Forged in the Furnace of Battle : The War History of 26 Cavalry Chhamb Operations*, Sang-e-Meel Publishers, Lahore, 2017.

Hamoodur, Rehman, *Commission of Inquiry with Respect to the 1971 War: As Declassified by the Govt. of Pakistan*, Vanguard Books, Lahore, Pakistan.

Jasbir Singh, Lieutenant General R.K. (Retd), 'Battle of Chhamb : Indo-Pak War 1971', *Journal of the United Services of India, vol. CXX, No 501*, New Delhi, July-September 1990.

Khan, Major General Fazal Muqeem (Retd.), *Pakistan's Crisis in Leadership*, Alpha & Alpha Publishers, New Delhi, 1984.

Lal, Air Marshal P.C., *My Years with the IAF*, ed. Ela Lal, Lancer International, New Delhi 1996.

Musa, General Mohammad, *My Version: Indo-Pakistan War 1965*, ABC Publishing House, New Delhi, 1983,

Saeed, Lieutenant Colonel Ahmad, *Battle of Chhamb (1971)*, Army Education Press, Rawalpindi, 1973.

Sandhu, Major General A.J.S. (Retd), *Battleground Chhamb : The Indo-Pakistan War of 1971*, Manohar Publishers, New Delhi, 2017.

Singh, Major General Jagjit, *Indian Gunners at War in the Western Front-1971*, Lancer International, New Delhi, 1994.

CHAPTER 6: BATTLE OF TOLOLING AND TIGER HILL

Bammi, Lieutenant General Y.M., *KARGIL 1999: The Impregnable Conquered*, Gorkha Publishers, NOIDA, 2002.

Kanwal, Colonel Gurmeet,

---*Kargil 1999 Bloods Guts Tears*, Lancer, New Delhi,2002.

---*Heroes of Kargil*, Army Headquarters, New Delhi, 2000.

Malik, General V.P., *Kargil : From Surprise to Victory*, Harper Collins India, New Delhi, 2010.

Resume of Operations, of units which took part in *Operation Vijay.*

Singh, Amarinder, *A Ridge too Far: War in the Kargil Heights,* Motibagh Palace, Patiala, 2001.

Singh, Major General Lakhwinder, *Chapter on KARGIL 1999,,* in the book 'Themes of Glory -Indian Artillery in War', Vij Books, New Delhi, 2017.

The Kargil Review Committee Report, New Delhi, 1999.

Unpublished Paper – *Operation Vijay* by Colonel Shafi Sheikh.

INTERNET SOURCES

Chapter 1: Introduction

Mukherjee, Lieutenant General Anjan, Thesis titled *Evolution of Indian Artillery and its impact on Comprehensive Military Power,* University of Madras, India, 2013.

Manucy, Albert, *Artillery Through the Ages: A Short history of Canon,* Gutenbug E Book, distributed Prof Team at http://www.pgdp.not

Chapter 2: Battle of Gettysburg

https:// www.nationalreview.com/ article/ 352377/great - battle - gettysburg-mackubin-thomas owens accessed on 13/02/2018.

https:// www.washingtonpost.com/ gettysburg - the - batlle - and - its - aftermath 2013/04/26/...accessed on 13/02/2018.

Chapter 3: Battle of Vimy Ridge

Battle of Vimy Ridge, available at http:// www.the canadianencyclopedia.co/ en/ article/ vimy-ridge/accessed on 05 March 2018.

The Battle of Vimy Ridge-Fast Facts, available at http: // www-veterans.gc-ca/ eng/ remembrance/memorials/ overeas/ first-world-war/ france/ vimy/batlle accessed on 05 Mar 2018.

How precision, planning made Canada's Vimy Ridge victory possible, http:/www.macleans.ca/news/Canada/ how-precision-planning-made-canadas-vimy-ridge-possible accessed on 07 July 2018.

The Battle of Vimy Ridge, available at http://veterans. gc.ca/eng/remembrance/history/first-world-war/fact-sheets/vimy accessed on 07 March 2018.

The Battle of Vimy Ridge, 9-12 April 1917, available at http://www.warmuseum.ca/the-battle-of-vimy-ridge-accessed on 05 March 2018.

When was the Battle of Vimy Ridge, available at http://thesun.co.uk/news/3218436/battle-of-vimy-ridge-world-war-1-centenary, accessed on 07 March 2018.

CHAPTER 4 : BATTLE OF BIR HACHEIM (PART 171)
Zobecki, David T., *World War II : North Africa Campaign* accessed from www.historynet.com//world-war-II-northafrica-campaign-htm.

Plate1: Lt. Gen. Robert Lee, Commander of the Confederate Army of North Virginia

Plate 2 : Maj. Gen. George Meade, Commander of the Union Army of the Potomac at Gettysburg

Plate 3: Brig. Gen. Henry Hunt, Chief of Artillery, Union Army of the Potomac

Plate 4: Brig. Gen. William N. Pendleton, Chief of Artillery, Confederate Army of North Virginia

Plate 5: Valley Of Death, art print by Dan Nance.

Plate 6: Painting depicting the famous Pickett's Charge titled The Gettysburg Cyclorama, by French artist Paul Dominique Philippoteaux, in 1883.

Plate 7: Gettysburg National Military Park

Plate 8: 6-pdr cannon on display at Gettysburg National Military Park

Plate 9: First Lt. Alonzo H. Cushing

Plate 10: President Barack Obama presenting Medal of Honor to descendants of
First Lt. Alonzo H. Cushing on November 6, 2014, over 150 years after the battle

Plate 11: Lt. Gen. Julian Byng, Canadian Corps Commander at Vimy Ridge

Plate 12: Captured German machine gun fortification at Vimy Ridge

Plate 13: Canadian National Vimy Memorial

Plate 14: British 6 inch Mk VII gun on improvised Percy Scott field carriage, firing in support of Canadian attack on Vimy Ridge

Plate 15: Sikh soldiers of Lahore Division Artillery, attached with 4 Canadian Division, in action at Vimy Ridge on 9 April 1917; painting by C Rawlins (Sikh Heritage Museum of Canada)

Plate 16: Perhaps the most well-known artillery image in Canada, titled the Taking of Vimy Ridge, Easter Monday 1917. It was painted by Richard Jack (1856-1952) in 1918 and the original is held at the Canadian War Museum

Plate 17: Pack horses transporting ammunition to the 20th Battery, Canadian Field Artillery in Neuville St. Vaast, France during the Battle of Vimy Ridge.

Plate 18: 85th (Nova Scotia Highlanders) Battalion on Vimy Ridge, by artist Richard Rudnicki

Plate 19: Mark VI 8 inch Howitzer being loaded during the Battle of Vimy Ridge.

Plate 20: Gen. Andrew G.L.Mc Naughton (then Lt. Col.),
Artillery expert in the Canadian Corps during the battle of Vimy Ridge

Plate 21: QF 18 Pounder Battery Gun Position

Plate 22: Canadian soldier returning from the trenches

Plate 23: Canadian soldiers go into reserve after victory at Vimy Ridge

Plate 24: 9.2 inch howitzer shells on their way to heavy batteries

Plate 25: 6 inch naval guns in action at Vimy

Plate 26: Canadians fix bayonets before going over the top

Plate 27: No Man's Land with bursting shrapnel and HE impacts

Plate 28: Lt. Col. Guy Horsfield, CO 2 Indian Field Regiment

Plate 29: Sikh gun crew of 7 Indian Field Battery (in foreground)
engaging German tanks at Point 171 (painting by German artist Langhammar)

Plate 30: Gen. P.P. Kumaramangalam, DSO, MBE, Chief of Army Staff India, from 8 June 1966 to 7 June 1969.

Plate 31: Gen. Tikka Khan, Chief of Army Staff Pakistan, from 3 March 1972 to 1 March 1976

Plate 32: Maj. Gen. Kalyan Singh, PVSM, Military Secretary, Indian Army from 8 June 1967 to 3 March 1969

Plate 33: Maj. Gen. A.S. Naravane, PVSM, Director Artillery, from 01 Jan 1965 to 19 Jun 1968

Plate34: Adm. Walter Cowan, attached with 18 Cavalry,
who was captured as P.O.W. at Point 171

Plate 35: Group photograph of officers of 2 Indian Field Regiment dated June 1941,
Trimulgherry. Maj. P.P. Kumaramangalam (front row right extreme), Capt. A.S. Naravane
(second row, 7th from left), Lt. Kalyan Singh (Last row, centre) and Lt. Tikka Khan (Second
Last row, Third from right)

Plate 36: Gen. P.P. Kumaramangalam interacting with ex-servicemen during his visit to 2 Field Regiment (SP) on 26 and 27 May 1969.

Plate 37: Author, then a 2nd Lt. (standing extreme right) with Gen. P.P. Kumaramangalam (sitting front right) during the latter's visit to the regiment on 26 and 27 May 1969

Plate 38: Author with the DSO awarded to Maj. (later Gen.)
P.P. Kumaramangalam, at the R.A.A. Museum at Artillery Centre, Nasik Road

Plate 39: 2nd Royal Lancers 2-pdr gun in action at Point 171

Plate 40: Gen. Erwin Rommel, commanding Afrika Korps (later Panzerarmee Afrika)

Plate 41: Maj. Gen. Jaswant Singh, VSM, G.O.C. 10 Infantry Division

Plate 42: Brig. K. Srinivasan, AVSM, Commander 10 Artillery Brigade at
Sakrana (near Chhamb) on 4 December 1971

MAJOR-GENERAL JASWANT SINGH—the
Saviour of Chhamb. "He fought a grand battle," said a senior staff officer of the Western Command. An important factor in our
victory was the high calibre of our commanders compared with the Pakistani generals who have for many years been doing
civilian jobs or playing politics.

EKLY OF INDIA, JANUARY 9, 1972   13

Plate 43: *Saviour of Chhamb.* Photograph in the Illustrated Weekly of India, 9 January 1972

Plate 44: Gun of 81 Field Regiment at the Sakrana Gun Position near Chamb

Plate 45: Gun of 18 Field Regiment blazing away at the enemy

Plate 46: Indian anti aircraft gun in Chhamb Sector

Plate 47: Maj. Gen. (later Lt. Gen.) Jaswant Singh (centre) with
Lt. Gen. Sartaj Singh (left) discussing the Counter Attack plan with Brig. (later Lt. Gen.)
K.K. Hazari, 52 Inf. Bde. on 10 December 1971

Plate48: Indian Artillery gun deployed in Chhamb Sector during the war

Plate 49: (L to R) seated in the Fire Direction Centre(F.D.C.) just after the war started on 3 December:
-B. M. Maj (Later Brig.) A.N. Suryanarayanan
-Cdr. Brig. K. Srinivasan,
-Svy. Tp. Cdr.-cum-GSO3 C.B., Capt. A.K. Kher
-Standing behind Cdr: I.O., Capt. C.K. Passi

Plate 50: Gen. Sam Manekshaw meeting Rifleman Padam Bahadur Thapa (of 5/8 GR) who was awarded a Vir Chakra. The CO Lt. Col. (later Lt. Gen.) A.S. Kalkat is on the extreme right

Plate 51: Col. Deepak Kaul with the cartridges with which he shot down a PAF Sabre over Chhamb on 8 December 1971

Plate 52: Capt. D.S. Jamwal of 81 Field Regiment at Burejal
(probably his last photograph before he was martyred on 4 December 1971)

Plate 53: Author re-visiting the battlefield in May 2014

Plate 54: Mrs. Ajit Jaswant Singh (4th from left) with then G.O.C. 10 Inf. Div. Maj. Gen. Tej Pathak (2nd from left) and the author (extreme right), after dedicating the Chhamb Memorial on 1 December 1999

Plate 55: Maj. Gen. (later Lt. Gen.) Mohinder Puri, GOC, 8 Mountain Division

Plate 56: Brig. (later Maj. Gen.) Lakhwinder Singh, Commander, 8 Mountain Artillery Brigade

Plate 57: Maj. Gen. Mohinder Puri, Brig. Lakhwinder Singh with Artillery gun crew

Plate 58: Bofors Gun of 158 Medium Regiment during the Kargil war

Plate 59: OP position of 197 Field Regt

Plate 60: Multi Barrel Rocket Launcher in action

Plate 61: Gen VP Malik, COAS, with troops of 158 Med Regt

Plate 62: Battery Gun Position

Plate 63: Gun of 286 Med Regt in action during OP VIJAY

Plate 64: Battery Gun Position of 197 Field Regt

Plate 65: Gunners Handling Amn at Apati Gun Position 2861 Med Bty

Plate 66: Photograph of Kargil Memorial with Tololing as a backdrop

Plate 67: Sub. Maj. (then Grenadier) Yogender Singh Yadav, 18 Grenadiers, who was awarded the Param Vir Chakra (PVC) for gallantry in the Battle of Tiger Hill.

Plate 68: Capt. Karnal Sher Khan, Pakistan Army, killed at Tiger Hill, who was awarded the Nishan-e-Haider for gallantry

Plate 69: Then 14 Corps Commander, Lt. Gen. Y.K. Joshi, with The Times of India Defence correspondent, Vikram Jit Singh, on Tololing Top with the Point 5140 ridge in the backdrop, on July 6, 2019. The battle for Point 5140 was the first of the two major battles fought by 13 JAK Rifles under Gen. (then Col.) Joshi's command during the Kargil War.

Plate 70: (Top) The Indian Express war correspondent, Vikram Jit Singh (in fawn trousers), in a tricky spot on the western cliff face of Khalubar ridge, Batalik, and coming under fire from UMGs and RPGs directed by Pakistanis lodged on the flanking Kukarthang ridge, July 7, 1999. He was accompanied by soldiers of the 12 JAK Light Infantry.(Below) During the climb to Tololing Top on July 6, 2019, as part of a 2 Rajputana Rifles commemorative expedition: Kargil War veterans, Hav. Rajinder Singh (Kirti Chakra) and Sub. Surender Kumar, along with the Times of India Defence correspondent, Vikram Jit Singh.

Index

10 Baluch: 195, 197

11 Cavalry: 131, 137, 160,
    180, 181, 182, 184,
    185, 187, 190, 195,
    207, 218, 232, 237,
    238

11 Field Regiment: 201

12 (Independent) Armoured
    Squadron: 221, 232

13 A.K. Battalion: 186, 187,
    189, 223, 224, 225,
    229

14 Punjab: 216

17 Artillery Brigade: 180, 200,
    226, 228, 232

19 Baluch: 182, 190, 232

20 Infantry Brigade: 182, 184,
    185, 232

23 Infantry Division: 163, 179,
    180, 182, 189, 195,
    200, 201, 209, 211,
    215, 226, 228, 232,
    234, 236

23 Artillery Brigade: 195, 200,
    226, 227, 228

23 Baluch: 190, 192, 193

26 Cavalry: 179, 180, 181,
    186, 232, 236

28 Cavalry: 185, 186, 190,
    192, 193, 195, 197,
    232

28 Medium Regiment: 193,
    201

33 Frontier Force: 229

39 Medium Regiment: 185,
    187, 198, 203, 208,
    212, 214, 215, 216,
    217, 221, 222, 223,
    230, 237, 238, 241

42 Punjab: 193

47 Punjab: 186, 187, 189, 222

50 Field Regiment: 201

51 Composite Mountain Regiment: 201

63 Field Regiment: 201

64 Medium Regiment: 201

66 Infantry Brigade: 180, 181,
    182, 184, 185, 186,
    232

71 Medium Regiment: 209

111 Infantry Brigade: 180, 181,
    182, 184, 185, 190,
    192, 193, 194, 195,
    198, 215, 227, 232

285 Division Locating Battery:
    201

Union Army of The Potomac:

1 Corps: 34, 35, 39, 40, 42,
    47, 49, 51, 52, 55, 56,
    61, 62, 74, 75, 77, 78,
    83, 88

Group Vimy:

1 Bavarian Reserve Corps: 94,
      124

1 Bavarian Reserve Infantry
      Division: 95, 124

Afrika Korps:

Ariete Division: 142, 143, 144,
      146, 147, 151, 152

15 Panzer Division: 140, 142,
      143, 144, 145, 147,
      151, 152

21 Panzer Division: 140, 142,
      143, 144, 146, 150,
      151, 152

90 Light Division: 147, 152

Ingram Content Group UK Ltd.
Milton Keynes UK
UKHW042026120323
418346UK00004BA/97

9 789390 917419